BANGALORED

BANGALORED

[the **expat** story]

ESHWAR SUNDARESAN

EastWest Books (Madras) Pvt. Ltd.

• Chennai • Bangalore • Hyderabad • New Delhi

EastWest Books (Madras) Pvt. Ltd.

571, Poonamalle High Road, Aminjikarai, Chennai - 600 029.
3-5-1108, Maruti Complex, II Floor, Narayanaguda, Hyderabad - 500 029.
53/2, Bull Temple Road, Basavangudi, Bangalore - 560 019.
A-10, Lower Ground Floor, Lajpat Nagar III, New Delhi - 110 024.

Reprinted 2007

Price Rs.350

ISBN : 81-88661-44-9

Cover design
J Menon, www.grantha.com

Printed at
Sri Venkatesa Printing House, Chennai - 600 026
E.mail: saiprints@saimail.com

Published by
EastWest Books (Madras) Pvt. Ltd.
571, Poonamalle High Road, Aminjikarai, Chennai - 600 029
E-mail : ewb@touchtelindia.net

In memory of
BALAM

Contents

Acknowledgments

All my stars who feature in this book, and also those who gave me their valuable time but could not be featured.

K. S. Padmanabhan for understanding the concept and being excited about it.

For providing me with contacts:
Srividya Ramesh, Thomas van Berckel, John Patrick Ojwando, Mohan Krishnaraj, Venugopal P. (ICCR), Claudia Romiti, Komala Ramachandra, Radio City FM 91, K. K. S. Murthy (Select Bookshop), Rev. Prem Mitra (International Cultural Youth Exchange & Voluntary Service, India), Senthil Rajaram, C. S. M. Kumar, G. K. Ramana, Maya Jayapal, Akbar Khaleeli, Heidrun Chandrakant, Adriana Vargas, Judith Mohr (CSB) and Suresh Jayaram (Karnataka Chitrakala Parishad).

For providing me with information:
Venugopal P. (ICCR), the office of the Commissioner of Police, Bangalore, Indu Venkatesh (Philips), John Patrick Ojwando,

Satish Suri, K. K. S. Murthy (Select Bookshop), Pushpalata Reddy and Ratheesh (Centre for the Study of Culture and Society), Prof. Ramaswamy, K. S. Vasuki (Narayana Hrudayalaya), Joyatri and K. T. Suresh (Equations), M. Hari and Sham Banerji (Texas Instruments), Balan Nambiar, M. S. Chandrashekhar (Taekwondo Federation of India), the HAL Sports Club, Lt. Col. K. D. Shelley (HAL), Dr. Sanjeev Jain (NIMHANS), S. Krishnamurthy (ISRO), M. N. Ramesha and Mukund Kirsur (Central Silk Board), M. R. Raju (Karnataka Silk Marketing Board Ltd.), Jomy Joseph Varghese (St. Martha's Hospital), Pushpa Dravid, Robert Walter (Joseph Campbell Foundation), Habib Aga, Akbar Khaleeli and Syeda Mirza, Ronnie Johnson and Dave Barnabus, Dr. Ambujakshi (the Karnataka State Archives), the State Central Library and Google.

BESCOM (Bangalore Electricity Supply Company) for their delightful inefficiency. Had it not been for their erratic power supply, I would have met all my deadlines and life would have been drab.

Partho Sengupta for his feedback.

Risha. For providing a new dimension to the book's gestation.

Finally, my wife Mumukshu who reviewed the material and provided feedback and encouragement while suffering me as usual.

Introduction

A light fog envelops the calm of the November morning. Inside the Indiranagar park, joggers and walkers of all ages are beginning their workouts. A couple of college students are holding hands in silence as they occupy seats in the farthest corner of the park. Suddenly, a volley of shrieking laughter pierces the heart of the fog and startles the mynahs into flight. The laughter-therapy group, too, has begun its workout.

I enjoy the cultivated histrionics of the group for a while, then get back to my motorbike and ride away. Turning into Old Madras Road, one of the important arteries of Bangalore, I find the traffic gliding along as if on autopilot. In an hour's time, this stretch would mutate beyond recognition. The fog will lift and be replaced by a heavy smog. People will be conversing in the language of honks and expletives. Sitting atop gearless scooters, confident women will celebrate their freedom by overtaking men. Not all will reach their office on time. They will have to negotiate long detours because roads are converted into one-ways overnight. They will be stuck in bottlenecks because it seems to take a lifetime to construct a flyover... These are just routine challenges for people living in a city mired by its own success.

Who would have thought that Bangalore would ascend to its current position of prominence on the global map? Did the British think it possible when they created the Civil and Military Station (known more popularly as the Cantonment area) in the nineteenth century? Quite unlikely. The Cantonment area I'm now driving through was designed to house sprawling bungalows, imposing churches, perhaps a few good schools and modest localities for the labourers.

And of course, it was built primarily to house the army. Today, the Cantonment has become a central part of the city. As a result, the defence forces occupy prime real estate even as the bigwig IT companies make do on the city's outskirts. Maybe it is an apt irony. After all, Bangalore is an important base for the Army, in addition to being home to the southern command of the Air Force...

I halt beside an army truck at the next traffic light. The young Sikh at the wheel seems to be gazing wistfully at the pavement. I follow his gaze and see a young IT professional, perhaps in his early twenties, knotting his tie as he waits for his company bus. He suddenly notices the army truck and freezes midway in his actions. Age-old romance meets new-age allure.

The traffic light changes; I soon reach Mahatma Gandhi Road (M. G. Road), park my bike and go for a leisurely walk in the sunshine. Over the years, M. G. Road has come to embody Bangalore. It is a commercial centre, shopping district, recreational spot and a historic place all at once. That is why, on peaceful mornings such as this, it becomes easy to imagine the road filled with soldiers taking a breather from the Second World War. If I try very hard, I can even picture the Dewan of the (former) state of Mysore riding past in a carriage...

I walk on and reach the circle named after Anil Kumble, a favourite son of the city, and not incidentally, an immensely talented cricketer. It never ceases to amaze me that a sportsman could be honoured thus while he is still playing the game. Perhaps this is a sign that Bangalore has plenty of available spaces for history that has not been fully written yet. And, perhaps, this is because the 450-odd years of the city's history sit shyly on the substrate. They hardly ever intrude upon one's senses. A mere toothpaste hoarding, for instance, might draw one's attention away from the remains of the Bangalore fort. Thus, modernity ends up occupying the space history politely declines.

'Just as well,' I tell myself as I get back to my bike and ride home. 'We, the Evolving, can certainly use the space.'

We need room for countless apartment complexes that will be purchased by, among others, homesick migrants who have come from other parts of India. We need room for crèches that charge dollar rates. For pizza joints that promise "gigabytes of taste". For new malls. For new localities with no infrastructure. For new or wider roads riddled with potholes that are outnumbered only by street dogs. Even then, we will run out of space. So we will fell trees in anticipation of projects that will never take off...

It is the best of times, it is the worst of times, to be a Bangalorean.

It takes me forty-five torturous minutes to reach home. I'm right on time to see the attractive girl next door return from her shift. She has spent the last ten hours helping customers from all over the United States. And for doing so, she had to travel thirteen whole kilometres to Whitefield.

* * *

In 1882, the area known as Whitefield was built outside the city of Bangalore by D. S. White, the founder of the Anglo-Indian Association of Madras. The nomenclature has an interesting double entendre – it was created to allow white men to selectively breed Anglo-Indian families. Today, Whitefield is home to hi-tech companies employing a burgeoning middle class. It is also home to white sports utility vehicles that continuously ferry call centre employees. Some of these employees are resolute, diminutive girls living in low-income colonies; they often return home late at night, perhaps to find proud and newly secure fathers waiting anxiously for them.

The IT industry itself, after experiencing two mini-recessions since the turn of the millennium, is back in form. As a result, salaries are touching unprecedented highs. And Bangalore has become one of the fastest growing cities in Asia. In the process, the city has redefined the global Indian. The Indian diaspora has spent decades working with their hands, driving cabs, serving spicy food, running cheap motels and helping NASA launch spectacular missions into space. But global recognition of the cerebral Indian has come only after the "offshore" engineers stepped under the spotlight. As soon as liberalisation (1991) made it easier for Indian companies to transact business with overseas clients, a few unsung software firms in Bangalore – Infosys, TCS and Wipro in particular – changed into high gear and have not looked back since.

Over the years, the Indian IT industry perfected its ability to execute projects across continents and time zones. Initially, the clients decided to offshore only tedious, "no-brainer" work. And since the millennium was coming to an end, there was an enormous amount of exactly such effort required. So every software company in India took on as much Y2K work as they could handle. Indian engineers sat behind consoles, pored over billions of lines of code and made them Y2K compliant. At the same time, the emerging giants of Indian IT persuaded clients that they could do more. Slowly at first, and later with an avalanche effect, the clients agreed to offshore their development projects. In return, they were given engineers who willingly worked during Thanksgiving and Christmas, took just a fortnight's leave to get married, didn't have to escort young Joe for choir rehearsal on a Wednesday afternoon, and pretended that tough deadlines were more fun than sleep. Their attitude lit up meeting rooms during crises. The humble Indian engineer worked his miracles; his company acquired a NASDAQ listing and quality certifications. By then, there was no doubt that the Bangalores of India could deliver. Enter Business Process Outsourcing, and along with it, a second wave of jobs. This time, the employees were not necessarily engineers. Just bright and responsible youngsters, comfortable with a headset and a colonial tongue.

Given the scale of success, it is hardly surprising that developing-world cities like Buenos Aires, Kuala Lumpur, Manila, Warsaw and Shanghai consider Bangalore worthy of emulation. But the city has many detractors as well. Dedicated websites depict the "menacing" advance of Bangalore. Self-proclaimed doomsday prophets make a good living by writing Indo-phobic columns. Forty states in the United States together introduced 112 anti-outsourcing bills in the first three months of 2005. All of a sudden, societies swearing by open markets are demanding protective padlocks.

The word "Bangalored" has, simultaneously, entered the American vocabulary. 'You are Bangalored' means 'You are outsourced'. And this phrase is made to sound as if a person has suffered a fate worse than being hit by a missile fired from a Bangalore torpedo (a weapon used by, among others,

the United States during World War II!). "Bangalored",
therefore, is a uni-dimensional word born out of hate and
fear. It is about time someone made it rounder, and the
expatriates based in Bangalore have the power to do just
that.

* * *

Many puzzling questions about expatriates prompted me
to write this book:

Why do I see them everywhere I go? Where are they from?
Where is Life leading them? How has India, and Bangalore,
affected them? How have they changed the city? Will the
relationship between them and Indians be symbiotic? If yes,
then how? If not, then why not? Do they yawn at
bureaucracy, tear their hair out at Indian paradoxes,
appreciate Bollywood, make Indian friends, better still fall
in love with them, repose faith in the local buses, sleep well,
rear children, agree to be taught, stand up to teach, protest
against prejudices, correct their perceptions, feel at home,
feel homesick, fall ill, get well, get employed, employ others?
Do they?

At the end of it, I found answers to most of the questions.
Sometimes, I found just the shadow of an answer;
occasionally, I could even see a clear pattern. And as I studied
the expatriate movement in Bangalore over the past 250-
odd years, I discovered an uncelebrated facet of the city –
its ability to assimilate.

But then, why talk about the immigrant population at
all? India, unlike the United States, does not rely on young
immigrant adrenalin to maintain robust economic health.
Point conceded. However, I believe that the guest more easily
notices the cracks in the ceiling and the fragrance of incense-

sticks than the host. In other words, I believe that the expatriates can teach Indians something about India. But to prove my theory, I had to first find appropriate teachers – dreamers, achievers, experimentalists and romanticists who have led fascinating lives. And I knew that by finding the right people, I could even attempt an answer to a broader question, that being: beyond certainties such as the survival instinct and evil streaks, do human beings share common characteristics irrespective of their origins? It is one of the most important questions in the world. It is also the most glossed-over question in the world.

With that in mind, I began my journey.

Tic-Tac-Toe

'This is where I broke my toenail,' says Thomas van Berckel. 'It was dark, yeah. And the sidewalk was being paved.'

'And you tripped.'

'Yeah-yeah!' agrees the Dutchman.

We are standing on M.G. Road, the weekend Mecca for pubbing pilgrims. The road is lit with sunshine after what seems to be ages of overcast conditions and piddling drizzles. The pavement is packed with Saturday window-shoppers. The two of us walk down towards the Brigade Road intersection. I look across at Thomas and find him immersed in his August 2003 toe-breaking caper, which was the highlight of his first visit to India. At that time he was working with Asha Niketan, raising funds for disabled children in Kerala, Chennai, Kolkata and Bangalore. But the stopover city had become special because—

'Bangalore is a very good place to break a toe,' he says.

Why wouldn't he? A helpful auto-rickshaw driver escorts him to a hospital in Infantry Road. His bleeding toe is dressed by a nurse named Lalitha. He gets interested when she dresses the famous toe again a few days later. He feels special, "an almost holy sensation", but one that leaves him reckless. In no time, he gives her a gift and to make matters absolutely clear, professes love to her.

He returns to Bangalore three months later, and gets married to Lalitha after three more. Fate, it seems, is not always fickle. Soon after this episode, the small orthopaedic clinic in Infantry Road closes and Lalitha moves beyond the purview of toe-breaking M. G. Road pedestrians. Thomas had wedged himself in precisely when the small window of opportunity was left open. Quite a task for a man of his bulk. As we make our way into the India Coffee House and find a table, I slowly realise that behind the smooth, open face lies a thinking, feeling mind. It is a mind that has urged him towards new adventures all the time.

'I have been to Africa,' says the Dutchman.

'Coffee. Two… Where in Africa?'

'Burkina Faso.'

'Huh?'

I certainly haven't heard of their cricket team, so it was probably a French colony. He smiles patiently at my ignorance.

'Here, let me write that down,' he says.

I look at his squiggles. 'How was it in Africa?' I ask him.

'Hmm. Pum-pupapam-pum.' At first, I think that means something in Dutch. It does. It means Thomas van Berckel is thinking in his delectable manner. 'Yeah. I went there three times. Yeah, three. But it's difficult to find a job there. Not so in India. And I can develop my spiritual side. India has a good balance of head and heart. The writer in me wants that.'

He isn't kidding about being a writer. He conjures up two of his works and lays them on the table. I look at the titles on the covers. *De Naakte Raam* says one.

'What does that mean?' I ask him.

'Naked Raam.'

I get the feeling that I'm being led into labyrinthine warrens by this man who looks as innocent as a bunny. I flip through the pages, half expecting to see a Dutch superstar named Raam baring it all. But the images in the book are beautiful black-and-white shots of clothed people.

'Raam is the locality I come from, in a city called Gouda,' explains Thomas.

'Gouda?'

He says something that sounds like *Gkhhou Da*.

'Gouda. We Dutch emphasise the G… we pronounce it very hard.'

'Yes, it's hard all right,' I agree and get back to the book.

Obviously, Thomas has put his heart into this project. It is his attempt to recreate the evolution of his beloved Raam over the past century. And although I cannot make sense of the Dutch words, the photographs speak my language. Thomas provides audio subtitles as I browse through the book – the exact reverse of watching a foreign language film, where the subtitles are in print and the visuals accompany unknown sounds.

'Gouda is a small city. Well, in the Netherlands we don't have big cities. The population of Amsterdam is 800,000; no comparison to Bangalore's 6,000,000 and rising. Gouda's is just 60,000 and the city is situated about 80 kilometres south-west of the capital. But Gouda has history…'

I see that.

'…great architecture…'

Agreed.

'… and is famous for its cheese.'

'Oh!'

'But ironically Gouda cheese is no longer made in Gouda,' he says.

We both pause for a moment to acknowledge the change. Change, I reflect, is most poignant when it is subtle.

'It looks like a hard-working city, mainly blue-collar,' I tell him. I get the impression from the buxom, much-midwifed women in long, thick frocks. They stare at the camera with a lively determination and impart dignity to their plain brick dwellings. Their happy children infuse the setting with joy.

'Yeah-yeah. It was mainly an industrial town to begin with. Now it's a modern city. But people still retain their values and their inferiority complex. They are very moral, very strict... Protestants most of them. So words mean a lot...are respected.'

He is alluding to the Bible. I nod, pick up the next title which reads: *De Wereld Keuken (gezien vanuit de Raam).*

'The World Kitchen (seen from the Raam),' he explains. 'Over the last few decades, the fabric of society has been changing in Holland. Diverse ethnic groups are being added to it, yeah. So we – me and a few friends – decided to write a global cuisine book by interviewing local Raam residents.'

Thomas not only embodies his country's refreshing tolerance and openness, he also celebrates diversity. True:

The Ethnic Right

Theo van Gogh, a descendant of the master painter, was shot dead by 26-year-old Mohammed B, reports the *Hindu* on 8 November 2004. The reason was van Gogh's recent documentary, which highlighted the plight of abused Muslim women, against the provocative backdrop of quotes from the Koran.

But, most shockingly, the young murderer was born and bred in Holland. Due to such events, ethnic resentment is expectedly on the rise. It is said that if a suitable right-winger appears in the political arena and says the right words, another Paradise would probably be lost.

sometimes, melting pots boil over and scald those in the vicinity. But in a world bent on becoming a village, there would be no hope for humankind without the Thomases. Thomas adds: 'I also write a weekly column for a Dutch newspaper, *Postiljon*, where I talk about my life here and draw comparisons for people back there. I have named it *Our House in Kamanahalli*.'

He says "people back there", not "people back home". So I release the question I have kept on a tight leash.

'What makes you seek a life outside Holland?'

He has been waiting for me to ask. And it is a point he wants to make accurately. He begins by rubbing his fingers together, as if feeling Lalitha's silk sari between them, then says, 'I believe some people are born in one culture but identify with another. A lot of Indians,' he points his thumb to the door leading out to the pavement, 'belong to the West that way.' On cue, two appropriately clad desi teenagers walk past. He continues, 'In my country, society is more or less static, and there aren't many opportunities for a man of my leanings. Actually the whole of Europe is quite rational. Brain, brain, brain. But to be happy, you have to follow your heart. Then you'll be on the right path; and even if you fail in every aspect, you'll be happy.'

In silicon-struck Bangalore, I've seldom heard these sentiments. Thomas leads me on.

'See, I used to be a lawyer by profession,' he says, 'and I worked under one in Maastricht. Long time ago. There I became friends with a man who was immensely talented. He was great in his profession, a wonderful painter and a terrific writer. One day, just like that, he committed suicide. I've been thinking about him... maybe he didn't have a sense of belonging. People without structure lose their way. I myself am not sure if I'm a writer or a social worker.'

Since the social worker theme has recurred, I pursue this line. It opens a new dimension in his personality.

'I want to do something for society, for children, mainly,' he says in a matter-of-fact tone. 'So I've started the Toe-2-Heart Foundation; the name is an allusion to how my broken toe led to a mended heart... and Lalitha. I want to build a school that uses holistic teaching techniques. In India, too, the artistic, sensitive side of the child is left undeveloped. I want to remedy that. And also see what I can do for the mentally retarded.'

Hmm. I'm reminded of the man called Br. Paulose, who lives in a small hamlet outside Belthangady in rural Karnataka. I had interviewed him for a magazine the year before. People say he has a shady past. But the Br. Paulose I know is an angel incarnate. A man who brings home to his Seon ashram every destitute and mentally challenged person he finds. He cares for them in the best manner possible. He never asks himself: how will I find the money? I remember writing that the Lord he believes in gets him grain when he wants it. And now, Thomas' words echo that rare charity. Rare because even kind-hearted people find it difficult to show kindness to the unthinking.

'Why specifically the mentally retarded?' I ask.

'Because they represent the heart of society. They have minimal needs, a basic outlook on life. They need our care.' Echo. Definitely an echo of Br. Paulose. 'My friends back in the Netherlands want to build a support base for me. Two of them are planning to go biking to China on a fund-raising drive. As of now, Toe-2-Heart has just three members there, all of them office-bearers! But let's see... I'll plant one seed in Bangalore and let it grow globally. Finally, social work is a creative exercise, just like writing. I have to find a solution... find money for my dream projects.'

'So that's why you play the role of a translator?'

'Yeah-yeah. I work as a translator for my sustenance. But once I raise ten to fifteen lakh rupees, I can be a writer and a social worker.'

The waiter, who has been extra-polite because of the colour of my friend's skin, hints that we've occupied the table long enough during the weekend rush. I apologise, pay him and leave an extra tip. The two of us walk out. Thomas is meeting Lalitha outside the Rex theatre and allows me to tag along. The walk down M. G. Road assumes an unfamiliar nature for me. A hawker confidently strides by, peddling a Bangalore map, unaware that Thomas is capable of riding a scooter from home to office without directions. As he fades with disappointment, he is replaced by a man selling flutes. The one selling Bermudas and denim shorts keeps away; he knows his clientele. I have never been offered a flute or a map on this road and I know where this is leading. But I'm neither ashamed nor indignant. I wait for Thomas to say something. Eventually, he does.

'You saw the young boy who put his hand in through the window in the coffee shop? He, and all these people, associate white skin with money. They think I'm stinking rich. When auto-rickshaw drivers can't find change, my colour is the reason.' He pauses. 'I think we are all racists at some level.'

'True. But maybe Indians are a bit more racist than the rest. We don't pause at nationality or skin colour. We go beyond. We sub-divide using regions, then languages.'

Thomas is surprised at my frankness. So am I. I realise that he has made me feel comfortable enough to share a few distressing home truths with him. Both on the streets as well as in world-class companies, I have seen my countrymen's affinity to regions and tongues take racism to a whole new level. Thomas looks at me, and wants to reply to my comment, but the Brigade Road throng interrupts us.

We have little choice but to concentrate on circumventing other pedestrians. My eye catches a large poster on a sports' apparel shop window. I beckon to Thomas.

'Do you know who he is?'

Thomas needs just a brief look at the picture.

'Shah Rukh Khan. Yes. Can anyone in India not know him? He can do no wrong, can he? It's always Shah Rukh Khan this and Shah Rukh Khan that. Indians venerate their stars like no one else can.'

'Thomas!' A shrill, excited voice calls from behind. Even before I see her, I know it is Lalitha, Thomas' own venerable star. She radiates happiness. I see that the family is just a couple of months away from welcoming another van Berckel. I have many more things to discuss, but for now leave the couple to themselves.

* * *

The phone rings the next day. Thomas asks me when I would like to complete the interview. We decide to meet the following evening at his house. At the appointed hour I avoid the unpleasant rush of the city roads as I ride towards Kamanahalli. But the Outer Ring Road is just as jammed with vehicles. If anything, the traffic lights take more time to change. The only consolation is that when the traffic does move, one can aspire to cover distances fast. The straight stretch after Banaswadi dips and rises in two parallel streaks of lights. In front of me are the sober red dots of taillights. The adjacent strip channels a harsh river of headlights. It reminds me of long drives on US freeways. And that sets me thinking: is it possible for a person who has seen more than his homeland to stop making comparisons? A sight, a stray smell, a voice can all trigger memories. Homesickness reversed. A desire to revisit known haunts and touch their solidity. Of course, it lacks the febrile intensity of homesickness. I hope the evening will give me more insight into the diaspora syndrome.

Soon, I reach the first-floor apartment Thomas and Lalitha share with their dog Max. Lalitha van Berckel nee Jayaraj welcomes me in an accent I have heard before, but can't place. As I rack my brains, Max decides to go out for a walk. When Thomas excuses himself to chase Max, it strikes me.

'You have begun speaking like him, haven't you? I mean, the accent.'

Lalitha is unsure. I realise I have handled it badly. But I mean it as a compliment and a vindication of the theory that happily married couples generally end up talking, thinking and even looking alike.

'I'm learning Dutch from him,' she replies. 'We are planning to visit Thomas' parents in Gouda next year.'

Darius, the Radio City jockey, keeps telling Bangalore city how he loves the glow on expectant mothers. I find myself agreeing with him. But before the glow came the love. I ask her about it. She faithfully reports the toe incident and the swift proposal that followed it.

'I come from a conventional family. My parents were shocked. But I told them that I would marry Thomas or nobody at all.' She assumes the stern look she must have given her parents. 'Finally they said, "Let us meet his parents then." His parents had no objections. And it all fell into place.'

'Did it help that both of you are Catholics?'

'I guess so.'

Thomas arrives holding the pet in his arms and deposits him on the floor.

'Did you tell him about the one-week anniversary?'

'What's that?' she asks.

Thomas turns to me.

'Before the wedding, my in-laws had said: no interference. But they promptly began coming every day to check on Lalitha. They stay close by, you see. A week after the wedding, they came to celebrate the anniversary and I had a terrible tummy-ache. I told them, rather rudely, that I wanted to be alone. Poor people. Even today, after I've told them to come by any time they please, they wait for invitations.'

He laughs.

'Yeah, we laugh over it now. But I realise now that India has clear principles when it comes to marriages. Roles in the family are well-defined. Lalitha insists on doing the housework. No maids for her. Yeah, I'm very impressed by working Indian women; they never lose the family focus. I've experienced relationships before... in Europe, and it can get quite complicated.'

A thought brightens him up.

'I'm writing a book about my experiences while living with an Indian wife. *Small World, Big World*. That's the title. That's because I've realised that I come from a big world and she from a small one.'

I think I understand him, but he wants to make it absolutely clear.

'Indian women are protected by the family in their youth, so their world remains small. I'm different, rougher. So in this marriage, I make her world bigger and she makes mine smaller. The trend nowadays is to wish for a big world, but then you lose your sense of belonging. Just like my friend in Maastricht. But again, one is challenged when one's world shrinks. The writer in me can only allow it so much; I can't always distance myself. I'm too involved.'

'What you're saying is that varied perceptions have to be accommodated.'

'Yeah-yeah. Most people have an idea that Life is about seeking comfort and happiness. But I like my life right now because it's not very logical. My Dutch friends find it hard to comprehend. I tell them that if people remain logical all the time, the world wouldn't change.'

'You have Dutch friends here?'

'There's been a Dutch club in Bangalore for fifteen years. And I'm the only member who's married an Indian. So in many ways my experiences differ from theirs. They get cheated here all the time, but Lalitha ensures that it doesn't happen to me. She does the dirty work for me. Like when I wanted to buy a PC, I went and finalised a model while she waited outside the shop. Then she went in and closed the deal for much less than what they had quoted me. See what I mean?'

I do. *The price of a product depends on the pocket of the purchaser.* 'But surely there's a happy side to being an outsider?' I ask.

'Yeah-yeah. It's nice to be special, get attention. And luxury. You see so many expatriates being chauffeured around. Back home, hardly any of them can afford a driver.'

'All in all, would you say Bangalore is a swell place to live in?'

'Bangalore is an excellent place to break a toe.' He laughs. 'Yeah, it's exciting to be part of a rapidly changing city, a very confident city. Culturally, it may be low-key… but did I mention that it's a damn neat place to break a toe? Ever since I broke it, life has been getting better for me!'

'You feel you can achieve your head-heart balance in Bangalore?' I ask.

'Well, maybe twenty years from now, it might become a mundane, moneyed city. The problem with materialism is that when you catch it, you want to have, have, have. Already family life has become less important. That's scary and I hope India retains its spiritual identity, and remains an example for the rest of the world. Like what Gandhi wanted.

But fifty years after Gandhi, nobody is even talking about his message. Even now, Indians are very spiritual. You can see it, feel it. But they can be quite aggressive too. I find that a profound contradiction.' He pauses, and then reflects on a connection that isn't easily grasped. 'It would be a pity if the whole world just develops in the aspects of dancing and drinking while there's still so much misery.'

I collate the angst in his views and redirect it to a more personal topic. Doesn't he ache for home? Or more specifically, for the established idea of home, which is more elusive than home itself? Before he answers, his eyes go soft.

'Wasn't it Georgy Konrad,' he says, 'who said the best emigrant is one who believes that everything he has left behind is tasteless, immoral crap? That's what I try to believe. Now, the problem with the outsider is that nobody in his new country asked him to come. So he has to show a good profile to his adopted people. Not too much as to invoke jealousy, but good enough. But I still have strong, enduring ties with my homeland – the language I write in and my Toe-2-Heart Foundation. Of course, there's my family. Having lived outside for ages, the ties have become a bit loose, paramount as they are. The truth is that people get used to your not being around. In a way, you have died a little bit. But when something happens, sickness or even death involving a friend or family, I'll feel lost here. In the long term, I'll always be a bit torn apart between two cultures. I accept it as my destiny and something I have to experience. But for how long, I can't say at the moment.'

I want to give the story a more conclusive end, so I ask him a direct question.

'Are you going to settle in India?'

It doesn't startle him.

'That's the plan,' he says. 'But I'm taking it a day at a time. Each day, I live through heavenly visual delights and hellish pollution and traffic and bureaucracy. I'm learning to respect authority for its own sake. By night, I get drained confronting the world and myself. So I've taken to praying. It helps me keep my balance.'

I try a mental summary of Thomas. A writer, a social worker, an adventurer who has ventured into a unique marriage with open arms, a translator for now, a humanist at heart, a practising philosopher and a sentimentalist who still keeps his worn-out soccer shoes in the cupboard for old times' sake.

'I wish you'd stay back,' I tell him.

He concludes in typical van Berckel fashion.

'All I can say is that I'm happy to have this corner in Kamanahalli and an Indian wife to go home to.'

I realise that one can ask for little more. I promise to pay another visit once the child is born and say goodbye. As I rev my engine, it strikes me that Max is the most appropriate dog for this family. A Dalmatian. Black on white. A furry white coat dotted with a unique black pattern that, perhaps, holds a family secret. Now, what could that be? True love? Or maybe it is an encrypted game of tic-tac-toe in which everybody wins.

Bangalore Safari

A week after I meet Thomas, my fingers are numb due to the incessant thumbing of the directory and the punching of numbers on the phone. Contacts are hard to come by. I get a whiff of a European involved in aviation and follow my nose only to find it slammed by a closing door. An Indonesian student assumes I'm a telemarketer and bangs down the phone. A Japanese translator working in an MNC is evidently disappointed that I'm not seeking weekend language lessons.

All in all, a bad week. I'm desperate. They are wary. Instead of imitation carpets, I might be selling them a plausible idea with the intent of swigging coffee or beer at their expense. And then, perhaps, I would lie in wait for further windfalls. That is why the databases maintained by bodies such as the Indo British Partnership and the Indo American Chamber of Commerce are sacred. Not to be shared. Some promise to help in other ways. But...

Click. Slam.

A disconnected line and a closing door sound the same. Of course, they are absolutely correct in being cautious. But where does that leave me? After thinking up numerous schemes, each more bizarre than the one before, I finally do something concrete. I call the Indian Council of Cultural Relations (ICCR), which oversees the student exchange programme. A gentleman named Venugopal answers politely and invites me for a chat.

The next day, as soon as the rush hour winds down, I head for Sankey Road. But at the City Post Office signal, my path is blocked. A traffic cop is manoeuvring the traffic into a detour via Cunningham Road. An auto-rickshaw driver riding beside me provides the reason for the blockade. Staunch Kannadigas are voicing a demand that the release of non-Kannada films be delayed by three weeks. They feel that this will help the ailing local film industry make money. Meanwhile, meetings are being held in other cities in Karnataka, and requests to reserve jobs for Kannadigas in the state government are being conveyed to the authorities. The mood seems to be: let the son of the soil till the land before others.

And we aren't even talking about foreigners.

Kannadigas are normally the most peaceful and the least vociferous among Indians. They have been an amiable foil to their volatile neighbours in Tamil Nadu, and have made few linguistic demands. But here they are, indulging in a show of strength. Is Bangalore's rapidly changing

---

Smashing Idea, This!

When the immensely popular Kannada actor Rajkumar was kidnapped, ardent fans went on a rampage. Some city eateries came up with a novel method to prevent their glass panes from being smashed: they pasted large photographs of the star over them.

And, of course, it worked!

demographics making them feel insecure? Or are they simply catching up with an unruly world? Perhaps the people I meet will provide an answer.

I shrug and reconcile myself to a three-kilometre detour via Cunningham Road, towards the Cantonment Station and then back to Sankey Road from under the Windsor Manor bridge. Upon reaching the ICCR, I apologise to Venugopal for being late. It isn't necessary. He welcomes me to his sparse office and says:

'I love meeting diverse people.'

'Well, that must be a definite asset in your job. How long have you served the ICCR?'

'Eighteen years,' he replies, 'the last seven of them in Bangalore.'

'And what kind of changes have you seen in that duration?'

'The number of students is increasing,' he says. 'It's much cheaper to get a quality education in India. And thanks to the IT revolution, more students come to Bangalore to study "silicon" subjects.' He rattles off the places from where the students hail. It reads like an unsorted list of countries under the UN banner. After a pause, he says: 'Quite a few of them would also like to stay back and work here. A Bangladeshi joined an American multinational a few days back and doesn't want to leave.'

Don't inform those protestors, sir, I think. It doesn't matter that the boom in the industry appears poised to absorb not just a Bangladeshi, but the whole of Bangladesh. But even otherwise, foreigners snatching Indian jobs seems such a First World problem. It *sounds* like a step in the right direction.

'Are such success stories a regular feature?' I ask.

'Last week, someone called from New York thanking ICCR for the opportunities it had provided him,' he says.

Pithy. I ask him another.

'Other than overseeing the student exchange programme, what does the ICCR do?'

'Well, we are a channel for showcasing foreign cultures here and Indian culture abroad. In fact, we're planning a bash on 11 December. It's the birthday of Maulana Azad, the freedom fighter and founding father of ICCR. We call it the International Students' Day.'

At this point, he picks up the phone and dials the number of a Kenyan gentleman named Patrick, the President of FISA-B, or Federation of International Students Association – Bangalore. When Venugopal passes me the receiver, I'm mildly surprised. If I ignore the slight accent, Patrick sounds like an Indian who talks at an unusually slow speed. He has spent twelve long years here. He sounds friendly over the phone.

And he is willing to meet me.

* * *

The Public Relations wing at the Sri Bhagawan Mahaveer Jain College is a single room strewn with computer terminals and yuppie students immersed in what's on the screen and what's blaring from a nearby speaker. The latter happens to be Bollywood hits at the moment. Since I don't see an African in the room, I enquire about John Patrick Ojwando and a student named Shreyas tells me "Pats" will be back soon.

'How do you know Pats?' I ask.

'He's almost an elder brother to us here,' says Shreyas.

I cannot decide if Shreyas means it or has been inspired by the Bollywood music. He goes on to tell me that Patrick is a man for every crisis, a great counsellor, fun to argue with, is known for his innovative ideas and has the ability to be completely neutral.

'He's more open than I am,' he concludes.

There. I feel I have a head start over Patrick. It is just as well because he soon walks in with his mouth filled with glucose biscuits and says:

'I can't afford lunch. So...' he points to his mouth. 'Surprised?'

It would take me months to realise that Patrick couches both his humour and earnestness in a deadpan look. And he often combines the two, leaving the listener thoroughly confused.

'I'm a big puri-bhaji fan,' he continues, 'but I find it difficult to eat any other Indian food. So... biscuits, chocolates and Fantas for lunch. You wouldn't guess I used to play soccer, would you?'

I wouldn't, I decide, looking at his generous midriff. My gaze then shifts to other salient features. Long fingers that end appropriately in large, fleshy hands. A head that is a few millimetres shy of a tonsure... but even in its scantiness, his hair retains its curls.

'My workday is not quite over,' says Patrick breaking into my thoughts. 'Perhaps you can begin the interview here while I work.'

I take a seat and ask:

'What do you do here?'

'I create content for the institute's newsletters and websites. The honorarium I'm paid for it sustains me. So... what do you want to know?'

'Let's begin at the beginning,' I say.

'Well,' he says, 'I'm the third in a family of four boys and four girls. I come from Kisumu in West Kenya. It's the third city in Kenya, after Nairobi and Mombasa. The rest are mere towns.'

Although in India, he is known as Patrick or its variations, in Kisumu, he is John. His parents, he says, gave him a

Catholic upbringing and sent him to an appropriate primary school.

'It's very interesting,' he says, using his trademark phrase. 'After primary school, both they and I assumed that I have a scientific bent of mind. So in secondary school, I studied Mechanical Engineering as an optional subject for two years before better sense prevailed. My natural inclination is towards the Arts... I was probably too young to recognise my calling in my innate passion for writing.'

'Do you have a natural inclination to travel as well?' I ask.

'Yes,' he says. 'Undoubtedly the backpacker in me helped make the journey to India, but it did not initiate it.'

'What did?'

'Education in Kenya is very expensive,' he says. 'So, many begin dropping out right from primary school for economic or other reasons. When the time came, I chose to continue my graduation studies in India and it has worked well for me.'

It was a different India he landed in, way back in 1992. The economy was just opening up and Udaipur in distant Rajasthan wasn't exactly the place to measure the effects of liberalisation. But that is where he did his B.A. with Sociology, English Literature and Public Administration as his subjects.

'I first landed in Mumbai,' says Patrick, 'and feared it on sight...the people are in such a hurry every moment... run to the office, run back home... it reminded me of Nairobi. Even Udaipur wasn't as laid-back as one might expect. But I found my peace in Bangalore. It's laid-back, secure and friendly.'

'Why did you come to Bangalore?' I ask.

'I wanted to do my Master's in Communications; I was looking for a place that has plenty of English newspapers. Rajasthan didn't fit the bill. South India, I felt, was apt for my pursuit.'

'Why not Chennai, then?'

'The weather is too hot for my liking!! Bangalore is just right.'

Again, Bangalore in '95 was a few generations removed from today's economic bustle and muscle. He dug his heels into the city and completed his Master's by '97. Although he hadn't seen home for five years, he felt India had something more to offer. A doctorate. Unfortunately, the same year, the government decreed that a simple student visa wouldn't do for students aspiring to do their Ph.D. Patrick had to get a research visa. Moreover, his father had retired and had serious doubts about a doctorate.

'Enough with it already, John! You're thirty now. Get your arse back home where it belongs and think about a vocation that'll add funds to the family coffers instead of the other way around!'

I admit that the kind Ojwando Sr. did not put it quite like that, but he said something along those lines and encountered a son who respectfully disagreed. Patrick even found a likely research position in the Mysore University. Now he had two problems: visa and funds. While the latter seemed more serious, in reality it was the other way around. Patrick ended up spending *more than two years* battling for a research visa. Why?

'It's interesting,' says Patrick.

It really is:

- The police wanted to see his research visa and a bona fide certificate of admission from the university before they would renew his permit.
- The university asked for a research visa before they would issue a bona fide certificate.
- And completing the circle was the Home Ministry in New Delhi that asked for a bona fide certificate before issuing a research visa.

A classic deadlock. It cost an innocent man in the prime of his life two years and some months.

'And nobody was willing to budge,' he recalls.

Finally, his guide gave him a letter. But then, he had to wait for one of her seven students to complete his doctorate before she could accommodate him! Patrick persevered. No wonder it annoys him to find people giving up their quest because they encounter obstacles. Today he is thirty-seven years old and just as determined a student as he was a decade back. And he is just as much in love with the college atmosphere. Give him a college festival, a young crowd, some noise and he will revel in it. He will even cover it for a newspaper like the *Hindu*, the *Deccan Herald* or the *New Indian Express*, all of which employ him as a freelancer. Looking at Patrick, I get the feeling that he has a happy-go-lucky streak in him, something that Shreyas describes as "languourous, but not exactly lazy".

Patrick has completed his official tasks. So we take lethargic steps, move out of the campus and occupy an unused bus stop in A. N. Krishna Rao Road. A nearby college loosens its vice-like grip on students for the day, and immediately the quiet tree-lined avenue assumes the air of a fair. Overgrown brats rev their bikes for fun and attention. Girls linger around to measure their popularity. One young couple particularly interests me. The girl with lovely brown eyes is looking away from the boy, into the setting sun. Something has gone so wrong that I feel the vibes on the other side of the street. The boy ventures an explanation; she snubs him and looks again at the light. She blinks an inchoate tear away and her lips sag a little.

'All I'm thinking of right now is completing my Ph.D by next year,' Patrick says.

Languourous, but not exactly lazy. I try to visualise Patrick's life. He lives with his girlfriend Joy in Kengeri

Satellite Town, some distance away from the city. He is researching the "Treatment of Development News Issues in the Print Media" in Mysore University while scraping a living in Bangalore. And: he is thirty-seven! I feel admiration for him, for his ability to fight against time while pursuing a lonely quest. Does he feel homesick? I try to ascertain this with an oblique question:

'When India plays Kenya, whom do you support?' I ask.

'No confusions there. Kenya, of course.' Patrick clarifies his point further. 'I keep telling guys here that no Indian plays for Kenya. Kenyans of Indian origin do.'

'Who's your favourite cricketer?' I ask.

'Brian Lara. I love to see the West Indies cricketers; they enjoy their cricket. The Aussies are too clinical.'

'And your favourite film star?'

'I hardly watch films. My all-time favourite idol is Thierry Henry.'

Hmm. Opens up an *interesting* topic. Dark-skinned people who have been hurt by racism tend to have dark-skinned superheroes. I ponder over this and peer at the changed situation across the road. Whatever sweet nothings the boy has murmured into the girl's ears have worked. She shares a laugh with him that brings the stars back in her eyes. She has regained her superhero.

I feel hungry and pull Patrick towards a snack joint. I order a Student Burger, hoping it would make me feel younger. Patrick orders cheese toast. I ask the taboo question as we await our food:

'Have you had racist experiences?'

He hesitates a moment, I cajole him to bare all. Slowly, he opens up.

'Well, I've had interesting encounters on the bus. See, people don't expect foreigners to travel in them and even the conductor has a funny, local quip ready for you. Mostly, being black is the issue. People call me *kalia* (black) or *kothi* (monkey). Many people just stare ...I've learnt to ignore it.'

It comes as no surprise to me. After all, India is the land of fairness cream companies.

'But how do you control your anger?' I ask, biting into the unappetising burger.

'This is life for every African in the city,' he says. 'What do you do? I used to get angry. And fight. Once, I and my friend were waiting in a bus stop in Mysore. The man standing next to us was entertaining his wife by his continuous mocking. She was enjoying it thoroughly, was laughing like crazy. It soon became obvious that he was referring to us. Finally we confronted him. The wife immediately began crying and attracted a crowd. When the situation turned tense, we started running. We rushed into a police station nearby, but the mob chased us even there. They accosted the duty inspector and insisted on pressing charges. The cop, after hearing both sides of the story, decided to let the matter drop. But the incident shocked me speechless. If the cop had been any different... do you wonder I'm careful now?'

'So what do you do now?' I ask.

'Mostly ignore... In the initial days I got a lot of help from an NGO named Samvada. Its Director Anita Ratnam had faced similar discrimination as a Master's student in the UK. And catharsis is a good option. I wrote an article on racism titled "The Hostile Dark Side of Hospitality" and got it published in the *Deccan Herald* in '97. The editor wanted numerous confirmations from me before he published it. My friends were worried too – about the possibility of a backlash once the article appeared.'

I ask him about a different backlash that's happening in the city. He replies:

'The Kannada Rakshana Vedike's censorship of non-Kannada movies brings forth a bigger issue,' he says. 'In any setting, locals see the aliens as taking things away from them. Like jobs and security. They never see what they add to society. I cannot understand why we don't fight to compete. Here the Kannadigas are fighting for their identity. Someone, somewhere else will fight for his language and face. In that place, a Kannadiga will suffer. In an open society this is disastrous. The same is happening back in Kenya. The Indian community there is quite strong. They're way more successful due to their hard work. But they're not open. I never could relate to them, even as classmates. You don't find a Patrick and a Hari going out together in Kenya. And it irks some of the locals.'

The theme seems to be universal. Expatriates stick to their own kind in an attempt to create a flavour as close as possible to the one they left behind. Sometimes, passage of generations does nothing to change this. Nothing wrong with that per se, as long as the demarcation remains innocent and doesn't invite resentment.

'But I've seen positives in India too,' continues Patrick. 'Many families invite us for dinners and weddings. This Diwali, the World Organisation of Students and Youth – that's the international student wing of ABVP – invited FISA-B to participate in a cultural event and dinner. Organisations like the International Cultural Youth Exchange and Voluntary Service never miss an opportunity to shower the international student community with their generosity. And – I find saviours in the same buses where I get assaulted. They defend me when others jeer, or at least let me know that not everyone is as mean. Some even offer me a cup of coffee!

'In fact I've been the recipient of greater acts of Indian kindness. In 2002, when my sister passed away, a few Indian friends sponsored my trip and enabled me to attend the funeral. Why, even my first return trip to Kenya in 1998 was sponsored by a couple of Indian friends. Such events confirm one's faith in friendship.'

It is just as well that his faith has been reaffirmed. A disillusioned Patrick couldn't have held the FISA-B fort together. Since it is his third one-year term as president, and twelfth as a student in India, there is probably no one with more experience for the job. In the entire country! Patrick often needs every ounce of his experience to counsel fellow students. And although their Kengeri residence is modest, he and Joy keep it open as an acclimatisation ground for new students.

'The worst problem is death,' says Patrick.

'What do you mean?' I ask.

'Students have died in my tenure. From road accidents or illnesses like tuberculosis, jaundice and HIV/AIDS… all issues that one associates with unmonitored youth. And then there's the third-year syndrome.' That requires some explanation and Patrick gives it. 'The trend we observe is that parents promptly remit money for the first two years. Often, the third year ushers in financial silence. Scores of letters evoke no response. What does a student do? He isn't even allowed to earn. I went through the same thing at Udaipur when my dad had a bad accident. It was the turning point in my life. I realised I had to do something for myself. So I now use my pen to survive. But what of those who don't have a marketable skill?'

Fund-raising, that's what. For example, when a student became mentally deranged recently, the fraternity and well-wishers pooled money to pay a two-month NIMHANS bill. *There are good reasons why birds of a feather flock together.*

After a long stint, Patrick understandably wants to pass on control of the FISA-B flock to someone else. And concentrate on other things. I ask him about his long-term plans again. He replies:

'I'm quite open to life's interventions ahead. I've no regrets so far about being a perennial student, but it's time to shed that tag. I want to go back home, although I'll still be the born traveller who thinks of home merely as a place for pillow and head to meet. However, the diversity of India is such that one needn't really see any other place after being here. I'm a foreigner here, but also a localite. I belong to Udaipur, Bangalore and Mysore in parts. And all this while, a part of me has been re-looking at my own country as an outsider. These perspectives will help me.'

'You'll be grateful to leave?' I ask.

'Grateful to leave, as I'm grateful to be here. I've participated in a media industry that's a lot bigger than in Kenya. And I learnt a lot in the informal settings of the *Times of India* during my internship. In every way, India has shaped my writing. I believe that wherever you are, you have to keep a sharp lookout for blessings. For instance, I could meet a Kenyan Vice-Chancellor when he came for a visit here, but he wasn't available for an appointment when I went back home...blessings are strange creatures.'

Strange indeed. I will count a new blessing tonight – this encounter. As I take leave of Patrick, I have no doubt that I will meet him again. The President of FISA-B is a handy man to have around when a clueless writer is looking for contacts.

Continental Drifting

'You'll love her,' says Patrick Ojwando. 'Sue's the name. She's a Trinidadian and a restaurateur.'

I take Sue's number, give her a call and am greeted by a singsong voice. When I tell her about my book, she invites me to visit her restaurant in Indiranagar. It is situated in a small alley off the Krishna Temple Road, which has, over the last two years, been transformed from a sleepy thoroughfare to a bustling marketplace. Close to the junction where callous shoppers double-park their cars and block traffic, I see the name, Sue's Place, written above a red-brick façade.

I enter the restaurant to a jangling of bells and ask for Sue. I wait by the bakery section and breathe the rich aroma of plum cake. Soon, a short, plump lady comes out from the kitchen and says, 'Hi! I'm Sue.' Her dazzling smile and mellifluous voice alone would set her apart from the hawkish breed of hoteliers. On top of that, she has a distinctive face.

Her skin isn't dark but in her features I see a hint of something that is... maybe African? I cannot decide.

Since it is not quite lunchtime, we easily find a vacant table. Once we are seated, she asks:

'So what would you like to know?'

I choose a broad warm-up question.

'How do you find India?'

'Oh, India is such a *paradox*. I tell you, I long to go home all the time, but the moment I reach there, I want to come *back*,' she says.

Yes, she stresses the last word of each sentence, so that it rhymes and rhythms with the music in her heart. And the moment I mention music, she is up and running towards the boom-box. She arrives back at the table accompanied by a melody that fills the air.

'Have you heard calypso before? Oh, it is so *Trinidadian*, I tell you; it's part of that *soil*. Most outsiders don't have a ear for it.' She pauses. 'There's this beautiful song by a calypsonian singer... he's a half-and-half... has an Indian and an African parent. He says: *When my mother/ father go back to India/Africa, they'll have to split me in two.*'

I'm aware of the Caribbean reputation for startling racial mixes. And since Sue looks like a racial mix herself, I inquire about her parentage.

'Oh, you won't believe it, *dear*,' she says, 'but I have a brother with yellow skin, Chinese eyes and an otherwise African face. And one of my sisters is so, *so* Hispanic. Our family has Spanish, Indian, African and Chinese blood. But we siblings feel we're so much like each other. And we grew up not knowing racism.'

Diversity begins at home? Well, it apparently has the potential to do so. In my imagination, I see someone with Sue's background announcing her pregnancy. And her family giving a twist to the banal boy-girl debate by speculating about the baby's looks.

'I bet it will be an African-Spanish girl,' says the father-to-be.

'Oh, out with you! It's surely going to be an Indian-Chinese boy!' replies the grandmother-to-be.

Sue breaks my trance.

'But a few Trinidadians, of Indian origin mainly, are becoming very aware of their race and segregating themselves.'

The talk slowly turns to the most famous Trinidadian Indian.

'Oh, Naipaul doesn't know where he's *from*,' says Sue. 'He can't find himself, dear. Have you read *An Area of Darkness*? Read it, and you'll know what he thinks of Indians. And ironically, some Indians want to claim him as their own.'

'That didn't go well with him, I believe.'

She shakes her head.

'I tell you, Indians are so star-struck! Do you know that Mervyn Dillon, the Caribbean pace bowler, had the naivety to assume he can stroll down Brigade Road? And – naturally! – he was mobbed back into his cab.'

'Speaking of cricketers, tell me about those photographs,' I say, pointing towards the billing counter. Sue beams. It is her favourite story.

'You know, we went to the Chinnaswamy stadium to watch a three-day match featuring the West Indies,' she says. 'Obviously our small group was the only one cheering the visiting Caribbeans and the team took note of that. We got introduced and they said they'll drop in here and have some authentic home food. I tell you, it's the highlight of this hotel's *existence*. I couldn't believe it. I came fluttering in here to announce: "The boys are coming! *The boys are coming!*"'

I laugh.

'Evidently,' I say, 'your favourite snap is the one where you're with Vivian Richards – the staff has not dared paste a business announcement over it.'

Were such a thing possible, I would swear that Sue's smile broadened. She says: 'When he kissed me, I said, "*Oh my God! I'm not washing my face again!*" It was so exciting, I tell you. And the boys were so cool... it's a trait the small islands have given them. I cannot think of Indian stars being so comfortable; they lack that luxury. Come to think of it, I guess I've amassed a little bit of Indianness myself. When I go back now, I'm wary of strangers coming up and conversing. But that's how people are at home.'

It is not surprising that she has adopted Indian virtues and vices. After all, she first came here in 1978! I ask her if she recalls having transition blues. The answer is a descriptive *Yes*.

'Oh, the vastness of this country is *overwhelming*. Especially so for a girl from an island of two million. My father gave me the best advice when I left: *They won't change; you'll have to*. So true...! I made adjustments, not least of all controlling my unlicensed, blabbering Caribbean mouth.'

'You're saying that frank and open behaviour isn't appreciated in India?'

'Dear, Indians are warm people. Having studied in England – a cold country with cold-shouldering people – I ought to know. But trusting Indians is walking a tightrope. In fact, I learnt to dislike people only after coming here. But to be fair, it could have happened in Trinidad had I not left it when I was so young.'

'What did you do in Trinidad before you first came to India?' I ask.

'Oh, I had a TV cookery show, *dear*.'

'You what?'

'It was called *Saucy Sue – Indian Delicacies*. Quite successful it was too. And in a small place, enough to make me a mini-star.'

Ah! Sue, the Star. That fits. I can believe it happening in "overwhelming" India as well. But …

'Indian delicacies? You got hooked onto India even before you set foot here?'

Seeing my point, she laughs.

'There's so much detail in Indian food; even the manner in which it is served is ritualistic. And the *variety*! But I'll be damned if I can get my cook to wear an apron. Speaking of adjustments, how's this – I dress like an Indian, I *try* to talk like one, I perform pooja and whatnot to fit in. Why, I even shake and nod my head while speaking (something I have to unlearn at my cousin's place in London on my way to Trinidad). Yet I'm not one of them. You see what I'm saying? I hate to be here. I love to be here. It's an *amazing* country, dear.'

'At least it seems to have suited you.'

'Oh, yes. I have a lovely home tied to a lovely business. A nice husband, smart daughters who got an education unthinkable in Trinidad… In fact, one of my daughters has become the Secretary of her Trinidadian company in a short time and she owes it to her Indian education. But there's a flip side to the success of Indian children – they get very serious at a tender age. They miss all the fun, dear.'

A couple of customers working for an IT company stop by to tell Sue how much they enjoyed the food and service. Once they leave, Sue tells me, 'The new generation is so affable and *refreshing*. They know what they're all about and it shows in their faces.'

'Perhaps that's because of enormous changes in the past fifteen years or so?' I ask.

'I can vouch for that. When I came, one couldn't find cheese or cornflakes in the market. Now, I not just have them, I have *choices*.'

John, her husband, passes us by and Sue stops him for an introduction. She then excuses herself to go on her rounds. She walks around tables, pats shoulders, ascertains food quality, enquires about life and work, and smiles incessantly. I sip my coconut water mixed with herbs and take the opportunity to pick John's brains. In his hurry, all he can give me is a quip:

'There's no cultural synthesis with foreigners coming here.'

That sums up what we've discussed so far. Now I feel like probing the other side. Surely Trinidad, Sue's sunny island, has a few warts? So when she comes back, I enquire about the problems India has helped her escape.

'I'm glad my children are drug free,' she replies. 'In Trinidad, almost every home has a druggie.'

'How's that?' I ask.

'It's an oil-producing nation, dear. Then there's tourism and sugarcane. You find wealth and so you find drugs. Also, the problem partially is that we're big copycats of America. That's one aspect of the story. The other is that my country has much poverty in the countryside that we're blind to.'

Amidst all this, the calypso is still swaying our minds. A song ends and another begins. Sue seamlessly integrates music into her next thought.

'The reason I opened this place is because it merges three of my loves – cooking, music and meeting people.'

I've sampled the last two, so I urge her to tell me about culinary challenges. She rolls her eyes, thinking about the bad days she has survived.

'When I began, I didn't know my arse from my elbow about running a restaurant! But those who attended the parties I threw kept goading me to open one. I finally took the plunge. John designed the place. We ferried cement in our Fiat and even broke bricks. One day the place was ready but we had no licence. I left John to deal with it and flew to Trinidad. While there, I worked in a restaurant for three weeks. Quit, went to New York, worked for two weeks. Quit, went to London, worked some more. By the time I had garnered some experience, the licence was ready. I came home, and told the staff: *"Boys, we're ready*!"'

They weren't because—

'I want to serve Trinidadian home food in a home environment. There's nothing commercial about what you eat at Sue's Place' – except the bill, I guess – 'but the professional cook I hired brought about a tandoori hybridism I loathed. So I fired him, and hired boys who hadn't seen a kitchen before. I didn't want people wasting time and effort unlearning. Even the servers were inexperienced.'

'And you seem to have pulled it off,' I say, as I hear the door swing open yet again.

'For twenty-three months after I began,' she says, 'I cooked *all day long*. That was the time when a new restaurant opened in Indiranagar every day. So I had to slog to keep adrift.'

Successful though she is now, Sue has not slackened her pace. She tells me that she wakes up at 5.30 a.m. to begin baking for the day. Bread, cakes, puddings, pies and even vegetables flit in and out of her home oven in an endless stream. Yes, she does her baking at home. Her infrastructural arrangements, in fact, retain a charming amateurism. For instance, refrigeration equipment is inadequate in her hotel. So meat, vegetables and other commodities are passed from hotel to home and back, through myriad processes, before they plonk on the customer's plate. Amazingly, it all works.

'Yes, it's going well now,' says Sue. 'We're almost booked solid for our Christmas meals. I'm so excited about it.'

She shows me a large notice next to a smiling Richards. It lists the menu for Christmas Day lunch and dinner. There is duck, there is pork... I read the endless list till I reach:

'...Jamaican Jerk Chicken? Where does the term come from?'

Sue laughs and a twinkle appears in her eye.

'I don't know, dear. It was probably invented by a jerk and there are so many of them in Jamaica, *believe you me*.'

I laugh. Sue retains her homeland citizenship, frequently lisps "they" into "dey" and is not averse to taking a friendly dig at Jamaicans. It fits. And it allows me an opening for a taunt.

'How is it that the Caribbean islands come together only for cricket and nothing else?'

'India,' replies Sue, 'has unified sports teams because of geopolitical integration. But then, India has not rid itself of linguistic, religious and casteist segregation. So you win some, you lose some.'

'Touché!' I mutter to myself.

I look around and find that the crowd has thickened. I seem to have divined the reason behind Sue's recent abstracted behaviour. So I elicit a promise from her to meet me again after Christmas and take her leave. The bell above the door rings me out.

* * *

Vigyan Nagar is a suburban colony that embodies Bangalore Unplanned. But it is one place in the city that doesn't have bad roads. Yes, half a mile before one reaches it, a horribly patchy road gives way to a rollercoaster. I would highly recommend it to gynaecologists who wish to induce labour. So not surprisingly, both my motorbike and I are rattled by the time we reach the office of an NGO named Equations, which stands for Equitable Tourism Options. Inside the office I find a cherubic girl who remains fixated on her monitor, oblivious of intruders. She is Claudia Romiti, an Italian who studies in a Swedish Institute and is currently undergoing a short internship at Equations. The most noticeable thing about Claudia is her open face that trusts objects to measure up to impressions. She agrees to be interviewed and we move to a small library filled with books on activism. I begin by asking how she feels about India.

'The first two weeks were terrible,' she says. 'I was shocked. Everything's different here, be it lifestyle or social structure. But now I feel that if I have to live in Bangalore, I can.'

'Wonderful. What brought you here?' I ask.

'I'm writing a report on the positive and negative impact of tourists upon environments, economies and ethics,' she replies.

What could possibly go wrong when tourists infuse blood into local economies? Equations is probably the right place to seek an answer to that question. Over the last two decades, this NGO has been fighting a gamut of issues that includes physical and professional displacement, loss of identity, loss of access to resources such as water, environmental damage, cultural erosion, exploitation of women, child labour, child trafficking and child sex tourism.

The stark issue of child sex tourism was brought to the forefront by the Freddy Peats case in Goa. Peats actually gives a sinister dimension to the presence of expatriates in India. He used to run a vast paedophilia racket and was so successful in masking his intentions that Goan moms were known to phone and request him to coax their children to sleep. Today, Peats remains an inspiration to generations of paedophiles who haunt prime tourist locations in the country. And he is just one of the monsters Equations is fighting against. Even a rudimentary study of the work done by this NGO convinces one that it requires a strong stomach and deep commitment. And it is not a matter to be glossed over. So I skip asking Claudia about her job, but come up with a question that deals with her personal interests as well as her current role.

An excerpt from an Equations write-up, aimed at mobilising people to act upon tourism issues.

Kochu's Life
What is India's answer to Mauritius?

Kovalam. The answer is clear as the brine in the beach that is Kovalam. The humblest website describes the locale in exotic, luring terms. The once sleepy fishing hamlet just sixteen km from the state capital is now a thriving tourist destination. A few lagoons nestle in its shores, tall palm trees sway in divine stupor and a tropical sun bakes clean sand into a mesmerising shimmer. Nature has been doped into unblemished beauty; no wonder the long-haired hippy rushed to claim it in the seventies.

Since then, supply-chain management techniques have taken over. The tourist is fussy. He prefers things just so. Just so it would become then. Water skiing, kayaking, windsurfing – what's your take? Or would you rather prefer parasailing? There's a lifeguard at hand, should anything go amiss. Country rafts await you, to take you offshore for a silent sunset, or to let you gaze at magnificent corals in the shallows. *Where there is demand, there would be supply. (Old Kovalam saying.)*

Explore the options at leisure. There are a few shocking ones lurking in the shadows. You've heard of the famous ayurvedic massages. Somebody just forgot to mention that sometimes, the hands that give them belong to seven-year olds. Kochu, the one that peddles you his service is that young. Observe – if your stomach can handle it. Applying scented oils on skimpily clad bodies may not be the only act he is up to.

The urchin rotates his gaze. With eyes that lack curiosity. A man, a domestic tourist by the looks of it, approaches him. Gives him a few sweet words, a

'Have you travelled in India?' I ask.

'Of course!' she says, 'As part of my job, I've travelled extensively in the last two months. I've been to Halebid, Belur, Shravanabelagola, Kerala and Mysore. And I've myself had a bad experience as a tourist... I was in Mysore during the Dashera festival, participating in the elephant parade. And... I didn't know women had a separate section...'

Men fondled her, crushed her against them. Till she managed to get out of their midst. If an independent woman

---

toothy smile. The lad has seen it all before. If the gentleman asks his company for a "walk", he won't refuse. Sigh! You're happy that the sequel is performed away from your shocked eyes.

What drives Kochu to this point? Poverty? Lack of opportunities? Dysfunctional family? All of the above is generally a good answer. Kochu is in a rut he defines as LIFE. If you catch up with him later and coax him, he might just give you his story. Especially if you carry a candy.

That's the reason he prefers foreigners. Not only do they give him chocolates, toys and (sometimes) nice clothes, they also pay a far sight better. Of course, they ought to be pleased. Then they might even have your house renovated and spend a pleasant couple of months in the company of very many children. If they are dissatisfied, they aren't averse to giving a sound beating.

Somehow, it all evens out. The thrashing and the toy. One can become the other too.

Where there is demand, there would be supply. (Old Kovalam saying.)

Demand comes from various quarters. There are a few five-star hotels sprinkled around. Associated with adult prostitutes, pimps, taxi-drivers and many more middlemen who are only too eager to act as the conduit between the esteemed tourist and Kochu.

Students from Karnataka think little of making an overnight journey to Kovalam for a weekend fiesta. Kochu isn't their meal of fare. But his sister is...

It promises to be a short, eventful life for Kochu.

could be so molested, then what would be the fate of vulnerable eight-year-olds? Thankfully the incident has not blinded Claudia to the charms of India. She has been to the *Bangalore Habba* ("*habba*" in Kannada means "festival") and has allowed herself to be mesmerised by Pandit Shivkumar Sharma's music.

'In places like the *Habba*, one can *feel* the Indian culture,' she says. 'You find happiness and curiosity. Indians seem to smile all the time. Even here in Vigyan Nagar,' she says pointing outside, 'the poverty-stricken find reason to smile while walking on bad roads. In Europe, lack of money leads to depression. Indians, on the other hand, decide to work for money.'

That is high praise coming from someone who has travelled extensively – to Japan, Australia, America, Puerto Rico and of course, much of Europe – in between taking up numerous jobs to support her education.

'Before this, I worked in a call centre,' she says. 'But I also campaign for causes. I've tried to enrol members for Greenpeace... And in Sweden, I play in a band that uses music to convey social messages. We even collaborated with the Gothenburg Social Forum and a few of my friends went to Brazil to interact with children.'

'What do you play in the band?' I ask.

'An agogo and drums.'

I look agog. She laughs.

'An agogo is a samba instrument having two bells that you beat with a stick.'

'A peon in my school played something similar to mark the end of the day,' I say. 'He was very popular. But seriously, have you always had the activist streak in you?'

She thinks about this.

'Well, I'm a confirmed leftist and you can quote me on that. It's that outlook which brings me to the NGO industry. In Italy, we've not forgiven or forgotten the right-wing Nazis and Fascists. My grandfather was forced to fight the war for Mussolini. Even today, I find right-wingers making many mistakes. The EU is supposedly trying to flatten the landscape. Eastern European countries like Poland are gaining and we're losing. People have started asking: "*Why*?" My father is quite fed up with the way Europe is shaping up. He nowadays dreams of settling in India.'

My ears perk up and I ignore the discrepancy of a leftist disagreeing with a flat landscape.

'Really? Is he staying with you? Good. Tell me a little about him.'

As I listen, I know one thing for sure – I will meet Franco Romiti. I have only one question left for Claudia, to which she responds:

'I'll definitely come back to India one day.'

* * *

I meet Miller (name changed) while I'm nursing a beer in a fashionable joint in the company of a rich friend from America. (Yes, he is footing the bill.) Miller is friendly. He moves forward on his bar stool for a chat as soon as my friend introduces us. He tells us he is from – here he mentions a place in the southern hemisphere – and he is yearning for company.

'You chaps are the first Indians to have taken the initiative to chat me up,' he continues. 'And I've been coming to India for twelve years.'

Most of the evening, the talk revolves around the comparative merits of various suds and the dangerous vocation of antagonising Indian women. In between, I gather that Miller, who works in a medium-sized IT company, has a few interesting insights on the Indian IT industry.

The next evening, I punch four numbers on a hotel phone, wait for his familiar voice, then say:

'I'm in the lobby.'

In response, he comes down and drives me to a classy terrace restaurant. We take our seats and experience a serene Bangalore. Muffled honking reaches us from the packed streets below. A tired sun is preparing its descent. At the moment, it is poised above the dome of the Vidhana Soudha.

'Been inside that?' I ask, pointing to the dome.

'What's that?' he asks.

'Oh, nothing important. It's a place where people meet to decide about nothing. We call that government in India.'

He roars with laughter.

'Bangalore has few tourist attractions,' he says, 'so I guess I'll check it out one of these days. Boy, this city is culturally dead! How can pubs be asked to close at eleven? But for the marvellous weather, this city might have fallen by the wayside. The airport and the traffic are bursting at their seams and the pollution is best forgotten. Mumbai's different. It's a seamless city, well prepared to accept global citizens like me. But one does agree that Bangalore has fewer beggars on the street; poverty is better hidden. So you feel safer walking the streets.'

'What do you think prevents Bangalore from becoming a global city?'

'I guess its lack of acceptance, mainly. I'm speaking as someone who's lived in America, Latin America, Africa, Europe and Southeast Asia. I'm speaking as someone who's run a successful business for a long time before losing out. And as one who has dual citizenship in countries belonging to separate continents, yet spends a lot of time outside both.'

'As a professional globe-trotter, in short.'

'Yes. And since a sudden chain of events has made me an employee of an Indian IT company, I've also seen the professional side of Bangalore. And frankly, I find it suffocating at times.'

I smile inwardly. I have a hunch about what he will say next and he proves me right.

'I easily work 50% more than I used to. In my country, the norm is to work eight hours, have fun for eight more and round off with eight good hours of sleep. But that doesn't work in the Indian IT industry because it has large elements of slave-driving. The more hours one puts in, the more one is appreciated. Very, very old-fashioned mentality. Why, the office looks operational during a weekend. It's a wonder these people keep their marriages.'

'Perhaps,' I jest, 'both the husband and wife work the same crazy hours, often in the same organisation.'

'I understand where this neurotic, misplaced energy comes from,' he says. 'Indians have to fight hard for a place in society, to provide security for the family. Family is so *embedded* in the Indian culture...outsiders find it difficult to comprehend this fight for survival... they're used to following their ambitions instead of restraining themselves for the sake of family.'

Miller's words recall the words of a wise Indian who said: 'Our scriptures propound four kinds of duties. *Swadharma, kuladharma, rajadharma* and *sanatana dharma*. Duty towards self, towards lineage (implying family), towards the state and the universal duty. But we understand *kuladharma* and nothing else.' Outside my thought waves, Miller expands on his observations.

'So IT companies in Bangalore, especially the one I work for, try to plant the idea that the company is an extension of the family and has the same values. Of course, they create an artificial edifice because business understands nothing but the bottom line. Everybody knows that. So what happens? Powerful survival instincts – organisational combined with individual – create an untrusting workplace, one in which there's not as much emphasis on building relationships.'

'From what you're saying, it must have required immense adjustments on your part.'

'Don't get me wrong. I don't see an aggressive society like India as essentially bad. The Indian attitude is what keeps Indian IT ahead. But yes, I've had to make adjustments. And working more is the least among them. What's difficult to cope with is the "kudos culture" that managements encourage. I have to deal with a lot of fence-sitters who'll jump into an effort just before it fructifies so that they can claim part of the credit! This whole concept of having to shout your achievements from the rooftops to get promotions... it's frustrating and unproductive.

'To answer your question,' he continues, 'from a business culture perspective, I ought to quit this job and work for a less demanding firm belonging to my country. But the opportunities here are extraordinary.'

'If you ask anybody in the business world,' I say, 'they'll swear that the creation of opportunities is all that matters. Maybe for all the sacrifices Indians make, we badly deserve that.'

'Yes, undoubtedly, you do. Yet, if you put your ear to the ground, you'll hear Mandarin. The Chinese are coming, never doubt that. From 2006 onwards, Indians will have to watch out.'

The sun has disappeared behind the dome of the Vidhana Soudha. In the pink and lavender sky, jet black birds circle and regroup with urgency. They want to get home before it gets dark. How many Indians, I wonder, live fearing the umbra of the dragon? How many IT professionals today have the sensation of working in twilight, wanting to reach home before it gets dark?

'But surely India, with its competitive streak and language skills, can hold its own?' I ask.

'Yes. It also has the infrastructure and philosophy in place to run businesses. In a sense, my presence here is an example of reverse colonialism because an Indian company is dictating rigid parameters of operation to a white man. That kind of maturity has fallen in place. But I see lacunae that need urgent filling up. Like it or not, the people I work with have little or no creativity. They cannot think outside the box. They're smart and they're hard-working. But I don't believe one can *work smart* for twelve hours a day, six to seven days a week. Or perhaps their education system is to be blamed for their lack of creativity.

'The problem is accentuated,' he resumes, 'because companies are looking for drones. Initially, I tried to act according to my high designation and assumed some creative freedom. But I soon discovered that it's like pushing against a wall. Much as my company is global in its presence, it is still fully Indian. Integration, which should start at the top, is absent because the top brass is Indian in word, deed and thought. I sometimes try to look at this from their viewpoint. The Indian work culture has a positive image abroad, and there's a valid fear that integration dilutes the power of that image. But it would surely help the long-term health of the company if Westerners also participate in image-building and other activities.'

We sit in the illumination of freshly lit lamps. The temperature has dipped and the traffic has thinned further. We're the only customers in the place and the staff is being given dos and don'ts by the *maitre d'*. That's a good idea. We Indians are great at following instructions. I wonder how these affluent restaurants keep afloat. As if reading my thoughts, Miller says:

'A different middle-class is coming up in Bangalore. Those who're getting used to cars and foreign holidays. The well of potential global citizens is getting deeper.'

I take leave of Miller on that note. As I walk away, I wonder: what kind of "sumptuous dinner" will he have tonight? Will he find a "hideout" catering to Westerners, as he sometimes does when he has absorbed enough of India for the day? Or perhaps he will find another way to compensate for an overdose of Indian conversation.

The Hungry Master

'To succeed, you need harmony, hard work and honesty,' says Master Lee Jae Ku. And I wonder: is his abrupt dive into a dictum of aitches a simple demonstration that he is a teacher above all else? Sitting across the table in his office, I get the feeling that I'm not as rapt as his students. But I manage to absorb his salvos all the same. 'We need cooperation to earn money. Autorickshaw drivers are as essential as software engineers. Bangalore has many North Indians today, but that was not the case ten years back. India being One despite its immense diversity is a wonder of the world. Within twenty to thirty years, India will be a top nation. I believe so. I love India. Love is about give, not take. An upturned map of Karnataka resembles South Korea in shape. Korea and India have more similarities than India and China.'

Before he can proceed further, a dutiful assistant brings us two steaming cups of black coffee. Master Lee briskly drains half of his before saying:

'During the Korean War, India sent us aid and soldiers via the UN. I want to repay the debt. Other Koreans are coming too – LG, Samsung, Hyundai!! In Korean culture, repayment of a debt is not optional. If someone has hurt me, I'm supposed to repay that debt too, although in a different manner.'

If debt is what has brought him here, he has more than worked that off in the past nine years. In 1996, Master Lee was the Director of the World Taekwondo Mission, a South Korean Christian organisation that sends instructors to developing countries to teach the martial art of taekwondo and carry out missionary work. That year, an instructor despatched to Bangalore informed Master Lee that there was much work to be done. Master Lee felt as if God were calling. Relinquishing his position and a comfortable life, he came to Bangalore. Since then, he has taken thousands of underprivileged kids under his wing. And taught them, without demanding a fee, what he knows best – taekwondo. They, in turn, adore him. Each time they meet him, they bow and respectfully greet him in Korean.

'*Ahn nyung ha se yo* (hello), Master Lee.'

I ask Master Lee what he is trying to achieve with taekwondo.

'Taekwondo,' he says, 'embodies a healing spirit. It instils discipline, which is necessary for these kids to rise in life. Most of their parents fight. School teaches them to be selfish. They end up developing bad egos. So we try and remould them. See, we have power flowing through our veins,' – he breaks the handle of his cup by way of demonstration – '*That* is useless power. If I can put it back, power finds utility. So we ask our students to channel their power. Carry water for old women, help someone cross the road, anything really. But when they act, they shouldn't speak about it. We want them to learn that with honesty they can not just survive but build upon the greatness of this country. They should learn not to hate Malayalees or Biharis. Control your impulses. If you can do that, everything from clean streets to a strong economy is within reach.'

'Master Lee, I find the idea of a nationalistic identity being repeated in your views. Why is that?'

In reply, he tells me that as coach of the Karnataka taekwondo team, he elevated them from the fifth position to the National Games champions. He then employed his skills at the national level. As a member of the selection panel and a coach of the team that India sent to the World Championships. But the team failed to qualify for the Olympics.

'Taekwondo may be an individual sport,' he continues, 'but one cannot win without team spirit. If I'm coaching the Indian team, we end practice sessions by clapping hands vigorously and chanting "India! India!" and then "Jai Hind!" The Karnataka team will chant the name of the state. That way, the team members subconsciously learn to appreciate their heritage. We need another Gandhiji and I want one of my kids to step up and fulfil the demand.'

He is half-jesting. Barely half. I think about what he has said. Nationalism as a promoter of culture? Definitely possible. But perhaps it is primarily a binder that works. I later pose this question to M. S. Chandrashekhar, the Secretary General of the Taekwondo Federation of India. He is as impressed by Master Lee's ability to instil nationalism in his students as by his grasp of the martial art. According to him, Master Lee has adapted to his role here.

And that, I learn, goes beyond mouthing the right chants. After coming to India, Master Lee had to reinvent his teaching techniques.

'A proper taekwondo workout would expend 1,100 calories,' he says. 'Some of my kids don't get that much nutrition in the first place. So if I go the full distance with them, they avoid attending practice for the next two days. I compromise… lighter training. Whatever works.'

Perhaps this empathy comes partially from firsthand experience. During his first three years in Bangalore, Master Lee seldom had money for food. He would travel to Kamanahalli, Cox Town, Banaswadi and other areas to teach eight batches of kids each day, some of them numbering 300. And upon reaching home at night, he would crash into his bed with exhaustion and hunger, and sing gospel songs.

'How did you manage?'

'No manage. Suffering. Hunger,' he replies inimitably.

He tells me that he has once fainted in the middle of a training session. He also remembers another occasion when he had wriggled in agony during a session in the gym. Sometimes, his students would offer him an egg *bonda*, or perhaps a morsel of birthday cake.

'Those three years, God trained me. For hours at a time, images of my parents and friends from Korea flashed past my eyes. I admonished myself for being a useless man here. No help, nobody looking after me. I asked myself why I shouldn't go back. During that time, an Omani student offered me a monthly fee of $500 if I taught him exclusively. I cannot describe the temptation I felt. Probably the most difficult decision I've taken is rejecting the offer. Once I did, I knew that I couldn't, and wouldn't, disown the kids who looked forward to my classes. God made me realise that I love India. And I promised Him that I'll die for this country and for Him. After the turbulent time passed, I got everything. A wife, sponsorship through the Full Gospel Nowon Church in Seoul, recognition… it was as if happiness broke the dam of sorrow to inundate me.'

'How did you meet your wife?'

Master Lee smiles. It is a story he relishes telling. And he tells it well.

'Ours is a marriage arranged by God. I was in India, she in Korea. One day, a young Korean girl, whom I recognised by sight because she also lived in Kamanahalli, approached me and gave a chit of paper. It had a name – Na-Soon Sook – and two Korean telephone numbers written on it. I was about to depart to judge a competition in Mumbai and was carrying five-hundred rupees for my travel. I asked God: who is the chit-girl? And more importantly, who is Na-Soon Sook? In reply, He asked me to call. So I went to the phone booth in my Sai Baba hairstyle and the only clothing I had – scruffy, dirty rags. I dialled the first set of digits and it turned out to be a wrong number. I came back to the hotel dejected. I guess I was a lonely soul and badly wanted to find a match for myself. Half an hour later, I went back to the booth and placed a call to the second number. Na-Soon's mother answered, told me she must be at her brother's house and gave me his number. I dialled a third time hoping the brother wouldn't give me a firing. But he just gave me another number...of a place where Na-Soon was living alone. Why was an unmarried girl living all alone? I almost didn't call her. But I did. And she was waiting by the phone. She told me that she had been fasting the past week and praying for my call. And – I had reached her on the last day of hope and waiting.

'"I want to meet you," she kept repeating. Turns out Na-Soon and Lee Young Mei, the chit-girl, were students in one of my courses. I had never spoken to them, not even asked their names. Na-Soon was on a short Indian trip then... I now told her I had no money to call. Would she write instead? Her first letter reached me five days later. Those days, letters took a fortnight to reach. It takes ten days even today. Without special stamps, how did the letters arrive so soon? Another small miracle. One day, I proposed over the phone, she accepted me in her next letter and we were married in

Korea in '98. We are proud parents of two boys now; both of them are born Bangaloreans.

'I thank God for giving my wife a beautiful heart... I'm successful by His Grace and her character. Girls like her are rare in my country and yours. She married me despite knowing I had no money. We married on faith, nothing else. I got the coaching assignment for Karnataka only after that. For the past five years, the state has been crowned national champs. And Bangalore has become the taekwondo capital of the country.'

Things have certainly improved. He is now the President of the Association of Korean Residents in Bangalore. The post requires energy. As does his coaching sprees for the national and state teams. And it has set him thinking that—

'The professionals will find other coaches. I want to refocus on my kids. They're the reason I'm here. I want to keep advising them to pursue taekwondo with a single-minded dedication. Be crazy about it, think about it all the time. No girlfriends or family. Just taekwondo. You have to flog yourself to reach the top. Never ever give up. I see kids sometimes giving up during the last ten seconds of a match and it breaks my heart to see that after months and years of training... be it taekwondo or life, these kids have the potential to be leaders of the world. Why give up? I'll not. It takes a century to build a great nation, and we've begun.'

By which, he means to say that India has begun.

'When are you planning to return to Korea?' I ask.

He gives me an incredulous look.

'I'm not as comfortable being in Korea any more. Bangalore is my hometown. I've given it my soul, mind, spirit and time. It's so amazing to see the city growing; it changes every day. Soon, we'll be one-crore strong and suburban towns will spring up and widen urban reaches. It'll be exciting.'

Does it mean he has transferred his love for Korea to India? There is an easy way to determine that.

'What do you think about the prospects of a unified Korea?' I ask.

His eyes flash with fondness and passion.

'It will happen,' he says, 'despite Chinese and American attempts to fracture the union. Ships and trains already operate between North and South Koreas. Flights will begin soon. We'll not integrate the German way. It won't be overnight. We'll take the gradual, economic route to merger. And when it happens, it'll upset the world geopolitical equations. Koreans will gain in strength. It's not for nothing that we're called the second Israelis of the world.'

If he is alluding to grit, he himself is certainly not playing second fiddle to anyone. Imagine this: he first quit his job in the then largest software company in Korea for taekwondo. He then braved life in an unknown country because he heard a divine call (which decidedly lies outside the audible range for most humans). Today, Lee Jae Ku, still just thirty-seven years old, radiates a still, firm beauty. I can see it. If I stay for some more time, I might start hearing those calls. And since I know my responses would hardly be so beautiful, I take his leave.

As he bids me goodbye, he says:

'Watch out for the new generation. It's *kicking* out ego and corruption. I'm really happy.'

Contrasting Encounters

It is 8.30 a.m. and I have motor-biked thirty-seven kilometres from home to arrive punctually at a resort-cum-golf course off Mysore Road. Over the last few years, such resort establishments have become part of a mature service industry in Bangalore. They provide corporate houses with a place to conduct seminars and employee training programmes. They can also be venues for the quarterly bash where the really young employee can retch freely after a few drinks.

The resort I have entered, additionally allows the honchos to tee off in quiet, brilliant sunshine. And it certainly is classier than I had expected. It takes two minutes to cross the parking lot. I see a caddy returning alone from the course. The sprinklers are on the job, as is an army of gardeners. I walk past the reception and stand outside Oleander, the conference room Philips has hired to groom its next generation of managers. The dumb sign that reads: "Do not disturb! Session in progress" is enough for a peace-loving Indian to stay put.

'Push!' calls an authoritative voice behind me.

I suddenly feel very pregnant. But the man in a canary-yellow shirt and cream pants has neither dilating nor dilatory thoughts. He pushes the door and heads inside as if he owns the place. That and badly-shot Page Three images confirm my suspicion that this is Bob Hoekstra. I still need to correct myself: 'Pronounce it Hookhstra!'

Once I follow him inside, the most famous expatriate in Bangalore and the CEO of Philips Software India, smiles affably and wonders aloud why he hadn't seen me yesterday.

'I'm not here to get trained,' I say. 'Not that it wouldn't help me, but I'm the writer you agreed to meet.'

His face lights up in remembrance, much like the bulbs and monitors his company sells. I explain my mission for the record: to shadow him through a couple of half-days before the grand interview. To know what traps to lay beforehand! Before he gets alarmed, I add: the truth is that I need to exhibit corporate efficiency during the interview. I cannot expect him to spare too much of his exclusive time.

As we stand speaking, the class pours in after a leisurely breakfast. All the participants look relaxed, perhaps because they are staying here for two days. It is practically a free holiday. The minor cost – sitting through eight hours of training sessions each day. With a speaker like Hoekstra, that becomes easy. Today, the theme of his lecture is "Deliver on Commitments". I take a seat and listen to a philosophy that reminds me of my past life. But Bob Hoekstra being what he is, keeps me interested with periodic nuggets of relevance.

'...it is hard to demonstrate the importance of good leadership, but the impact of the absence of good leadership was excellently demonstrated by the Dharam Singh government in Karnataka.'

...

'Indians are bad at promises. You don't mind coming late, right? 8.35 is fine with you.'

...

'I was born in Southern Holland and raised in the north. The south is Catholic, laid-back. Sin and beg for forgiveness. In the north, you face the consequences. Business environment, right? More than anything else, we need *cohmittment!*'

...

'Dogs can be given instructions, not cats. In manufacturing, it's mostly about setting processes in place. But knowledge workers in the service industry have to be allowed the freedom to execute.'

...

'While in Taipei, I rode a scooter. Why? It was easier to park.'

...

Each sentence rings out in his loud voice. 'These Dutch are loud people!' confides one of his employees during the break, at which time I also catch up with Bob. Although his smile lines, which are as mesmerising and alive as his eyes, disorient me, I somehow mumble my wish to tag along when he goes golfing after his training session, as a caddy if need be. I feel the grass and sun will allow some rare viewpoints to surface. Unfortunately, it is not to be. Rules do not allow non-members even to sniff the grass. I thank Bob, and leave the opulent environs of the resort at noon. My day has just begun. There are other promises to keep...

* * *

The KHB Housing Colony in Kengeri and the resort I have just left seem to be in different planets. Surprisingly, a sixteen-kilometre stretch of the accident-prone Mysore Road is all that separates the two worlds. The very air in this colony appears to have a different consistency. And the residents seem to be milder versions of those occupying *chawls* in Mumbai. The one-bedroom home, the back-slapping neighbour who may bite you the next day, the pettiness and the magnanimity – it is all here. The last thing I expect to see in Bangalore. I ring the doorbell in a second-floor apartment separated from others by thin walls. A wiry 23-year-old woman answers. She is Joy Bilha Wangari Maina. She is *also* Patrick's girlfriend. (I will burn my fingers before I learn that Joy detests labels that steal her individuality.) Patrick's at work, she is studying at home for the day.

The living room I enter is almost entirely taken up by a large double-bed. A leaking roof above the inner bedroom has just been fixed and the bed, I'm told, will soon be lugged back where it belongs. But despite the lack of space, the room has everything a couple would need: a fridge, a computer desk, a small TV, a shelf scattered with books and papers, and a couple of swivel chairs. Three captivating photographs of the lady hang on the wall opposite. Two of them show Joy carefully dressed in Western outfits. But what captures my imagination is the one in the middle.

'That's a Maasai outfit I'm wearing,' she says, 'although I come from the Kikuyu ethnic community.'

As I take a chair, I sense her wariness. After all, I'm a total stranger. I fidget, look around some more. A large poster above the bed laments the exploitation of women. It shows a pageant in which Miss Displaced, Miss Domestic Violence and so on stand on pedestals. Miss Infanticide is conspicuous by her absence. It is a powerful message. I lower my eyes to reduce the shock. They fall upon a soft teddy bear lying on

the bed with its arms outstretched. It heartens me to discover
that agony and innocence can coexist. And I feel I know a
little more about Joy. Emboldened, I ask her about her studies.

'This is my fifth and final year as a law student,' she
tells me.

'But Kenyan law would be so different!' I exclaim.

Joy almost rolls her eyes to a question that she has
answered a million times before. No, she explains. Both
Indian and Kenyan laws are based on British law. Statutes
differ, but otherwise they are nearly the same. Kenya too
does not have a uniform civil code, just like India. Islam
came to Kenya through its ports and now they have Muslim
law. And each ethnic community has its own customary laws.

'Our countries suffer from the same absurdity,' I tell her.
We have found our first point of intersection. The
conversation picks up.

'I feel strongly about human rights, especially women's
rights,' she says.

We talk about that. And it slowly dawns upon me that
beneath her slim exterior, Joy is a plucky woman.

'I want to pursue further studies in the UK,' she says. 'But
at a recent seminar, a dean from a Queensland college tried to
show me the advantages Australia provides. And he added:
"We're both Africans. You should come to Queensland." Since
he had pure British looks, he had to reveal our common African
connection – he was born in Malawi. It felt surreal to discover
such a bond in Bangalore! Now Australia is a possibility.'

'Wouldn't you like to stay on in India?' I ask.

'Well, after five years here, I want to experience another
culture and a different mode of learning.'

'So you're also a born migrant?'

'You can say that. I've been in boarding schools since the
age of ten. So coming to an alien country at the age of
eighteen didn't feel so uncomfortable.'

The younger Joy came here in search of opportunities and found "something different from Kenya" and "new friends, a pedestal for life to begin".

The ice has been broken; I suggest we lunch out. But she is fussy about what and where she eats and her kitchen doesn't have vegetarian fare today. So I watch Australia thrash New Zealand while she casually observes the match during her meal. Once she has finished, we proceed towards an Udupi restaurant. The moment we hit the road people turn their penetrating gaze on us. I mutter a curse under my breath, but there is no circumventing the topic. I might as well ask her about racism.

'It's unnerving when the staring doesn't stop,' she replies. 'We've been here for ages and people still stare and laugh. Back home we have whites, blacks, Indians... and everyone's accepted.'

'And what's your pill against the malady?' I ask.

'Not knowing the local language is my protection,' she says. 'That way, I'm spared the details of the insinuations or abuses flung at me. But otherwise Kengeri is a fine, quiet place. It allows me freedom... My former landlady in Rajajinagar had no problems with my Indian girlfriends, but she was not happy with my African friends dropping in. She started making rules, such as: no guests after 8 p.m. When I prodded her, out came the truth: *we do not like to entertain foreigners...*' What Joy says next makes it even more interesting: 'Otherwise everything else was fine and she treated me like a member of her family. Anyway, I moved to Kengeri with Patrick. I've known him since my early days here.'

As we walk on, a man leers, yes, unnervingly. Joy, who has been getting angrier by the second, says:

'At times, I feel like asking, "*What are you laughing at?*"'

I almost snap at her in defence of my countrymen. They haven't been exposed to outsiders. They don't know better. They need time to adjust. But over and above the rationalities, they are *my people*, Joy! I stop myself just in time. What the hell just happened? Thomas' words echo in the sunlight: *We're all racists at some level.* When Patrick raised the issue softly, I was fine. When Joy displays her raw anger, I get angry myself? Mercifully, her next words help calm me down.

'Denzel Washington, in his Oscar acceptance speech, said: "I look forward to the time when people will be judged by their character and not their colour." I admire him so much for saying that.'

'That makes three of us. You, me and Patrick,' I say, and immediately switch to the live-in angle.

'It's quite accepted in Kenya,' she says. 'And we've been friends first.'

'You must have shared a lot of experiences. He too recounted similar abuse stories,' I say as we sit down for lunch.

'Did he tell you about his Mysore episode?'

'Yes.'

'He was supposed to return from Mysore to meet the Vice-Chancellor of the University of Nairobi that day and imagine his plight with a ruined shirt!'

I don't recall the mob tearing his shirt off him, so I ask her to clarify. I learn that we are talking about separate episodes. In this one, Patrick was rudely woken up when someone threw cow-dung at him through the bus window. Question: how many other research students in Mysore have faced similar occupational hazards? Answer: none. Patrick is perhaps the only foreign research student shuttling between the two cities and his road to Mysore seems fraught with danger.

'But he's mentally strong and keen to reach his goal. He won't let the obstacles win,' says Joy.

Amen to that. We let the topic die. Next, Joy states that the Western media don't seem to have anything nice to say about the rest of the world and that, sadly, their Indian counterparts seem to be following suit. Back home that night, I hear Joy's words all over again and this time I listen better. Because in the dark, your eyes, too, participate in the listening. I think about Joy and Patrick's house in Kengeri. I think about the bolt on their main door. About how it guards their fragile peace even though it is broken in the middle. I hope they never lose that. Neither their fragility, nor the peace.

* * *

Meanwhile, after I finish my lunch, Joy escorts me to meet a family of five. They come from a country devastated by ethnic strife and genocide in the previous decade. The man – let us call him Miller – answers the door and reluctantly admits us in. But when I explain my project – that I'm there to find out how a student supports a large family with a nearly nonexistent stipend – he politely declines to be interviewed. As we exit the wife resets the volume on her TV. *The Bold and the Beautiful* resumes its bold illusion over a disillusioned family. Opium, I notice, comes in various forms.

Joy speculates on the reasons Miller kept mum. Most probably his embassy doesn't like him talking. Or perhaps he distrusts Indians. Whatever the reasons, the short meeting has left a profound impression on me. Their bare house and defeated body language tell a lucid story. Perhaps, just as in the marathon soaps, their story will end with an unexpected, happy twist.

Winning Hearts

On the day I visit the Narayana Hrudayalaya (NH), two contrasting items in the newspaper catch my eye. One: 101 Indians are arrested in Karachi for fishing in Pakistani waters. Two: the Pakistani cricket team lands on Indian soil to play the home team in an honour-or-death series. Strangely, one doesn't feel the irony. India and Pakistan have starred in such thrilling comedies for five and a half decades. They are known to brand the other's back with a hot iron while smiling for Western cameras; and to make visible preparations for war while furtively seeking diplomatic solutions. Hence it is natural for the fishermen soap opera to go through another dull rerun while star sportsmen hone their skills in a strikingly different "net session".

What takes me to NH, I ask myself? Oh yes, the innocent face of Noor Fatima. In 2004, this two-year-old Pakistani girl mesmerised the Indian media the moment she crossed the Wagah border. From there, she travelled south for a cardiac operation at the Narayana Hrudayalaya in Bangalore. And the city went berserk. Every cameraman with ambition clicked her and every scribe recorded her repetitive heart murmur for eager readers. No exaggeration. Legend has it that a few days after his arrival at NH, Noor's father, finding the hospital's PRO waiting at the gates for a VIP, is reported to have asked in all earnestness:

'You mean someone other than me?'

Why wouldn't he ask that question? People recognised and stopped him on the streets for a *salaam*. Hoteliers fed him free *biryanis*. National politicians sent his daughter bouquets, local ones came visiting for a photo-op. And school children wrote her a boxful of greeting cards.

Yes, I decide, the Noor Fatima phenomenon deserves closer inspection. So I bike into Hosur Road, cross the Silk Board junction and travel the dangerous stretch towards Electronic City where employees, dollars, computers and dreams are immured in a bitter-sweet world of corporate fantasy. After crossing Electronic City, I continue riding towards the Tamil Nadu border till I reach Health City and find the buildings that house the Narayana Hrudayalaya. Inside, in a large waiting room, announcements are being made inviting relatives of a patient, or patients of a doctor, to proceed for their appointments. The busy façade masks the anxiety felt by people who would rather be furthering life than preserving it. Soon, I gain entry to the office of the Public Relations Officer. But before entering it, I'm made to wear cloth covers over my sneakers. I'm entering restricted space, but one that Noor Fatima's fairytale has made its own.

'In the fifteen days of Noor's stay,' says the PRO, K. S. Vasuki, 'we got more publicity than in the two preceding years.'

Fairytales are like that. This one has an ingenious plot. An innocent Pakistani girl will die unless a skilled Indian doctor takes a scalpel and patches her heart. At the right moment, the diplomatic skies open and the sun shines for her all the way to Bangalore. Add a few songs, a comedian and racy dialogues and you are ready to threaten Bollywood records.

'Noor was the beginning of a new era,' says Vasuki. 'in the sense that before then, patients had to fly via Dubai and lose precious time, not to mention money. With improved relations between the two countries, flights, buses and even trains are operational. And Noor ushered in a new era in NH too. We got 62 patients from Pakistan before her and 212 since.'

The chief protagonist of this tale is Dr. Devi Shetty, founder of NH and one of the best paediatric cardiac surgeons in the world. He and his peers frequently operate on hearts the size of a one-rupee coin. Imagine that! And imagine having scant regard for their fees.

'If you take the average profile of the parents,' says Vasuki, 'you're looking at a mother in her mid-20s and a father in his early-30s. Most of their savings have been spent in getting married. Some parents, upon hearing the cost of surgery, are not averse to thinking that it'd be cheaper to just have another baby and let this one go. After all, they're young. Since we understand this mindset, we charge a reasonable fee and even then show leniency. Dr. Shetty also charges no fee for children who're operated upon within the first month after birth. The logic's quite simple – parental bonds blossom only after regular contact with the child.'

In other words, the worth of a child increases with time. No wonder the Bangladeshi patients who turn up at NH revere Dr. Shetty. One of them has reportedly said: *Humne*

Khuda ko tho nahin dekha, Devi Shetty ko dekha hai. ('I haven't seen God, but I've seen Devi Shetty.')

'Bangladeshis,' says Vasuki, 'begin and end their consultation by touching his feet. 95% of all cardiac cases in Bangladesh come to NH.'

According to Vasuki, India is the only country in the whole of Asia where paediatric cardiac surgeries are performed. And that too in five different hospitals! In NH alone, four surgeons on an average perform eight to ten surgeries per day. NH also has tie-ups with a voluntary organisation in Tanzania and a government hospital in Yemen.

'Do you get patients from the West?' I ask.

'They're trickling in. I feel our reputation will soon bring in more. When insurance covers the cost, money becomes a non-issue. Only specific problems in their health care systems, like with the NHS in England, bring them here.'

Vasuki's assistant Bimesh soon arrives to take me around the hospital. He informs me that NH currently has fifteen

---

George Marshall Comes to Town

George Marshall, a violin repairer from Bradford, England, was diagnosed with coronary heart disease. He was asked to wait six months for a bypass surgery, or shell out £19,000 for immediate treatment since he wasn't in the SOS category. Marshall took the plane to India and finished the deal within £4,800 at Wockhardt Hospital in Bangalore, travel charges included.

Marshall belongs to an ageing Western population facing the brunt of elevated health care costs. Economic and quality considerations together brought 150,000 patients to India in 2004. With a 15% growth, 2012 should bring in a revenue of Rs.100bn (£1.21bn), according to a study conducted by the Confederation of Indian Industry (CII) and McKinsey consultants.

Ironically, public health care in India is simultaneously declining in quality. With just one hospital bed per 1,000 people and four doctors for every 10,000 people, health care is becoming increasingly inaccessible to the Indian poor even as the global rich discover new options in India.

Facts sourced from the Guardian.

Pakistani patients, most of whom are housed on the third floor. And all of them are under the care of Dr. Rajesh Sharma. We begin with the Ilyases. Mohammad Ilyas is a 39-year-old father who works as a newsagent for *Jung* in Lahore. He is a visibly relieved man because Dr. Sharma has successfully operated upon his five-year-old son Waleed.

'Places like the NH should proliferate,' says Mohammad. 'The two governments are opening their skies and borders. We're playing cricket matches. Now let's do some important things. Let the Dr. Sharmas travel across the border as they please. Allah should create a fate where Pakistanis will come to India for enjoyment. Shop in malls, see Hindi movies and experience this diverse culture, instead of travelling under this burden of fear for a son's life.'

'Have you had an opportunity to see India?' I ask.

'The only trip I made outside the hospital is to report to the Foreigners' Registration Office in Infantry Road,' he says. 'I wish there was an FRO desk in the hospital. One is tense as it is; things can be made simpler. But anyway, the anxiety associated with a trip to India is unwarranted. Only people with evil in their minds need fear.'

He lightens up when I ask him what he feels about the Bangalore he has seen.

'It looks like any Pakistani city. How different can it be really? Before the partition, my family had a successful business in a village close to Ludhiana. What I've seen of Bangalore, and of Delhi, is exactly as my elders had pictured it for us. It saddens me though that my visa does not allow me to travel to Mumbai. Next time, I'll not miss that great city.'

He hopes for a next time!

'Shoaib Malik, the cricketer,' he continues, 'is getting married in an Indian city. Families are distributed on either side of the border. Businessmen want peace. Everybody's tired of war. People want to visit places that have been out of bounds for too long. Too long. But... it all depends on the governments.'

Two thoughts strike me. Firstly, a parade of such forward-looking, hackneyed phrases shouldn't always be discarded as rhetoric. Maybe it will serve as hypnotising Newspeak. Second, and this has been evident ever since I began the interview, Mohammad Ilyas is speaking with deliberate, even exaggerated, care. By now, an Indian would have discoursed at length about political nuances and historical twists to the border jamboree. Pakistanis seem to have learnt the coercive logic of silence. And since politics is taboo, I resort to cricket, that ultimate sub-continental buffer. I ask him to predict the outcome of the upcoming series.

'It looks as if they decide beforehand how many each will win,' says Mohammad. 'Not exactly match-fixing, you know... it makes sense to control the tension. Split the honours and everybody goes home happy.'

I turn to the silent wife, Shazia Ilyas, whom I've ignored to maintain decorum. Just one question: how does she feel here?

A Zimbabwean Troupe

In NH, I also meet four Zimbabwean patients, three of them children. A member of the Lions Club of Khumalo and Mzingwane has sponsored the group that is accompanied by a few close relatives and a physiotherapist.

Randall, a 16-year-old boy, is slated for a high-risk surgery because a crucial artery on the left side is not visible in scans. Princess, the daughter of Ntombiyosikon had been operated upon successfully the previous day. Sukoluhle finds Indian food hot (and comical, apparently) as she waits for her son Abel's operation.

The adult is 64-year-old Premji Bhikha who has roots in Gujarat. This erstwhile shoe salesman cum cobbler now owns a small bicycle shop, three blocked arteries and a damaged fourth. Other than hoping to go back and resume his association with ball bearings, he wants to visit Gujarat.

'At home,' she says. 'Religious barriers don't exist at all. In the evenings, we ladies – Pathani, Mumbaiya, Sikh, all of us – hold chat sessions. It's as if I never left Pakistan.'

Clichéd imagery indeed. But who would prefer intellectual blabber to cool clichés that click?

* * *

Three times during the interview with the Ilyases, Raahat Bibi has ventured into our circle to see if I'm done. Finally, her daughter Naheed Jamshed herself appears and escorts me to her room. She *has to* finish the interview before going down to the ITU to spend time with her three-month-old baby. It is clear that she sincerely wants to share her story.

Naheed is a Pathani woman from Rawalpindi who doesn't look as if she has borne four children. Slim as a girl, she exhibits only one sign of stress – the multiple folds in her eyelids end in crow's feet. Parisa Jamshed, dozing in the ITU, is her fourth child. She lost her firstborn, a boy, and then a girl to cardiac irregularities. The third-born has been blessed with good health (she frisks around us and has evidently become the apple of every passing eye). Just when Naheed assumed that the worst was over, Parisa came as a reminder that blood needs pumping and an absent valve doesn't help the process. This time, Naheed, along with the child's resolute grandmother, decided that the solution lay in Bangalore. So one day, they simply travelled to NH without notifying their native doctors.

Naheed places a delicate kiss on a book with calligraphy on the cover before speaking further.

'We're so happy and thankful to you,' she says. 'Oh, we're thrilled with Indians. When we landed in Delhi, an ambulance was waiting for us. Airport personnel carried our luggage, ignoring our protests. We were given food, the baby was put on oxygen, and then we were helped to board the Bangalore flight. And the process was repeated in Bangalore.'

Raahat Bibi echoes her daughter's sentiments in a louder voice.

'Allah gives life, but the doctors and nurses here are great. That two unescorted ladies could come to a supposedly hostile nation and receive such tremendous treatment... May all mothers bear children like Dr. Sharma. This hospital will be the engine for peace, just watch. Pakistanis from all over the country are coming here and witnessing personal miracles. When we go back, we'll shout our tale. Can peace be far then?'

'And,' says Naheed, 'the hospital said: "Don't worry about the money. Pay as much as you can." Oh, this has been great. Even the visit to Shivaji Nagar. We didn't shop – that can wait till our child has recovered. But we had to buy a few things for this naughty girl here because we packed for winter when we left. The shopkeepers insisted on huge discounts... oh, everything's been great. Even the Indian Embassy in Islamabad stamped our visas the same day we applied...'

'There's even a mosque downstairs,' continues Raahat Bibi. 'Oh, there'll be peace one day... if Indian entertainment and medicine works for the Pakistani, where is the need to fight?'

I leave the cliché driven world of palpable happiness before I completely forget ground realities. But two Pakistani families have changed me a little bit. The next time I'm fatalistic about Indo-Pak relations, I will remember them and the Narayana Hrudayalaya.

Conscientious People

*I*n a small hut in rural Maharashtra, Komala
Ramachandra, a tall, loose-limbed girl with dark,
translucent skin is deliriously ill. But at the crack of
dawn, she wakes up to the gentle prodding of the lady of the
house. Duty beckons. Carrying a small earthen pot, she
follows the elderly lady out of the house and down the muddy
path towards the pond. The path is already wet and slippery,
telling her that she is far from being the earliest riser in the
village. It is shivering cold and she struggles to fill her pot.
The lady has meanwhile filled her two larger pots and, piling
one on top of the other, starts walking up the incline. The routine
chore for the older woman proves to be a struggle for the young,
unwell girl. By the time she returns to the hut, precious little
water remains inside the pot. Komala lightens her load and
looks at her companion with newfound appreciation.

Komala is seated in front of me in the India Coffee House,
that wallet-friendly M. G. Road haunt, when she narrates

her story. I smile, but not at her ineptness in an alien rural environment. I'm simply amazed that she intentionally became part of that setting. What other sane Telugu American would want to do that?

'Nice initiation into rural life,' I say. 'But surely you didn't say that you spent one whole year in rural Maharashtra, did you?'

'Of course not!'

'Phew! For a moment I thought...'

'But I stayed for a year in a village named Manchal in Andhra Pradesh,' she says with her ready smile. 'Except the time I took off for bimonthly meetings with other members of the NGO I worked with – Indicorps.'

That is longer than most urban Indians have ever been in a village. It would have taken some willpower and training. The fetching-water-at-daybreak incident, she tells me, happened during the orientation programme organised by Indicorps. All volunteers were assigned a villager to shadow for one whole day; some were fortunate enough to be assigned a child.

'As luck would have it, I got the homemaker,' says Komala. 'Not the easiest person to emulate when nursing a fever. Anyway, we also had an orientation programme in Mumbai before that with a lot of well-formulated exercises. For instance, the first lesson was a demonstration that the language barrier did not really exist, that we could communicate in myriad ways, particularly with children. So each of us were given the responsibility of entertaining four underprivileged children in an amusement park. That was easy. All play. Another day, we went on a scavenger hunt.'

'What's that?' I ask, intrigued by the terminology.

'Well, we needed familiarisation with urban Indian life. So we were asked to travel a particular bus route, buy a particular book from a specified bookstore, buy a particular brand of soap from a specified store, place a call to a particular number from a specified phone booth...'

'That's particularly interesting now that you specify it.'

Even though she laughs vigorously, her black-framed, broad spectacles remain firmly fixed on the bridge of her nose.

'We left our homes with no idea of what we would deal with,' she says. 'Words like sanitation, health and education draw different images in Western minds... hence the orientation. We were given a historical, social, and economic introduction to India. We got to meet individuals who are making changes in their communities, like Dr. Kurien.'

'And after a month of training, you were ready to become a full-fledged social worker?'

'Hmm. You can learn language and rudimentary survival skills. But finally, you have to go to the field, jump in and take control. Which is so different from the hands-off US approach... ground reality is so different.'

'And shocking?'

'Yes, that too. I think I've myself changed more than anything else that's happened.'

'But Komala, I'm unable to digest this small detail: one year in a village?'

'One year is barely enough time to accomplish anything unless you are partnered with a solid grassroots NGO. Perhaps a year is enough to complete a small segment of a large project; and to learn a great deal about development, India, rural life and yourself. Indicorps works that way. On one hand, they filter applications and select a few Americans and Canadians – it's normally less than a dozen – for their programmes. On the other hand, they identify Indian NGOs to partner with. My programme, for example, was affiliated with the Jana Shikshana Samstha in Hyderabad.' Then, in a lighter vein, she re-answers my question: 'Village life is boring, I have to admit. Women have to stay indoors after 7 p.m. The highlight of our day used to be sitting outside a shop and having a Thums Up around sunset. And it used to taste fantastic.'

Apart from downing colas, Komala worked on issues related to water, women's health, education and vocational training. And experienced both success and failure. She tells me about her attempts to get villagers to harvest rainwater.

'I've learnt that unlike in a corporate setup, you cannot control the environment and the process, in social service. Potential of failure is high. Unplanned activities are unavoidable. But the more you try, the less frustrating it gets; I doubt if it gets any easier.'

Coming as it does from a 22-year old American, it amazes me. Why is she allowing dust to accumulate on her graduation certificates? Do I smell a mild aroma of corporate disgust? Again, she laughs. I ask her to hold the answer in abeyance because I have sensed something else – the waiter's impatience to see us leave. Komala gulps a glass of plain water without qualms before we oblige him, cross the road and settle under a tree on the other side of the purple-and-pink bougainvillea streak. Disengaging her two cloth bags, she sits cross-legged, Indian style, on the platform beneath the tree.

Who's the outsider?

And with that question in my mind, her answer takes an interesting dimension.

'I'm planning to go back and study law in the fall of 2005,' she says. 'Since that's ridiculously expensive, I'm sure to be neck-deep in debt by the end of it. So I'll have no choice but to stay in the corporate world. For a while at least. But I don't see myself sustaining it. One of the reasons I committed myself to social service now is because I'm unsure if I'll be able to do it later on in life. And of course, I'm here for the experience. No point denying it.'

And partly for exploring her roots. Although she used to speak shattered (not just broken) Telugu at the time, she chose a village in Andhra Pradesh.

'In my house there is a confluence of many languages,' she says. 'Mainly Telugu, Kannada and English. My parents used to think we girls, me and my sister, were deaf to Kannada. But we were just dumb to it, if you know what I mean. So growing up, we were privy to a lot of conversations we weren't supposed to overhear. Now, of course, both my Telugu and Kannada are in better shape.'

'And how did your parents react to your decision to come to India?'

Komala gives me a Cheshire cat grin. She has retained the traits of an American teenager after all.

'They were like: "No, you cannot do this!" My decision breaks their idea of a linear life – education, career, marriage, children, etc. So I eased my mother into the idea. Step by step. At first, I said, "I'll apply for the position and then won't accept the programme." Then I said, "I'll attend the interview." And finally, after I got it, I informed my father. He finally agreed for a one-year hiatus. But after a year in Manchal, I decided to come to Bangalore for a year more,' – here, she displays her entire array of teeth – 'and they're realising that it's difficult to argue from overseas.'

This strengthens my notion that first-generation Indian Americans come to India solely on nostalgic trips. Somehow, they seem reluctant to adopt a holistic outlook while here, and therefore feel out of place after a few weeks of vacationing.

Komala's veterinarian father left Bangalore for Winnipeg, Canada, in 1985. Seven years later, when Komala was just nine, he migrated yet again. This time, it was a hop across the border to North Dakota. Komala has since followed her family to rural, "animal-rich" places like Oklahoma, Iowa and Nebraska. Interestingly, the venues turned increasingly rural before her days as a student in Chicago.

'But I was born in Bangalore,' she says. 'And we always came visiting once every four to five years. It felt different each time. I remember being amazed at seeing foreign cars here in '95. Now this place,' she says, looking at the idle crowd, 'doesn't even look like India. You know, I did not feel a culture shock coming to India and even going to Manchal. But after Manchal, Bangalore gave me a big culture shock. It's fun being here, though. I've forged many lasting friendships. If I had any fears about relating to people, they've been buried.'

She stays with her maternal grandparents in Jayanagar. 'They want me to stop shuttling around the country. Like tomorrow, I'm off to Kolar to have a look at a few NGOs working there. Then, I'm planning to go to Pondicherry to work with Auroville in the tsunami relief and rehabilitation efforts… it's hard to see them worry so much on my account.'

It is a lucky family that finds itself worrying about having reared an excessively compassionate girl. Other Americans her age are walking into rehab centres to get detoxified. Komala, on the other hand, dropped everything and spent most of January in tsunami-struck villages in Tamil Nadu.

'Working in such villages is a different ball game,' she says. 'It's tougher, of course. I was coordinating a needs-assessment survey in a few villages using a standard process called Participatory Rural Appraisal. It's an attempt to get the villages to own *pucca* records. For example, a street-level map that details the materials used for constructing each house. Having these records will help the villages claim damages.'

'Komala, when we first met, why did you tell me that you do nothing?'

She laughs.

'I'm into, like, a million things. But nothing that I can label.'

That is modesty speaking. I refuse to believe that people who have shrugged off educational and professional labels to follow their heart would suddenly want a label to feel accomplished.

'Complete a label for me now. While in Bangalore, Komala is a what? I know this is your home in India, but still...'

'To explain that, I'll tell you another story. After completing a year in Manchal, I was planning to go to South Africa. I've heard fabulous stories of NGO successes there and it's fast becoming the world's NGO capital. One of the reasons is that the government and the NGOs work in tandem. It's supposed to be exciting and enriching. But a young village boy I know changed my plans. He held a painting exhibition in Hyderabad around the time I was preparing to leave Manchal. Seeing his wonderful pictures, it suddenly struck me that in gaining a rare rural experience, I've completely missed out on cultural India. I found it unacceptable to leave India without experiencing this dimension. So I decided to base myself out of a city. What better place than Bangalore? I disagree with the opinion that culture is dead or dying in Bangalore. The *Bangalore Habba* was exciting; so was the *Rangashankara* theatre festival. I've come across people who've quit IT to become theatre artistes and writers and filmmakers. And to my surprise, I discovered a tremendous activist culture. I never associated that with Bangalore. At first glance, it seems to be a congregation of shopping malls and wedding halls. But believe me – Bangalore's full of people who're making a difference. I came here knowing just one social worker and now I know dozens. The NGO movement is strong, and has mature models working locally as well as globally. And... there's a personal reason to be here...'

Boyfriend? But since we're speaking of culture, I shrug off my philistinism and keep the thought to myself. Komala herself offers the explanation:

'I will soon begin an internship with an NGO named the Alternative Law Forum. The stint might give me a better idea of how to use law to uplift society. Otherwise, it's easy to get lost inside a career maze and never get back where one desires to be.'

'Komala, why do I get the impression that you're finding your way out of Uncle Sam's reach?'

She thinks carefully before defending herself against my googly.

'In many ways, severing ties with America is impossible. That's where I have my family, friends... and memories. But I wouldn't rule out settling outside. Politically, the US is in the doldrums. You should know that I'm very anti-Bush... I don't know what he's trying to pull. Keeps talking about upholding democracy, but it's just the oil money. A lot of Americans have a condescending attitude towards the rest of the world... some think they're actually helping Iraq. And I'm going to sound condescending now – they're unaware of the world's diversity. Be it in clothing, food... anything. They think different is worse. I have a hard time believing 9/11 justifies Bush. He's just plain lucky to have so many things going for him. Any hostility other countries show America works in his favour. And he's backed by the right-wing neo-Christianity movement... Bush portrays himself as being a family man before being the President; "man of God" kind of rhetoric. As the traditional notions of family and home are being challenged by, say, gay marriages and abortion, Bush gains. There are people who think: "My parents vote Republican, so will I!" It's shocking that citizens of a world superpower don't think for themselves.'

'It's time the whole world voted to elect your President,' I say. 'The White House impacts us as much, if not more. Komala, if ever you feel like leaving America and it's a toss up between South Africa and India, I'll find you an Indian boyfriend if that's what it takes. One more in a billion makes no difference to us. We need you here.'

Komala giggles.

'You know, Indicorps is a very conventional organisation. No smoking, no drinking, no relationships either!'

* * *

A steady diet of FM waves feeds my radio receiver as I sit and work one fine morning. Amidst the clickety-clack, my mind does not register the beginning of a snippet programme named "Karmayogi" – loosely translated, it means "one who performs his duties like a saint" – till a voice arrests my attention. It is a foreigner's. What he says and what is said about him makes me grab a pen and get ready for the number. Two minutes later, I call the number and apologise for not knowing the man's name. The lady on the line informs me that it is Father Hank Nunn, and that he is a Canadian. When she patches me through, Fr. Nunn readily gives me an appointment.

The next morning, I head for Bannerghatta Road. Since it is the rush hour, I prefer to take the longer route via the Outer Ring Road. The portion of the ORR that I drive through has light traffic and few lights. Yet it is late by the time I reach Hulimavu and find myself outside a stout stone building with a sign that says: Athma Shakti Vidyalaya. It is the institute Fr. Nunn has been running for the last twenty-six years.

Fr. Nunn greets me cordially and leads me upstairs. The solid interiors are lighted in patches by a skylight. Stuck on one of the doors on the first floor is a large greeting card, created on the occasion of Fr. Nunn's recent seventy-fifth birthday. It reads:

H – Humble
A – Affectionate
N – Noble
K – Kind

Later, when I ask him if he agrees with the adjectives, he replies casually:

'Oh, the Affectionate sounds about right.'

For now, he leads me into a large room in which mattresses are lined along the walls. More than twenty people – a mixture of staff and inmates – are seated randomly upon them. Hank and I take a seat and the meeting begins with staff announcements.

Mark has gone to buy his tickets, Kasthuri has taken the day off and the timing of the Sunday night medication has reverted to 8:30 p.m.

Next, one of the inmates reports her morning's activities. When she is finished, the staff grill her.

'You say you woke up at nine, but I saw you in bed till around ten.'

The inmate is confused, tries an explanation and then another. She is soon unclear about what transpired as recently as the morning. Finally, she attributes her late rising to insomnia. It is decided that the root cause would be discussed in detail later. The agenda shifts to the next inmate who is a brisk, middle-aged lady. She clears her throat and provides a status report for the last two weeks. Most days sound routine. But she is evidently anxious about the computer courses she has enrolled for. Her problem, I learn later, is that she is overwhelmed by her problems.

'The good thing is I practise daily on the computer. Word, Excel etc... yes, I know I can go back home when I clear my exams, but I don't know if...'

At this point, a very intelligent-looking man comes into focus because of his vacant expression. The staff ask him to summarise the happenings of the last ten minutes, which he does with concise precision. I'm glad I have some idea of what constitutes mental health problems; I might otherwise be wondering why normal, bright people are being put under the microscope.

Nobody else is in a mood to share their thoughts, so Fr. Nunn leads me back downstairs to his simple office. He has kept quiet during most of the meeting except to give a couple of soft suggestions. I ask him why he chose stone for building Athma Shakti Vidyalaya (ASV); he tells me it is because of the strength and stability it conveys. Meanwhile Gina, his dog, also signs off from the meeting and joins us in the office. I look at the organised litter around us and begin.

'Father... er... that came across as a trifle unconventional. The meeting, I mean... A newcomer ought to be forgiven for thinking that unreasonable demands are being made of the inmates.'

'Oh yeah,' replies Fr. Nunn. 'It seems harsh. We'll even restrain the kids – that's what we call them here – when required. My staff is challenging the kids to think; and most importantly, to take responsibility. For their emotions, thoughts and behaviour. We are telling them: you can control your feelings, you can know why you feel a certain way and once you've acted upon your impulses, you have to explain what you did, why, and what changes are required.'

The attitude of mainstream society makes the transition steep. Taking responsibility means letting go of coping mechanisms that have "worked", although they have placed the kids at the dysfunctional end of the mental health spectrum. And mental health issues by their intrinsic nature allow the affected person to believe that it is the outside world that has changed. That the instability is not within. So, suddenly being treated as an equal can be threatening.

'They require warmth and physical reassurance. We give them that; *sure*. And we also use techniques like Transaction Analysis Language, Neuro Linguistic Programming and Behaviour Modification. And *sure*, we use medication. In moderation, because it makes people artificially docile. I'd rather say to my kid: show me what you've got and we'll try to solve it. I believe that being mentally ill is just like having diabetes or a heart disease. *Sure*.

'I've noticed that kids with a violent history usually direct their anger at their parents. Why? There might be many reasons. It's plausible that they missed a strong bonding with their parents during their childhood or later. Many of them search for father figures, so I encourage them to call me *Dad* if they feel like it. Sure.'

He takes the title to heart and showers them with love. That explains why his rehabilitated kids turn up to celebrate his birthday and write touching letters long after their days at ASV turn hoary. I read through one such letter as Fr. Nunn responds to the ringing phone. It is written by a medical practitioner who is now married, has children, and enjoys being on the other side of the healing process. When I finish reading, my eyes fall on a pencil sketch of Fr. Nunn. It was drawn in the morning by the hesitant girl who, even now, is sitting on the bench outside the office, waiting for her Dad to spend a few minutes with her.

I look at his image on paper and then at him. Striking as the resemblance is, the sketch fails to convey the silver in his still thick hair, or the unruliness of his bushy eyebrows. It remains mute to his measured voice that has reduced its pace to cater to a special audience – he cannot switch off his patience even when talking to arguably sane people like me. ('Gina, her name is Gina. G-I-N-A.') When he completes his phone conversation, I show him the letter to indicate that I have absorbed its contents. He picks up the thread, and moves on.

'Our goal is rehabilitation, not custodial care, though we have four kids who're residents for life. Their families have disowned them.'

'How many have been rehabilitated so far?' I ask.

'Let's see... I think around 160-170.'

Thankfully, his haven is not run by corporate barons with impersonal, stringent targets. 170 people in 26 years can sound pathetically inefficient or astonishingly high, depending on who is hearing the numbers.

'We have capacity for 24 kids. And in any therapeutic community – that's what we are: a close-knit community engaged in therapy – the optimum strength is 20-25. Everyone has to know everyone else. The numbers might climb now that we're attempting to replicate this model in Chandigarh...'

But funds are always an issue. ASV relies on "random donations and hard-earned one-time grants". The ten thousand rupees charged per kid is a flexible amount and it is routine for the trust to show red balance sheets. His wonderful staff keep the show going, says Fr. Nunn. Some of them, including a few cooks, have been around for twenty years. And on salaries that might put off staunch socialists.

'*Sure*, it's the spirit of the place that keeps them here,' he says while escorting me for lunch. I am soon chewing on my noodles thoughtfully. The skein on my plate is a smooth braid in comparison to the complicated journeys people make for reasons that defy articulation. Notions and consequences crisscross these journeys in time, and only someone with a clear mind will be able to untangle the neural mess and show a long double strand of reason and passion. Something tells me Fr. Nunn is one such man. I quickly devour my food and get back to my interrogation. And slowly, the man emerges from his halo, but the halo realigns above his head.

'What's behind the title of Father? I'm a Jesuit priest,' he says. 'No, I don't give sermons. Jesuits prefer running schools to churches and I'm associated with the St. Joseph's community nearby. We involve ourselves in activities that'll help people. Sure.'

'Were you always religiously inclined?' I ask.

His answer reveals his life-story. He was 21-years old when he joined the religious order in 1951 after graduating in Arts. Four years of training in Toronto, followed by two years of philosophical studies in Montreal landed him in Addis Ababa as an English teacher. Three years later, he was in Darjeeling. It was 1960.

'I would say I was deputed to Addis Ababa to work alongside French Canadian Jesuits. Darjeeling and India, I prefer to think, I chose. I was deeply interested in Indian culture, diversity and spirituality. (Canada, if you think about it, is a bland country.) And coming to Darjeeling also meant working with English-speaking Canadian Jesuits. That helped... This was the time when I was slowly getting convinced that my personal religious path was to save people and answer their needs. To make the best use of myself. To further that, I undertook my theology studies and became a priest in 1964. Then between '64 and '68, I taught in different schools including those with Nepali as the medium of instruction. After that came the headmastership of the Darjeeling St. Joseph's. I held the post from '68 to '75. That done, I went back to Canada for a sabbatical and to study spirituality...'

'The Christian way?'

'Oh yeah. And at that time, Bangalore happened. A friend of mine asked me to come to Ashirvad to teach courses on spirituality and counselling. Once there, I gradually found myself getting increasingly into counselling and psychotherapy. Actually, I was very much interested in psycho-spirituality. I still am. When a person takes a decision, it's his spirit you encounter. However, the root causes and consequences of that decision fall in the realm of psychology. Psycho-spirituality smoothly marries the two inexact sciences. In such approaches, I was influenced by the American philosopher Ken Wilber. It was with this mindset that I came to Bangalore in 1979. And gradually started meeting families who wanted help with loved ones who were seriously ill.'

And, knowing that some people needed help was sufficient motivation for him to start a registered trust.

'Athma Shakti Vidyalaya,' says Fr. Nunn, 'is a loose translation of the Freudian term "cathexis". C-A-T-H-E-X-I-S. Which means being able to shift your energy, to go from knowing your feelings to being aware of your thinking. That's the basis of our therapy too. That I'm responsible for my own anger, which doesn't originate from the other person. And that I have to know how my present and past attitudes and beliefs affect me.'

'Father, may I ask how your past shaped your present?'

'I led a careless teenage life. Some people might call it rough; way too much sports. I was part of a four-member rowing team. Those were good days... We were crowned champions of the Nova Scotia province...'

'Were you Olympic material?'

Ken Wilber

Ken Wilber is a serious connoisseur of different approaches to philosophy and has created his distinct perspective by blending Oriental and Occidental notions. His Buddhist leanings, together with the Western psychological and psycho-therapeutical amalgam, make him wish that Freud and the Buddha could be integrated.

Interestingly, Wilber was born nineteen years after Fr. Nunn.

'Oh no. We were not up to the mark and quite aimless. I even flunked a year in B.A. When I turned twenty, it was touch and go. Could have gone under. Till a professor of mine thought it worth his while to have a long chat with me.'

'What did he say?'

'He said: "You're a bum; you're messing up your life." And I said: "Oh yeah? I'll show you. *I'll show you!*" That pride ignited a flame of ambition and reversed my life. I turned away from my alcoholism. I stopped fighting my father. Oh yeah, sure. He thought of me as a bum too! Once I resolved to change, I sensed the change in myself perceptibly. I knew I was making a lifelong commitment, was dedicating my life to God. And I never went back, never regretted it, not even having to live in bachelorhood. No, never had temptations either.'

'And of course,' I supplement, 'the question of loneliness is redundant when you're surrounded by so many people you love and who love you.'

'Exactly.'

Exactly. That is the wrong word which miraculously fits. People who choose un-trafficked paths are seldom fans of exactitude. Hank Nunn, the one-time twenty-year-old rower and tippler today sits almost incongruously in Bangalore and the picture fits. And he isn't in a mood to leave, despite the city having mutated beyond recognition in his time.

'Oh, what a beautiful city Bangalore was in '79,' he reminisces. 'Smaller. Quieter. People seemed to know each other. Ashirvad used to be in St. Mark's Road and you could see those quaint little bungalows all around... and there was a nice little hotel in the corner of Mallya Road... my memory fails me with the name... I remember the name of the steak joint though. The Only Place, at the corner of Brigade and Residency. Haroon, the proprietor, has shifted his business to Museum Road now; he still looks the same and serves equally excellent steaks. He used to run it primarily for hippies then and his joint was a landmark. During those days, when I came to Bannerghatta Road to visit St. Joseph's, BTM Layout was a complete jungle. Can you believe it?'

I want to tell him: 'I've seen you. I'm in the mood to believe anything' Aloud, I ask: 'What makes you tick?'

'At seventy-five,' he says, 'I just want to get the energy flowing and keep busy. Yoga four times a week, daily walks and the next heart attack is halted in its tracks.'

'No, I mean – Bangalore's changed. The world's changed. You seem to represent static solidity. How?'

'Well, the same things that kept me going fifty years ago are valid now. While I've kept up with the happenings, I'm always grounded in the basics. What is essential to a human being is what I know. That's being practical, and for me spirituality and philosophy are the most practical of things. Because my subject is the most important – the human being. Come to think of it, the New Age is seeking exactly the same thing by consuming popularised versions of meditation, yoga and stuff like that, *sure*. So long as people derive personal growth, sure.'

Sure.

Have I distilled the quintessence of Fr. Hank Nunn? Surely not. So what do I do? Easy. Take the help of someone whose life he has deeply graced. Mohan, for instance. He is a former kid who, after rehabilitation, began helping out in a small centre for autistic children in Chennai. In the postscript of a letter he begins with "Dear Daddy", he says:

P.S: This is to say – I got A Best Life – New Life, Changed Life, Being A Different Person Altogether Life – All clubbed in ONE.

Due to having known you well – understood u altogether – having belonged to u – loved U from bottommost of my heart – the credit goes to The All The Member of ASV community.

No one, I feel, can improve upon Mohan's words. He succumbed to a brain tumour in 2003. But for the grace of Fr. Nunn, he would have died without owning a cause.

* * *

It is early afternoon when I leave Athma Shakti Vidyalaya. A misplaced belligerence in the February sunshine converts my helmet into a mini air-conditioner unit. My next destination is Fireflies, an NGO on Kanakapura Road. I get back into Bannerghatta Road and turn left, away from the city. I'm advised by local auto drivers to continue till the gates of Bannerghatta National Park, after which I can take the road that connects to Kanakapura Road.

As I leave urban Bangalore behind, Bannerghatta Road – it seems to me, with almost wicked glee – becomes smooth and motorable. I reach the National Park, easily locate the link road and ride down it. Just a few miles away, the Deccan plateau lies subdued by the city; here in its outskirts, it asserts itself. Small and medium-sized rocky hills lift up their hot heads and stare with hostility as I ride past. Their presence makes my road serpentine. If a tyre punctures in this stretch – which is a distinct possibility given the state of the road – a long walk awaits a weary man. Eleven lonely kilometres later, I reach Kanakapura Road at the point it passes through the town of Kaggalipura. I find the Vinayaka temple dressed in garish colours and take the mud road leading to Fireflies. Three kilometres and a packet of glucose biscuits later, I alight inside the Fireflies compound.

Caroline Mackenzie has already made an impression by giving precise directions. She soon appears in person and begins strengthening it. Hers is the second silver head I encounter today. Another pair of light eyes and another patient smile...

'How was your meeting with Hank?' she asks. 'He's something of a legend in the NGO circles.'

'He's certainly a phenomenon,' I say, following Caroline down a narrow path cut across by drip irrigation pipes. We hear the chisels before the workshop comes into view. Three artisans are caressing, chiselling and brushing debris off different slabs of stone in an attempt to make granite reflect the image in their mind. The roof of the wall-less workshop is made of dried coconut-tree fronds; work areas are rudimentarily separated by opaque-blue plastic tarpaulins. Caroline introduces me to the chief artisan and surprises me by breaking into Kannada that, but for the accent, sounds wonderfully chaste to my untrained ear. I feel humbled that I'm asking a Scotswoman to mediate for me in a conversation with a fellow Indian.

'*Neevu yeshtu warshadinda ee kelasa madidiri*?' asks Caroline on my behalf.

'I've been a sculptor for thirty-odd years,' replies the man. He tells me that the granite has come from a quarry near Devanahalli and that the new team is taking it slow and steady.

'Firstly,' says Caroline, 'we're using soft granite during the period we get used to each other. Once we deem ourselves ready, we'll graduate to harder granite; it's tougher to sculpt but...'

'...produces finer results?' I ask.

'Correct. As of now, we're experimenting with this stone. I have my own interpretations of Indian mythology. You may call it a modern version of the symbols and figures. I use unconventional proportions and they – the proportions – mean something to me. So these artisans, who're exceptionally skilled, have to understand me and make fine adjustments in their work. And as we work, they sometimes come up with suggestions for improvement. But don't mistake it as Art for Art's sake. Our goal is livelihood... Anyway, first thing in the morning, we plan the day – course corrections, the next step...'

I can straightaway see her innovations. For example, she is capturing the birth of a goddess in the sculpture she is working on. It is almost never done (whereas depicting the birth of a god is common). Why not? By asking the question, Caroline is trying to challenge obsolete notions using archetypal images.

'Depicting the birth of the divine feminine,' she says, 'is a celebration of femininity, which doesn't exclude the feminine side of men. Stone can bless us with a new worldview. But let me say no more. I find that when I speak about what I intend to do, it dilutes the effect... dissipates energy that could have been channelled into my work.'

We take leave of the artisans and their smiling faces and walk to a roofed terrace above the Fireflies library. From here, I get an unobstructed view of the countryside. The sun shines over a muddy pond set amidst an enchanting array of green. Rustic, hollow shouts that signal distant and nearby activities mingle with birdsongs. The birds are completing their meals in preparation for bedtime, which is a less than a couple of hours away.

'We'll have to wrap up by six,' says Caroline. 'I'm conducting the bhajan session today, which begins at half past. I need thirty minutes to compose myself.'

Time is short and I begin without further ado.

'How do you speak fluent Kannada?' I ask her.

'Oh, I was in Melkote for six years. It's a predominantly Hindu village thirty-five miles outside Mysore and since I was the only foreigner around, I had to pick up the lingo.'

'When was this?'

Caroline frowns imperceptibly while sifting memories. 'It was from '82 to '88, I think. I came to India first in 1976 and worked with Jyoti and Jane Sahu. They lived in a village off Tumkur Road called Siluvepura. Jyoti is a well-known artist who specialises in myths and symbols. I studied under him and earned my keep by helping in the care of the garden and cows, and doing a bit of shopping. During those six years, I carved six small granite pieces, all of them inspired by my visits to temples. These included images such as Umashankar, Ranganatha, Hanuman, Nandi, Linga-yoni...

'And then I went to Melkote for another six-year stint. During those twelve years, I visited home just twice for a couple of months. Of course, it was easier for foreigners then. Citizens of Commonwealth countries could stay without a visa. That changed during my eighth year. By then I was studying Sanskrit and got my professor's help in applying for a visa.'

It makes sense that she has shown interest in the language of her stone figures; she has to talk to them to understand their visceral needs. By way of explanation, she adds another reason for learning Sanskrit.

'I'm deeply interested in Indian mythological texts. The Ramayana in particular. During my initial days in India, I used the translations I could get hold of and drew a series of pictures while looking at the epic as Sita would have experienced it. Rather, as I imagined Sita to have experienced it. These interpretations were so different from the ones I heard from my Hindu friends that I wanted to check my ideas against the original text. For that, I had to learn the script. You perceive, don't you, that not having been brought up with the text, I saw the epics with a different eye? For example, Sita being the incarnation of Lakshmi intrigued me since Christianity does not believe in divine female incarnations.'

'You seem to have an all-encompassing interest in ancient India. Where do you think it all began?'

'Well... tangibly, I would say during my art school days in London. I joined the course in 1972 when I was twenty and within a year, I was disillusioned by consumeristic, fad-based art. During the first year, a student has to select a section of the London Art Museum for sketching. I was interested in both Chinese and Indian art. Both seemed to transcend the commercial dimension. I chose Indian art because I'm a naturally gifted sculptor. The stone figures pulled me towards them with their mythological, archetypal quality.'

'May we go further back with your permission?' I ask. 'Perhaps life decisions are based on even earlier events?'

Caroline smiles, pauses and continues.

'In retrospect, I can see patterns in my life that lead further back. For example, my interest in psychotherapy has common linkages with my love for mythology. One doesn't have to have a problematic life in order to learn and practise psychotherapy; some people substitute it for religion...'

'You spoke of a common linkage.'

'Yeah. Take a deity like Narasimha who's devouring... dangerous. At the same time, it's understood that his danger has a saving value. He uses his power to overcome the egoism of Hiranyakasipu. That kind of ambivalence is quite common in Hindu mythology. Shiva is ascetic and erotic at the same time. He seduces the wives of sages, but drags his feet in tying the knot with Parvati.

'Psychotherapy is similarly ambivalent. It involves bringing out repressed parts of one's personality to the surface and allowing it to heal. Seen in that light, neurotics are simply people who keep facets of their personality repressed. Now here's the crux – worshipping a deity like

Narasimha is valuing its ambivalence and in some way, accepting your own ambivalence. If you're familiar with the works of C. G. Jung, you'll know that he propounds similar theories. In fact, his famous fight with Freud, his one-time good friend, was on their dissimilar opinions on mythology. Jung thought there's spiritual meaning in them while Freud believed in their literal interpretation.'

I'm thrilled at the oblique connection Caroline makes between two apparently disparate topics. I prod her to go deeper down memory lane.

'What do I recall about my childhood the most?' she continues, 'I guess spending a lot of time with ponies and having a rural upbringing. My family is from Scotland, but my father worked in England his entire career. We were based off a small village – Bramerton – in Norfolk near the east coast. When I shifted to London as a student, it was the early 70s. A chaotic period... I caught the toe-end of the Flower Power revolution...'

'Were you caught *inside* the vortex of the hippie movement?' I ask without polish.

'I was quite influenced by it, though not too involved. But I was frustrated in not feeling "liberated" or "happy". I found

---

Jung versus Freud

Jung's disagreement with Freud is related to the latter's theory that the instincts of self-preservation and sexual preservation (later he added the destructive instinct) govern all aspects of a man's life.

Not surprisingly, Jung's metaphysical interpretations contrasted greatly with Freudian theories. The two differed while interpreting almost every aspect of psychology, including dreams and symbols. The following Jungian quote about the artist gives a good idea of how removed his thoughts were from gratification of the instinct:

The artist is not a person endowed with free will who seeks his own ends, but one who allows art to realize its purposes through him. As a human being he may have moods and a will and personal aims, but as an artist he

the movement inhuman and alienating in some ways. In contrast, I was looking at Indian sculpture as having tradition behind it... a rare coherence... I tried out many ideas during that time. I even took philosophy classes, but gave them up because they were dry and logic-intensive; quite contrary to the subjective hippie philosophy of "expressing oneself".'

So she related to neither conventional nor experimental philosophy. But Indian sculpture—

'... is part of a much bigger worldview – scriptures, spirituality... the whole gamut of ideas. I appreciated it even more because at the same time, the hippie movement was unsuccessfully trying to convince me that I was having fun.'

So she decided that sculpting would be her path to nirvana and boarded a flight to India. She was just twenty-four when she came to Bangalore.

'Since I was based close to the city, Bangalore became my backyard. Oh, I walked the streets with a swagger in my step and happily visited friends. I wouldn't do that now; the traffic's turned awful. Yeah, it still has bookshops and some reminiscent glimpses but the horrible traffic nullifies all that. Bangalore seems to be in full-fledged celebration of consumer freedom.'

---

is "man" in a higher sense - he is "collective man", a vehicle and moulder of the unconscious psychic life of mankind. (from 'Psychology and Literature', 1930)

It is said that Jung wrote in a 1912 letter to Freud:

If ever you should rid yourself entirely of your complexes and stop playing the father to your sons, and instead of aiming continually at their weak spots took a good look at your own for a change, then I will mend my ways and at one stroke uproot the vice of being in two minds about you.

Despite all their differences, many believe that Jung tried to integrate his theories with existing Freudian concepts by, among other means, borrowing Freudian terminologies.

'What was your impression of Bangaloreans of yore?' I ask.

'Somehow, one feels that they were more focused on family and familial values. And for the first time in my life, I met seriously religious people. I had to come to Bangalore to make my first Catholic acquaintance. Yeah, I hadn't met even *one* in Britain. And the Christians in Britain left no impression on me. On the other hand, religion played a pivotal role in the lives of some of those Bangaloreans. And I have a vivid memory of this English family I knew in Rhenius Street; they lived in a bungalow. Houses and lives like that don't exist any more. If you own a downtown bungalow in Bangalore today, you'll not catch the sun rising or setting. You'll just see tall buildings frowning down upon you. A lot of essential Bangalore seems to be lost...'

Speaking of a sense of loss, I wonder how she stays separated from family, especially her spouse, for long periods.

'I'm a spinster for life,' she grins. 'Why? Hmm... the strongest reason was that in my generation, if a woman was serious about her career, it was made clear that marriage wasn't possible.'

'We're in the British context here?'

'Most certainly. Regressive thoughts aren't an Oriental prerogative. End of the day, the economic throttle is held by men. To a frightening degree, even today the situation is the same. I still see young women curtail their talents and take up lesser jobs. Boyfriend first. Or hubby first. Men might have opened their minds now, but only moderately. Look at working Indian women, doubling up and stressing themselves at home after a full day at work.'

She herself offers the reverse image.

'Two years back, I made an oak carving for a parish church in the town of Caerphilly,' she says, handing me a copy of a report from *The Times*. 'Notice the bull enshrined in the Nativity scene. Let's be clear about this – it's inspired by Nandi, but it isn't Nandi. The bull's presence serves a purpose. It's a fertile, violent animal that has the power to become the image of peace. I've approached the symbol in a respectful, accurate manner. I fear misinterpretation of my work as disrespect of any religion. That would be totally false because I respect Hinduism a lot.'

The engraving, adorning a church in the Welsh valleys, has a very Indian imagery. The central figure is that of Joseph, transformed into a caring father while holding the infant Jesus. Lying down, Mary looks on, trusting her husband with this fragile new life. *After 2000 years, Joseph holds the baby*, runs the title of the piece. 'The reason I'm telling you this is because there are middle-class men in Britain today who make sacrifices in their career to spend time with their children. Facing the situation as is – including nappy changes and all that – instead of having a glamorous, hands-off approach to fatherhood. They're called Fathers Direct. These men deeply appreciated the work. So there's hope that the subsequent generations will see equality.'

I suggest that many women in the Bangalore IT industry have no choice but to be serious about their career or get kicked out of work. A coercive corporate force stronger than machismo is forcing young Indian men to adapt, to become metrosexual. Perhaps that change is happening in India at an earlier stage of economic maturity. The talk turns to the Indian IT revolution and I ask for her opinion.

'I'm not a mechanised person, so I hardly have an opinion about the IT movement,' she says. 'It will be interesting, though, to see how the situation develops beyond consumerism in the next five to ten years. The message in current circulation is that consumerism is progressive. Since this idea is at its crest, it's not advisable to analyse it right away. But bear in mind that I've just flitted in and out of Bangalore during the last decade. I've seen the change in spurts while passing through the city on my way to the villages that called me.'

'Why did this village call you?' I ask.

'Oh, it's a long story,' she says. 'Siddhartha – the founder of Fireflies – had an idea about working with existing craft in a new way. In India, you find amazing levels of skill, but the end-product is often kitsch. Also, there's a fear that these skills will die without patrons. Augmenting this fear is the fact that sculpting itself is changing. You'll find trendy shifts in medium like using stainless steel instead of stone. Even in stone, machine grinders and cutters are taking over. The artisans who work with machines might contract silicosis because of the fine dust they breathe in. And at the same time, a beautiful manual art is led towards extinction. Traditional stone is not used even in temples nowadays because of an incorrect perception that cement is cheaper.

'Last year when I was here, someone told me about these seventy-odd talented artisans. I visited them and found their work to be of high quality. I then asked them to sculpt the scene of Joseph and the Nativity. Other than gauging progress regularly, I took a hands-off approach. When I liked their work, I spoke to Siddhartha…'

And the artisans were eventually roped in to work with Caroline. She now hopes that the initiative results in images that can help the artisans grow. That it would empower them.

'If the project succeeds in creating beauty, the next step would be to inform people that this great art form needs support. As of now, it mechanically caters to the tourist trade, on the fringes of creativity. To change the scenario, this project would like to link with the Jung Centre in Bangalore and thereby have a modern context through which to find patrons, specifically middle-class people. And we hope they will value the creations. More ambitiously, I would like these very people to come and try their hand at sculpting; that might inspire them to retain their patronage.'

A flurry of cawing and screeching overhead reminds us that the sun is setting. Caroline has to get ready for prayer. I have fifty kilometres to travel back. We say goodbye, but not before she tells me how she relates to her chosen art form.

'Working on stone,' she says in a soft voice, 'is a slow, transformative process. It has a therapeutic effect, involving the whole person. Since it grows at a human pace, one really has to engage.'

Weeks later, I'll stumble across another Jungian quote concerning the artist; it is one that fits well with the image of Caroline working in Fireflies:

The creative process, so far as we are able to follow it at all, consists in the unconscious activation of an archetypal image and elaborating and shaping it into the finished work. By giving it shape, the artist translates it into the language of the present and makes it possible for us to find our way back to the deepest springs of life.

* * *

I revisit Kamanahalli one fine morning and see signs of it becoming a preferred residential locality among budget expatriates. I reach Thomas' home and present a homemade teddy to Eva van Berckel. She was born a few days ago and has just returned home from her baptism. While the young lady, representing a cultural amalgam she doesn't understand or care about, wails in protest, I snap her into film. Over breakfast, Thomas tells me that his parents have hopped a continent to see their granddaughter. He then casually informs me that he had gone to Cuddalore for some tsunami relief work before Lalita summoned him back to wait on her.

'Rightly so,' I say.

'Yeah-yeah.'

'So what else is new?'

'Piri Piri,' he says, sounding quite excited.

I learn that it is the name of a new café that has opened near his house. It is owned by an Indian and his Portuguese wife. Thomas takes me to the place and orders black coffee. We sit in the portico and look around with self-satisfied grins. Change, I reflect, is the subtle springing of one café at a time.

* * *

I meet Megan Sullivan, an American, when she is on the verge of going back home. There is no time for a comprehensive chat. So we keep it short. She tells me that she came to Bangalore as a volunteer for the I-to-I Foundation.

'I had to come,' she says. 'I then had an Indian boyfriend of more than two years. And the Indian courses I took in my college were fascinating.'

After spending five months teaching hearing-impaired kindergarten children in the city, she went to Tamil Nadu to do her bit for the tsunami victims. Only then did she take a month's vacation in Thailand.

'I came back a bit disappointed,' she says, 'I found Thailand touristy compared to India.'

'That's a popular opinion,' I say. 'Many people find the rest of Asia er... unusual after India.'

'You bet. India is a stimulating assault on the senses.'

We have heard that somewhere before.

Minding Their Languages

It is a lazy afternoon when I arrive at a small boutique-cum-tailoring joint in Indiranagar. Vidya, the lady who runs the place, is busy sewing clothes. Seated on the other side of the cutting counter is a man who spends his afternoons chatting with her. He is dressed in a patterned blue, green and yellow beach shirt, semi-casual trousers and beige shoes with zippers running through their centres. His large grey eyes seem familiar because he has passed them down to his daughter Claudia, the girl I met at Equations. Franco Romiti welcomes me in a rasping, half Don Corleone voice and offers a chair. He speaks good English, but with a strong Italian accent.

'How do you find Bangalore?' I ask upon taking a seat.

Bang! Just like that, he begins his prodigious comparisons.

'The climate is the same as the Canaries, the traffic the same as Napoli.'

'Napoli?' I ask.

'Yes. Napoli is probably worse; nobody notices red lights there. Although you don't find cows on the road. In Bangalore, men may not evoke respect, but you cannot imagine running down a cow.'

Ah, the classic cows-on-the-road image! It appears to have overtaken snake-charmers and rope tricks as the image foreigners most associate with India. But Franco has a rounder view of the country. Not just because he has spent a whole winter here, but also because—

'I see things in India just as they were fifty years ago in Italy,' he says. 'In the forties, I've experienced water scarcity and utmost poverty as a lad. It was only in the mid-fifties that things began improving in Italy.'

'When were you born?' I ask.

'1942.' That means he was burping, toddling, and finally measuring the world with clumsy steps while Europe was experiencing the gruesome horrors of World War II.

'So you were already a teenager by the time things began looking up?' I ask.

Franco nods.

'In 1960,' he says, 'mine was the first family in our neighbourhood to own a fridge. I used to love having a rock of ice in my mouth, savouring its freshness... life is best when simple!'

His past sounds compelling. I ask him to tell me more about it.

'I was born in Anagni (pronounced Ananyi) in the province of Frosinone,' he says, beginning at the beginning. 'I started my professional life as a tutor in an educational institute. My job was to help convicted juveniles reform themselves after serving their sentence. After that, I enrolled for the mandatory stint in the military. You couldn't find proper employment otherwise... you may be summoned for duty any time, you see? So I served my time there before joining an airline company where I worked till my retirement six years ago.' He adds with all humility: 'It was an administrative position.'

'I hear that you've found a new profession in India. How does it feel to teach Italian?'

'Oh, I'm just helping a friend,' he says. 'In an informal capacity, I teach a few Indians basic grammar. Colloquial tips, that's all.' As an afterthought, he adds: 'It's a joke!'

He means it is light work, made lighter by students who smile a lot and like to see him. It strikes me that six years after retirement, Franco has been surprised by a new sense of fulfilment. That serendipity, perhaps, has stoked the wish to start a new life in India. I ask him about it. He tells me that the chief reason is something else – he "feels well" about the cost of living here. Because back home, his life is controlled by the European Union.

'Britain, Germany and France are very powerful members of the EU and they want to force the others. That's all I understand about the concept of EU,' he admits. 'But I know that the cost of living has skyrocketed because of the EU. They fixed the exchange rate at 1936 lira per Euro. So even a 0.05 Euro price swing is large.' His body distorts into an expansive and fatalistic shrug. 'In Italy, I'm just a pensioner. In India, I can be called rich. On a conservative estimate, I can live five comfortable months here for every month there. Isn't the main problem for people everywhere their economic situation? So there. Now, if only I can convince my wife about this...'

That, he says, would take some persuasion. After all, he nearly didn't come to India himself. When he finally made the trip as Claudia's escort, it was meant to last a mere week. The elastic week has become a season and here he is, speaking about an alternative future.

'But,' he adds, 'one cannot reach a decision solely on a mathematical basis. There are other considerations.' He means cultural differences. To prove his point, he narrates an incident he has observed near Trinity Circle. 'There was this man picking crumbs, mere crumbs, from garbage cans when a worker came out of his fast-food joint, dumped waste food in front of a dog and totally ignored the man. That people here don't see such things is unbelievable! For God's sake, give the food to the man... the dog will survive!'

Before I can ask him the next question, Vidya, who has been working furiously in the inner room, comes out. She has heard her husband Anup arrive.

'Maybe we should finish that chore,' she tells Franco.

Franco responds by displaying great energy. He galvanises Anup into driving them to the cooking-gas dealer, then heaves an empty gas cylinder to the waiting car. I stand guard at the boutique and watch the unlikely trio head out for a replacement. I wonder what onlookers would make of them. Would they guess that they are flat-mates? Because that is exactly what they are. Anup and Vidya occupy one bedroom, Claudia and Franco another in a flat in Malleshpalya.

In fifteen minutes, they are back. I make them tell me how they met. It turns out to be a heartening tale of true globalisation. At six a.m. one morning, the Italians were looking for an auto-rickshaw while the Indians drove by. They stopped. And offered a lift when they discovered a common destination – the railway station. Franco, who finds everyone in India friendly except for "insufferable auto-rickshaw drivers" (which is why he prefers the Bangalore buses), immediately accepted. En route, someone mooted the idea of sharing an apartment. And wonder of wonders, it was enthusiastically accepted.

'One hour after we met, we found common interests,' says Franco. 'Now, we're like brother and sister.'

'We don't want them to go back,' adds Vidya. 'Initially, we were sceptical about staying with foreigners, but they're so much like us.'

Franco nods.

'In Europe,' he says, 'people use rudeness as currency to buy privacy. Whereas Indians are openly curious about other people. Such traits are responsible for this Indo-Italian partnership working. Plus...for me, everything happens casually. Just like my visit to India. I repeat: life is made of simple things.'

It sounds deceptively simple. He occasionally cooks a tasty Italian meal for all. And in turn has no issues eating spicy Indian meals. Somehow... it is working.

'What started as a financial solution has led to a good friendship,' he concludes.

So mathematical solutions do have a knack of working out. Perhaps that is an omen for Franco.

* * *

Seated in a meeting room in Kazumasa Kuboki's office, I observe his precise movements, black-white-brown hair and polite smile and hear him say:

'As a Senior Investment Advisor of JETRO (Japan External Trade Organisation), I help the promotion of trade between India and Japan.'

'Let's begin with how you became associated with India,' I suggest.

'I think it happened when I opted to study Hindi during graduation,' he says while pouring out two cups of black tea. 'The Buddhist culture had always intrigued me. By learning Hindi, I felt I could understand the country that produced the religion. And frankly, the major languages like

Arabic, Russian, Spanish, French and Mandarin had stiff competition. Only upon landing in Delhi in 1968 to spend a year learning Hindi on an Indian government scholarship did I realise: "Hey, these Indians speak good English. They don't need a Hindi to Japanese translator!"'

Apart from studying, Kuboki also utilised the year to travel extensively through India, paying particular attention to the Buddhist sites of Sarnath, Bodhgaya and Sanchi. And Indian hospitality impressed him wherever he went.

'Athithi devo bhava (the guest is akin to God),' he says in staccato Sanskrit, 'was till then an incomprehensible sentiment. It's quite different from Customer is King, right? In Japan, people who cannot afford servants find it difficult to welcome guests to their homes.'

After Kuboki went back home, job opportunities were understandably scarce for a Hindi specialist. But he found one at the Indian desk of an automobile company. The job brought him back to India for four years.

'I stayed in Kolkata between '78 and '81,' he says. 'I love the Bengalis. I was in Dhaka briefly in '73, so I knew some Bengali.'

'That would have made them your fans,' I say. Kuboki's reply tells me that he finds the Bengali's linguistic pride natural.

'We Japanese find it difficult to understand why Indians who can speak English feel superior. That makes me worry for Indian culture.' After a pause, he adds: 'I'm glad you're writing this book. Indians seldom write about their own mentality as Japanese do. You people are an optimistic, cheerful lot.'

I laugh.

'I wish I could see India from your perspective,' I say.

'Let me explain,' he says. 'I'm sure you're aware that the Japanese are polite people. We employ a lot of Excuse Mes and Beg Pardons in our speech. When somebody asks for a favour and a Japanese replies: "I'll consider", he means "No, never!" But soon after getting this reply, an Indian would cheerfully call up to enquire how the consideration went. Part of my job is to explain such nuances to visiting delegates. They normally find Indians to be quite blind to their faults. And they feel that Indians make excuses for their short-comings. For example, the infamous "Indian punctuality". But I'm glad to see the present generation eliminating those faults.'

'But we still need to do some catching up, I suppose?' I ask and get an indirect reply.

'Today, you'll hear an announcement in our railway stations if the train is a minute late. At one time, we weren't punctual either. In fact, the Japanese were notoriously tardy two hundred years ago. Why, before the Second World War, we were a nation producing inferior quality goods for a cheap price. The war eliminated the old guard and we changed. We realised that we don't have sufficient natural resources, so the only solution was to import raw materials, make quality products and export them. Everybody who could get an education did. And a culture free of nepotism and favouritism emerged. The economy picked up and as a teenager, I saw my family acquire a TV, a fridge and a car. All through EMI payments. At the same time, we saw a movement similar to what's happening in Bangalore today. Trains coming from the rural parts of northern Japan were filled with young, enthusiastic people. They got recruited by giant companies... and Japan soon became an urban country.'

'Do you think it was the nation's response to Hiroshima and Nagasaki?' I ask.

Kuboki is alarmed that I should think of attributing success to hate.

'The World War was fought by a monarchy and an army that controlled everything,' he says. 'The war finished that bad social system. Had we not been defeated so soundly, we might still be limping within that system. I don't imply that we have forgotten past lessons, mind you. But practically, look at what happened after the war – the Americans set up their defence bases in Japan, and that was good because it reduced our budget for defence. Till date, Japan has a rudimentary defence force; there's no "official" army.' He, resumes after a pause, 'Many Japanese feel the time is now ripe to have better defence infrastructure. And we would race towards that, were we as casual in amending the Constitution as Indians are.'

Ouch! This man has a way of pinching when and where I least expect it. To change the topic, I ask him about his presence in Bangalore.

'Two reasons pulled me back to India,' he replies. 'Firstly, I wanted to spend more time here. Secondly, I wanted to hone my skills with an MBA. So I joined a course in Delhi at the age of fifty-six. Three months after I enrolled, I saw this opening in JETRO. It was an offer I couldn't resist. I now work towards increasing Japanese investment in India.'

Of course, the current migration entails sacrifices. Kuboki stays all alone in a service apartment in Bangalore while his wife, Takako Hirose, teaches South Asian politics in the Senshu University.

'Her affinity for India,' he insists, 'was the initial attraction for me.'

'You are seriously besotted by India, aren't you?'

He smiles and says:

'It's a nation of a billion people living in peace, generally speaking. Admirable. I want to see how it works out for these hard-working people. I'm still pondering over what I should do after this stint. I'll either resume my MBA or learn more about Indian sociology. I would like to know, for example, why you retain surnames that give away your origins. Intriguing. It's a system that promotes differentiation. But then, that's India.'

Statistics

The Foreigners' Registration Office (FRO) is situated in the same compound as the office of Bangalore's Commissioner of Police. Today, I'm on my third visit here. After doing a few vain rounds of the compound during my earlier visits, I had learnt that unless I get Commissioner Muniswamy's permission, I will not be given any data. So I meet the gentleman who readily signs my application for some statistics on expatriates. That leads me to DCP (Intelligence) Krishna Bhat who, in turn, redirects me to the officer running the FRO, Assistant Commissioner of Police (ACP) Jagadeesh Prasad. In between, I have been witness to the sunset stirring of a thousand bats that roost in the trees shading the compound, and I have stood at attention along with constables during the lowering of the flag.

And now, sitting outside the ACP's office, I hear the traffic bellowing past Infantry Road. But the FRO waiting-room is pleasantly filled with expectancy. It has the bearings of an ad hoc cultural classroom. Seated next to me is a bearded man from the Middle East. In front of me, I see a diminutive pigtailed Asian, probably a Sri Lankan, and not far on my right is a white lady shushing her two naughty boys. Outside, close to the threshold of the FRO, are a group of young African students. A tall, balding white man walks in wearing a grey suit and an expression of resignation. A phone rings, my bearded neighbour answers and I hear the Arabic intonations of a weary man unburdening his heart to a sympathetic friend. A wail from behind alerts me to the presence of an infant; he is probably the only one in the room who doesn't care which country he is in.

Soon, my turn arrives and I'm led into Jagadeesh Prasad's office. Within moments, my instinct informs me that the room I've entered is bereft of khaki fear. I'm not surprised because I have had similar experiences in the Commissioner's and the DCP's office.

'How long have you been running the FRO?' I ask the ACP.

'Two years now. But during the two years preceding this stint, I dealt with state intelligence matters pertaining to foreigners... I believe you're looking for some statistics...'

'Yes.'

The ACP picks up a couple of files lying on his table and says:

'Well, we currently have 12,000 to 13,000 registered foreigners from 97 countries in Bangalore alone. *That's nearly half the expatriate population in the whole country*! It's difficult to provide an exact count because we made the Exit Permit optional. Instead, we ask the foreigner to simply surrender his Residence Permit at the airport before departure, and it takes around three to four months for that to reach the FRO that issued it.'

Predictably, the number of registrations is on the rise.

'We saw a plateau in registrations for three years from 2001-03. It was 6,121 in 2001; 5,914 in 2002 and 6,134 in 2003. But the number for 2004 is 6,943. And if I consider January to be a fair reflection of how the year would pan out, we'll have around 8,000 registrations in 2005.'

The United States heads the 2004 list with 1,600 registrations. Sri Lanka is a distant second with 890. Bronze is bagged by a dark horse – Iran, with 584 registrations. The fourth place goes to Bangladesh which, with 525 registrations, has seen a steep decline over the years.

'That's definitely because we conduct intense scrutiny of Bangladeshi applications ever since the then Home Minister L. K. Advani admitted that the Pakistani spy agency, the ISI, is infiltrating India through the Bangladesh border. So we've begun using the local police to verify the address given by applicants and also periodically check on them. When you consider that we had as many as 1,596 Bangladeshis registering here in 2001, you'll agree that our vigil is certainly not misplaced; the figures tell a clear story.'

Another nation that is on the FRO watch-list is Pakistan. The relations between the neighbours being what they are, visa violations are not easily tolerated. And Pakistanis who overstay might end up in prison.

'Overstaying is our biggest issue,' says the ACP. 'Last year, 157 foreigners overstayed whereas 608 registered themselves belatedly. Housewives are the biggest culprits – their reason for overstaying is simply that they forget to extend their stay. Professionals, on the other hand, have corporate memory reminding them to file extensions. Right now, we're lobbying to change the penal rules for overstaying because defaulting foreigners get away with paying a $30 fine. Unfortunately, this is encouraging them to abuse the system. A few of them think it's their prerogative to overstay. They talk cheaply about our rules and regulations. After all, they're paying the fine, aren't they? Whether you miss your extension by a day or months, the fine remains the same. As one of the amendments, we want to have incremental fines, so that their oversight will hurt the pocket. We welcome them to come to our land, but they should not violate the law. I believe we're very fair and polite while treating them. We don't chase out people like some of the Western countries would.'

That appears to be a fair statement. The FRO prosecuted just 20 people in 2004. These were extreme cases of overstaying or violation of multiple rules; there have been a couple of cases of forgeries too. He lists the countries these "extreme violators" come from – Iran, Jordan, Nigeria, Kenya...

'And nearly 75% of the violators are people of Indian origin! We find that once stringent action is taken against a person of a particular country, all fellow nationals immediately rush in to get their documents in order. So it actually helps streamline the system.'

Students seem to dominate the violation lists. Around 3,000 students registered in Bangalore in 2004, half of whom were from the Middle East; around 500 hailed from Iran alone. A good number of the students are prone to change their residence, course or college, or sometimes completely give up their studies without notifying the FRO. As I find out over the succeeding months, these are potential loose canon balls. I imagine that with so much young, alien blood, the FRO would be regularly dealing with cases of violent scuffles.

'Not at all,' says the ACP. 'I can remember just one case of a drunken brawl between men of different nationalities. Other than that, it's been peaceful.'

'Reports of racism from foreigners or Indians?'

'Oh, none that I'm aware of.'

That is a statistical glitch. Racist incidents are seldom – make that never – reported in police stations. Unfortunate foreigners who get mired in racism find other coping mechanisms... I turn my attention back to the ACP... So far we have spoken about foreigners who have been brought here by business and employment opportunities, and good educational institutes. But there is another important category: tourists.

'Yes,' says the ACP. 'Bangalore has a good number of temporary tourist visa holders at any time. It's valid for six months at the most.'

'Do tourists overstay too?'

'Sometimes. But they don't have to register with us. They're handled by the Bureau of Immigration.'

'Including the tourists, how many foreigners do you estimate in the city?'

'Well, my gut feel would put the estimate around 20,000 people.'

Over the next few months, I learn that a surprising number of tourist visa holders are staying back to work on the sly. And they are not just Bangladeshis or Sri Lankans. It sounds more like a problem that a developed nation would face. Perhaps India is coming of age.

'Globalisation has brought in an increased influx of foreigners,' says the ACP. 'And this trend is here to stay. Many foreigners are opting to stay back in Bangalore. They're quite happy except for the traffic. They get a handsome salary, the weather is lovely and the people friendly. What more could they ask for? Yes, this trend is moving in just one direction. Up. I can vouch for that... the workload in my office is increasing.'

I take that as a positive omen and take leave of the ACP. Outside, in the waiting room, the scene has barely changed. It feels like a model of the globe seen from a different angle.

Campus Round-up

All Patrick has to tell me about Brindavan College to get me interested is that it boasts of students from forty-two countries. Forty-two! In the mission I have undertaken, this piece of news is like discovering the means to get airdropped to the summit instead of climbing the mountain.

Two days later, Patrick and I start from Basavanagudi and head north towards Bhoopasandra. En route, as we wait for the Town Hall signal to change colour, I see dozens of pairs of eyes directed towards me. I compliment myself on my clothes before realising that the object of their attention is my pillion rider. Truck drivers lean over their helpers to have a better look; a well-dressed housewife in a small family car casts discreet glances from behind dark sunglasses. Passengers of a nearby bus peep at us as if inspecting an invisible accident. This has been Patrick's world for fourteen years! I'm hard-pressed to tolerate it for 140 seconds.

Mercifully, the signal changes and we reach Bhoopasandra without further incident.

Bhoopasandra is located not far from the Hebbal interchange that links the city with the Outer Ring Road. Despite its recent urban makeover, it is still a rustic locality. To reach it, one has to actually cross a short stretch of open fields basking in the sunshine. From that point, locating the college is easy – one just needs to follow the chatter and youth.

Once inside the college, we seek Raed Sabha. His brother and the Palestinian Founding Trustee of the institution, Majed Sabha, is on an overseas trip. It is only the mention of Patrick's name that has ensured an appointment. We wait in the corridor and look at the spotlessly clean interiors and pleasant ambience that the Bangalore airport would gladly accept. The college is twelve years old and already looks flush and distinguished.

When we are ushered into Raed Sabha's presence, I put forth my request to him. Step one of the mission is to meet a handful of students. I draw up a list of countries I would prefer them to be from, which includes Vietnam, Palestine, Malaysia, Brazil, Kazakhstan (or any other Central Asian nation), Russia, South Africa, any European country and New Zealand. Step two would be to interview Majed Sabha when he is available. As I study Raed Sabha's face for a response, I'm reminded of a haughty peacock in the thick of a thunderstorm. Once he satisfies himself that his college will come to no harm by harbouring a busybody like me, he lets the Secretary of the college handle the details. The Secretary, a meticulous man named Anantharamaiah, studies the list and informs me that the college has no Latin Americans and very few students from developed countries. He, however, promises to do his best and we set up a rendezvous two days later.

At the appointed time, I'm back in the campus. I wait and worry about the students' response. My fears are soon put to rest with the appearance of a student group which seems just as eager as I am. I have decided that we should have an informal group discussion – an open house, which will allow points and counterpoints to float around harmlessly. And also allow anyone in the group to pick up a floater and steer.

Although the group is not as diverse as I had hoped for, the lively discussion that follows teaches me an important lesson. That diverse individuals make up for the lack of diversity in their origin. In other words, hailing from different places is good; but what makes a journey truly exciting is travelling with people going different places.

Of Dogs, Debates and Diversity

Setting	:	Brindavan College, Bhoopasandra
Dramatis Personae	:	*(all play themselves)*
Rifard Faizal	–	Sri Lankan
Abhirup Sarkar	–	Bengali Indian
Jiten Joshi	–	Tanzanian
Debanjan Chatterjee	–	Bengali Indian
Mohammad Radhi	–	Bahraini
Miriam	–	Ugandan
Safa Sharif	–	Bahraini
Khulood Ali	–	Bahraini
Zainab	–	Sri Lankan
Sameer	–	Indian
Eshwar	–	Indian

Act I, Scene I
First Impressions

| Rifard | The first day, I mistook a Kolkatan for a Chinese *(looks slyly at Abhirup)*. But having 120 Sri Lankans in the college smoothened the transition to India and the college. |

Jiten	Incredible, my first day. The question "Where are you from?" took a whole new meaning – my class is *so* diverse. I'm still asking the same question today. My great-grandfather left India and travelled to Africa, so don't be fooled by my looks... I'm not Indian at all, not even in shades. But I prefer not to tell that to auto-rickshaw drivers here. And they never overcharge me!
Safa	Oh, we can handle those "auto-guys" now.
Rifard	I was once ferried by an auto-guy who didn't know Hindi. But we found a better alternative to communicate – we both knew Tamil!
Debanjan	Language is the first hurdle in our classroom. English, de facto, becomes the common denominator. I'm tickled to have international friends... when people in Kolkata sympathise with me for being away from home, I tell them how far my friends have travelled.
Mohammad	After five years – I'm doing my MCA now – I can laugh over my first day. But it felt disastrous then. Because in Bahrain, we're used to colleges having a front gate and a back gate.
Eshwar	Ok...? And which one did Brindavan lack?
Mohammad	The college was being constructed when I joined ... the front gate looked like the back gate. And a contented cow was passing by. "Is this the college?" I asked my father, and almost returned to Bahrain. But in my case too, the company of my countrymen helped. One of my friends went back because he couldn't tolerate the mosquito bites! We Bahraini have to learn about mosquito repellents after we come here... now the Bhoopasandra mosquitoes don't scare me.
Eshwar	(*grinning*) Do you talk them out of the room?
Mohammad	I can speak Hindi! And a few words of Kannada too. You may not believe it, but Kannada has a few words in common with Arabic!

Miriam	For me, the fear factor was canine. But dogs don't scare me any more. And I love India for the independence it gives me... unlike in Uganda, here I'm the queen of my own life. A few minor problems like not understanding the Indian accent or not being understood by Indians can be overcome. In shops, I simply point out the commodity I want to buy. And now, there are supermarkets everywhere; I can just pick what I need.
Eshwar	Is staring an issue?
Miriam	(*sighs*) You bet! And people want to touch my hair wherever I go.
Mohammad	In Bahrain, we have countless cats, but no dogs. India has countless dogs, but few cats. During the first year, I and my friends purchased a monkey for around 200 bucks. Our favourite sport used to be throwing it from the second floor balcony and catching it in the first floor!
Safa	(*resuming the original "First Impression" thread*) It was my dream to come to India. My education in Bahrain was in an Indian school where I even learnt Hindi. Now, I can somewhat comprehend Bengali, Telugu and Kannada. But frankly, I almost went back too... and I hadn't even seen the college when the doubts surfaced ... one look at the Mumbai airport did it. But a few days later, I saw M. G. Road and decided to stay on! For a spoilt girl like me, India is a multifold experience. I learnt even simple chores like opening tuna cans only after coming here. But I'm still not used to people in Bhoopasandra stopping me on the road and asking:"You're from Saudi Arabia? Give me five rupees!"
Mohammad	Some locals ask if I can help send a relative to Bahrain.
Khulood	The first day, I was amazed at the distance between the airport and the college. In Bahrain,

everything is just 5-10 minutes away. Then I met Safa, and she became my roommate and best friend... despite her heroics with tuna cans and... well, the first night we were together, she was muttering in her sleep: "India... Bhoopasandra..." I almost moved out.

Mohammad	Speaking of airports, my first Indian experience was during immigration... the official baking of my passport...
Eshwar	Baking of the what?
Mohammad	We have observed that the immigration official, after clearing the formalities will flip the passport from one side to another. It means he wants 150 rupees. Corruption is the biggest problem in India...
Safa	Even auto drivers want extra money. One night, we refused to pay more, came in and closed the gate to our house. The guy threw stones at our balcony and even abused us in chaste Arabic!
Eshwar	Maybe it was Urdu...
Safa	Not at all. It was Arabic.
Rifard	Initially, Bhoopasandra was safe. Now, foreigners are being targeted. Since we're mostly out, our homes are ideal hunting grounds for burglars.

Act I, Scene II
When Perceptions Change

Rifard	I'm a Muslim living with a Christian, a Sinhalese and a Punjabi Hindu. So I now understand a lot of other customs, and it has opened my mind. During my younger days in Sri Lanka, my best friend was a Tamil. Here too, I have a Tamil friend who hails from Jaffna. He tells me his side of the story...we talk frankly about our country's political conflict. Students are young

	and hence flexible. But we're human after all. Once in a while, one senses undercurrents, and even plain animosity. Maybe that's why many seek the comfort of groups. Most Tamils stick to themselves and Sinhalese do the same.
Zainab	I agree. I've been friends with my roommate since my childhood – for seventeen years – without really knowing her. There are immutable facets to people... I like to see myself as a sociable Muslim Sri Lankan. Like Rifard. And we love hanging out with Indians.
Abhirup	*(speaks in a measured tone)* The college has Bengali groups too, and I'm the odd man out who interacts with friends from all over. I used to be careful initially... you know, not to be overly and overtly intimate with foreigners. I wanted to keep everybody happy.
Debanjan	People aren't open to discovering mental compatibilities with others...
Eshwar	Have any of you attempted to cajole people out of their shells? *(The group looks around the semi-circle, and intuitively conjures up an uncomfortable, muted consensus.)*
Everybody	We try and avoid issues where we sense a difference of opinion.
Rifard	*(partially rescinding his earlier stance)* Finally, a political mess like the Sri Lankan North-East conflict is not worth discussing. Will it serve a purpose?
Zainab	Political and cultural differences don't matter. All one needs to preserve is the bond with an individual.
Miriam	I avoid conflict... this is an alien land after all. Back home, I would stand up for my rights.
Mohammad	*(smiling as ever)* I keep smiling and keep the peace.

Sameer	It's best to respect each other's differences and avoid debate. Cold Wars are unnecessary.
Jiten	Yes, debates lead to Cold Wars. I've seen that when Arabs from Zanzibar and Africans from the Tanzanian mainland discuss secession. At the same time, I'm an ICCR student; a part of me tells me that perhaps we're here for exchanging ideas as well as gaining an education. We owe it to ourselves to talk on neutral land.
Eshwar	That's a wonderful blessing isn't it? Having a neutral ground to stand in and orate?
Rifard and Zainab	(*together*) But every nuance of debate has been exhausted. All everyone agrees about is that we've had enough of the war.
Eshwar	That, perhaps, is the greatest agreement possible.

Act I, Scene III
Bangalore Mine, Bangalore Thine

Khulood	It's the best place in India. Why? Great weather, educated people.
Safa	Very cosmopolitan. Comfortable. I go out, even to Bahrain, and a string pulls at my heart. I want to come back to Bangalore. And especially to find myself seated in a Barista!
Mohammad	If you're looking for Arabs, look in coffee shops! Sipping caffeine is our favourite pastime.
Safa	But for the few problems with security and medical care, I would have been planning to settle in India right now. But I'll go back home for my MBA after all.
Miriam	But for the dogs, Bangalore is a swell place.
Mohammad	I once saw a dog in the casualty ward of Bowring Hospital... relaxing *aaram se*. You cannot trust doctors in India to do the decent

	thing. I went back to Bahrain to get my slipped disc treated.
Debanjan	Rains unpredictable, high cost of living. But easy to live here.
Jiten	Bangaloreans are smart people. Top management positions in Tanzania are held by South Indians. The Bangalore night life is good...But doesn't *anybody* want to solve the stray dog menace?
Safa	But I miss the cows and the dogs while vacationing!
Zainab	I like the idea of buses having a section reserved for ladies. And mostly, I love Bangalore for having nutritional options when I'm broke. With CDs and cellphone requirements, one does go broke often...
Rifard	Most of Bangalore University is corrupt. It's impossible to get our documents without bribing... exam papers are sold at the university gates, revaluations always results in reduced marks. Papers aren't corrected sincerely...

(*The curtain falls*)

We say goodbye. When I'm alone, I reread the play and try to find substantiation of the claims made by my anonymous source. According to this person, resentment against the college students is silently brewing among the Bhoopasandra locals. And the closed cauldron might one day explode. Upon making further enquiries, I find the fears misplaced. The locals are quite happy with the students as they contribute to the local economy, in fact *make* the local economy. Landlords are a happier lot. Rents have multiplied six times in three years. Whereas they used to charge a rent of Rs.1,000/- for a two-bedroom house, the going rate now is Rs.3,000/- for a single-room. Land rates have meanwhile seen a five-fold increase. Coffee shops, cybercafés, pharmacies and restaurants have sprung up in this once sleepy hamlet. Even furniture dealers are a contented lot because students seldom bargain while buying and always dump their belongings at throwaway rates when they leave. Shops in the vicinity of the college sell quite a few packs of imported cigarettes and even offer a choice of foreign chocolates. The rates are exorbitant, even for local products. The students look affluent and behave likewise.

When resentment makes its intermittent appearance in Bhoopasandra, the actors are the students themselves. Due to the college's diversity, simple issues are likely to take political, communal or nationalistic hues. Take for instance the college cricket team. Since the college has a sizeable student population from two nations with strong cricketing traditions – India and Sri Lanka – the selection of the captain becomes a geopolitical issue. Some tussles involve Arabs.

As I loiter around the campus and pick brains, I get to hear about some of them. Arab boys, a student tells me, are prone to taking minor issues seriously and blowing them out of proportion. A couple of years back, a boy from the Indian subcontinent teased an Arab girl. The Arabs retaliated by directing their ire against all the compatriots of the boy.

'Don't dare mess with an Arab girl!'

The message was unambiguous and unified. Of course, human nature being what it is, a totally different issue or situation might easily divide the Arab consortium into nationalistic colours. Some divisions are economic in nature as well. Most Omanis, for instance, are less well off than Saudi Arabians and Bahrainis. And non-Arabs observe that students from these nations do not treat the Omani as an equal.

A college like Brindavan, therefore, is a dynamic environment where treaties are rewritten daily. And some of the rewrites lead one to conclude that divisiveness is not always more dangerous than unification. For example, a minor fight between two students – a Bengali Hindu Indian and a Muslim Indian – took unification beyond established parameters and redrew the political map of the college. The Bengali allegedly made a derogatory reference to Islam in the heat of the argument. The Muslim boy is said to have reported the incident at the mosque located within the campus. That did it. The Arabs closed ranks with the Indian Muslim.

At such times, the college management takes a firm stand and quashes the uprising with well-aimed warnings. It is as well. The agitators are young and occasionally reckless. As I get to know more about intra-college issues, I begin to appreciate the task the college management has on hand. And I look forward to meeting the Palestinian Founding Trustee, Majed Sabha.

I wonder what he feels about running an institution like the Brindavan college. True, it is a place where emotions run high. But what an ideal training ground it is for young people who want to take on the world! Forty-two distinct value systems coexisting in an Indian setting. Classrooms that mirror reality. Adjust or perish. It cannot get better than this.

Long after the students turn professionals, the Bhoopasandra lessons will stay.

Germane Matters

Heidrun met Chandrakant in her hometown Heilbronn in Germany while playing badminton. They got married and came to Bangalore in 1980 when she was just twenty-four. She has been living in a joint family ever since and finds life very agreeable.

'In the initial years of my marriage,' she says, 'I adopted a happy-go-lucky attitude. My mother-in-law took care of the household while I played shuttlecock with my husband. Responsibility came with the birth of my children.' She adds, 'It helps Indo-Western marriages if the Indian man or woman has a Westernised bent of mind. And I think it helps if he or she belongs to the upper strata of society as well.'

'Do you feel homesick?' I ask.

'Initially, I did,' she says. 'Especially during Christmas. But there comes a certain point in time when you can't go back. Now I visit once every two to three years and find it shocking to pay two Euros for a bus ticket. Things change and so do perceptions. My biggest worry when I got married was my mother's welfare – she was widowed by then. But she used to come down for three months every year and I discovered that I spent more time with my mother than most Germans do.'

* * *

'I first came to India – Kolkata to be specific – in 1958,' says Wilfried Vogeler, 'as a consul in the German Foreign Service. While there, I married a Gujarati girl in 1963 and then went back to Bonn.'

Over the years, Wilfried was posted in Bangkok, Cairo, Port-of-Spain and New Delhi. His last assignment was in Kuala Lumpur. After retirement, one would have expected him to accompany his wife periodically on nostalgic trips to India. But he chose to do more than that.

'The idea of enduring harsh German winters appealed neither to my wife nor to me,' he says. 'So in 1994, we began searching for an ideal location where we could spend the cold months. Preferably a neutral country. We considered Lebanon, but it was politically unstable; we considered Afghanistan and thankfully decided against it. Then we saw that the Narasimha Rao-Manmohan Singh combination was making India more welcoming for foreigners. Liberalisation seemed to be working. So we said: "Let's try out India." And went about finding a suitable city in this vast country. We eliminated the four metros for many reasons, mainly climatic. But we found Bangalore very appealing. It has lovely weather and a great intellectual climate. We purchased this apartment a year later.'

'It's a good buy,' I say while studying the interiors of the house. Located in downtown Bangalore, it seems equipped with everything an elderly couple might need to live in comfort. 'What's your yearly routine?'

'We arrive in Bangalore in the beginning of November and return by around the first week of May. My wife has a Person-of-Indian-Origin card, so our tourist visas are valid for fifteen years. But we are very careful about the 180-day stay limit lest we get trapped in taxation issues. My wife owns the property, phone and credit cards, and she files a tax return every year to account for the small bank interest accrued. That simplifies everything.'

'Is it easy imitating migratory birds?'

'One does compare the two societies a lot,' he says. 'I get frustrated by the power-cuts in India, for example. I have to live with the UPS and the generator, not to mention uncollected garbage, perennial honking... I'm sure you are familiar with the list. But in Germany, I get angry at the over-regulation of life. I have to wait for the pedestrian red light to change before I cross the street even if there is no traffic. And I cannot stop just anywhere and ask for directions, or change lanes at whim. It's stifling, especially for one who has known a laissez-faire existence in India and the Caribbean! The net result is that I look forward to coming to India and then I look forward to returning. Overall, I find living in India quite satisfactory. We can even afford a live-in maid.'

'And this arrangement probably has the added advantage of your wife being on her turf half the time,' I say.

Wilfried smiles.

'One of the reasons we chose Bangalore is that she, being a Gujarati, has no linguistic advantage. We both are in an "alien" environment. That's the great strength of India. It's more like the European Union than a single nation. Germans keep asking me: "Do you speak Indian?" and I have to explain to them that their question makes no sense. There's no such thing as "Indian" language, or "Indian" food. The diversity has kept me fascinated. Let me tell you an interesting anecdote from my days as a diplomat. During an Embassy luncheon, three people from diverse backgrounds – a Muslim representative of India, a Parsee representative of Pakistan and my wife, the wife of a German diplomat – found that they could converse in a common language. Gujarati!'

I tell him I'm delighted to discover that Indian languages are not always divisive, and then ask:

'You said you were posted in New Delhi for six years. You must have handled sensitive information during that time. Did you, at any point, feel that there might be a conflict of interest since your wife is Indian?'

Wilfried responds with a diplomatic answer.

'Diplomats,' he says, 'work towards building bridges. We, I and my wife, have built a bridge by becoming a family. Can it get any better?'

'And how has the marriage been?'

'It's lasted, so it can't be too bad, can it? Marriages between European girls and Indian men fail more often.'

'A German lady happily married to an Indian for the last twenty-five years told me the same thing,' I say.

'Yes. Being an Indian daughter-in-law is very difficult. Love quickly fades and the daily chores take over. The tensile strength of Indian women helps sustain marriages of the other kind. And, of course, it's easier being an Indian son-in-law. You get unheard of privileges.'

'Do you think the male ego gets a boost in such marriages?'

'Well, Indian women who go abroad don't salivate over their foreigner husbands if that's what you mean. But yes, there are perks when the wife is Indian. Visiting the in-laws can be a holiday experience!'

* * *

During my first meeting with Astrid Abbrecher, we begin by talking about unemployment in Germany. Astrid attributes it to the carry forward effect from Germany's reunification, the German's reluctance to relocate, and the shifting of jobs to Asia and Poland. We then talk about her work as a language specialist in a multinational organisation, the many familiar travails and joys of an expatriate, her unending search for a lifetime partner and the challenges of living in India. We also touch upon racism, which is to say she provides the rationale behind a typical German's demeanour and passionately argues why it should not be misconstrued as racism. For some reason, she saves the most significant facet of her personality till the end. When we are saying goodbye, she announces:

'By the way, I play in the Bangalore School of Music Chamber Orchestra.'

It is too late to continue the conversation now. So she rides off on her gearless scooter and I look forward to our next meeting. It happens months later in an Italian eatery in Indiranagar. Upon taking our seats, I try summing up her appearance. Blood-red shirt. Sharp nose. Expressive eyes. Brown hair tightly pressed against her head. Brisk hand movements. It is a very pleasing sight and it makes me remark:

'You're still here.'

'I have no plans of leaving,' she says. 'I can cope with the chaos. Moreover, I feel comfortable and happy in India.'

'Is it because of the music?'

'Well, if it were not music, I might have found something else. But yes, music makes my stay enjoyable.'

I try to picture her playing in the orchestra. I can't; I need more details.

'What instrument do you play?' I ask.

'The violin. I'm not skilled enough to be amongst the first violinists. So I play a second violin. That means I provide support to the primary melody.'

'How did your association with the orchestra happen?'

'When I came here,' she says, 'I had not touched the violin for ten years. But I brought it along because I had resolved to resume my lessons. Soon after I reached, I searched the Yellow Pages, called up people and got to know about the Bangalore School of Music. I learnt that it conducts both beginner and advanced-level classes. So I went to enrol myself and met Aruna Sunderlal who used to be a singer and now runs the school from her residence. She first had a chat with me. It was almost, though not quite, an interview.

The Bangalore School of Music (BSM)

Western classical music has always been a passion in Aruna Sunderlal's family. Her father, a civil servant from the British days, was known to throw black tie dinner parties in which the musical compositions of the European maestros played a central role. She later learnt the piano in a Nainital boarding school under excellent German and English teachers. It is, therefore, not surprising that she founded the BSM in 1987 after permanently settling in Bangalore. The objective of the school is the promotion of two great classical systems of music – Carnatic and Western. Today, the school has permeated every square inch of Aruna's private residence and at its current saturation point accommodates roughly 280 students who learn under twenty-six teachers for an affordable fee.

Expansion will now be possible only after the completion of the modern facility being built in the aptly named locality – Rabindranath Tagore Nagar. But even with its current infrastructure, the BSM has many things to be proud of.

'We are the only school in India to have a resident conductor,' she says. 'His name is Narayanaswamy, a very talented musician. And a cellist from the Chennai film industry comes here every weekend to teach as well as play in the orchestra. We have also received enquiries from Singaporeans and expatriates based in the Gulf – they want to enrol their children with us. And oh – a few of our students have been offered scholarships to learn music in Portugal, Switzerland and Australia.'

The school is earnest about recruiting, as far as possible, only those who are keen about music. Anyway, I was accepted as a student. And I'm still learning under my teacher Manoj George.'

From the outset, Astrid proved to be a zealous student. At the end of each month, she would ask her teachers the same question: 'Can I play in the orchestra now?' For many months, the answer remained the same: 'You need a little more practice'. Finally, she was ready. Till date, she has played in two concerts – one in Alliance Francaise and the other in the premises of a software company.

'Sounds like you were impatient to play in the orchestra,' I say.

The spanner in the works, as always, is money. It keeps the studentship small, delays plans for expansion and cuts the budget for everything. Instruments made in China are purchased because they cost one-third the European models, and are of a comparable quality.

Some funding comes from bodies such as the Indo-Swedish Cultural Collaboration and Exchange Project. A great part of this money is channelled into outreach programmes – the school is making attempts to bring the gift of music to over 250 handicapped and underprivileged children. Additionally, the Alliance Francaise de Bangalore, the Indian Council for Cultural Relations and embassies in India lend support to the BSM. Interestingly, all these bodies deal primarily with expatriates.

'A number of expatriate parents,' says Aruna. 'often drop in on detail-level fact-finding missions. Their increasing presence is good for us. Because many Indians, unfortunately, do not view Western classical music in the right spirit. In our country, the North-Easterners somehow display the keenest interest. Perhaps because they are huge rock-n-roll fans. And people from hilly regions tend to be naturally gifted musicians and singers anyway.'

When I finally ask her about Astrid, she says:

'Astrid is a very committed and enthusiastic student. Good energy. But she needs to be more confident. One rainy day, we had very little attendance for the orchestra rehearsal. The conductor, finding her reluctant to play a first violin, had to gently force her. Once she began playing, she was perfectly fine.'

'Because it's sublime,' she replies. 'I don't get the same thrill playing alone. And some members of the orchestra are so talented and totally in love with the music. They know much more about it than I do... Indians are dedicated to whatever they attempt. As a result, and considering that Western classical music isn't indigenous to the land, our output is of a high quality.'

Limitations, however, exist. In full attendance, the chamber orchestra is just twenty-member strong (the youth orchestra, which also includes children aged seven to sixteen, has thirty-four members). And at the moment, it plays only violins, violas, double basses and cellos. Wind instruments such as clarinets, flutes and trumpets are conspicuous by their absence. That means the orchestra has a restricted repertoire.

'India lacks the proper facilities,' says Astrid. 'Our Chamber Orchestra is one of just four or five in the entire country. You see, India lacks a large knowledgeable audience... it's difficult to sell tickets for a pure classical concert. The few halls in Bangalore that are suitable for a concert are expensive. How do professionals make a living? No wonder many musicians try to earn money by playing for the film industries or music albums, or in marriage ceremonies and luxury hotels.'

'Carnatic music seems to be doing better. So perhaps the perception needs to change,' I suggest.

Astrid shrugs.

'Perhaps. Indians are otherwise more musical than Germans.'

'Don't you come from the home of Western classical music?'

'Yes. But I know what I'm talking about. Just see how important a part music plays in Indian films. Coming to India has rekindled my love for music. I'm certain that I won't stop playing hereafter. I won't ever be a professional because

I don't consider myself disciplined enough and... well, it would be a hard life. But I feel lucky when I compare myself to people in Germany. Those who don't turn professional simply give up playing altogether.'

'Still, it's amazing that a *German* girl finds an avenue to pursue Western classical music in Bangalore. Tell me, were you always interested in it?'

'Always. And my father used to play the trumpet as a young man.'

'So music must have come naturally to you.'

'Not quite. It happened only when I changed schools in my fifth grade. The one I entered offered free music classes and that's how I began at the age of ten. My family couldn't have afforded to pay for my classes.'

'How long did you attend the classes?'

'Seven years. But I felt my music teacher didn't like me much. And as I said, I was never disciplined enough to practise regularly. Yet, I had a good base when I came to India. And I'm now more disciplined. Friday evenings, I attend class at the school. I go back on Saturdays to play in the orchestra. A fellow player comes to my home on Sundays for a two to three hour joint practice. And I also try to squeeze in an hour's practice on weekday mornings. Okay, sometimes it's just half an hour. All right, sometimes I skip that too...'

I smile.

'Do you have time left for anything else?'

For the nth time, she readjusts her hair around the hair band. As usual, a few strands escape the cluster and droop down on the side of her face.

'I have a full-time job.'

'Any problems working with Indians?'

'It can be difficult at times. It's frustrating when positive criticism is taken as a personal affront. Or when a hierarchical mindset keeps people from taking responsibilities. But for the most part, it's wonderful working here.'

'What else do you do?'

'I read on occasion – I love Rohinton Mistry. I exterminate cockroaches in my kitchen, and I spend time with my soul mate...'

'You found one?'

'Yeah. It's this Indian girl with whom I can share many confidences.'

'So a soul mate needn't necessarily be a person you're romantically involved with?'

'Not at all.'

'And what about that life partner?'

'Still looking,' she says. 'It's difficult to meet the right man in India. In Germany, I can find a lot of eligible singles or divorcees. But most of the Indian men who are my age are happily married. You know, the longer I stay here, the more sense arranged marriages make. They require an entirely different mindset... And they may be the reason why Indian men are so sweet – they really like to take care of their women. And when interacting with them, I don't get the constant feeling that all their efforts are directed towards sex. They may still be looking for the same thing, but they take the highly chivalrous route.'

A Hilltop View

When I finally end up at Bob Hoekstra's residence one sunny morning, he is sitting with a cup of black coffee and an open newspaper. It is eight, but already warm. Bangalore has been unusually summery since the year began, and lavender jacarandas are blooming in heart-stopping profusion. Putting aside the pink newsprint of the *Economic Times,* Bob invites me for coffee. I enquire if his grandchildren made his Christmas and New Year memorable. They did, but—

'The first morning after they were gone, my wife and I were sitting here peacefully, and the sun was pouring from the windows just like today and we decided we'd manage not to miss them for a few days. Maybe even a few weeks!'

I laugh. Vijay, Bob's chauffeur-cum-assistant, enters the house and carries two bicycles down to the car. Soon, we're on our way. The agenda – cycling to the top of. Nandi Hills. Bob performs this healthy ritual every crisis-free Saturday morning that he is in Bangalore. The small twist today: I will be pedalling alongside him instead of Vijay.

Despite it being the weekend, we contend with heavy traffic on the way to Bellary Road. In 1999, Bob must have seen a similar view out of his window. I have read a popular version of his first impression and ask him to substantiate it.

'An airport with staircases instead of escalators,' he says, 'as if it's an African destination catering to charter tourists, isn't a good first impression. The Customs area was roofless, and there was a cow inside it!' Ah, I had begun missing the cow. 'I said: "I'm not sure if I want this. It's funny!" My wife Geraldine coaxed me. She saw it as an interesting challenge. It is, because when you reach the fantastic Taj West End hotel from the airport, you feel the full impact of different Indias. One thing you'll never find in India is the boring organisation Singapore characterises. The conventional Chinese method of hanging laundry on sticks out of windows – the Chinese launder every day, you know, and I don't know if it makes them clean people or dirty – is not allowed in Singapore. Whereas in Bangalore, you see cows being milked on Airport Road... our infrastructure is bad enough as it is.'

'Was all this new to you?'

'Well, I was in Taiwan between '96 and '99. So I was used to the long hours and traffic. But it's a dog's life there; the weekends tend to be drab. Especially when you relocate there from the US.'

'Why did you relocate from the US anyway?' I ask.

'After nearly five years in the US, my wife asked me what I wanted for my birthday. I replied: a Dodge pickup. So she gently hinted that I was turning into a hillbilly and it was perhaps time to move. When I asked my company for a change and they assigned me to Asia, a friend gave me a reality check. He told me that Asia's choc-a-bloc with people. It is true, right? Each millimetre that isn't protected by a barrier – a gate or a wall – is packed. Traffic accidents are avoided by a whisker and that's accepted with a fatalistic shrug. One morning in Bangalore, a BMTC driver almost killed a scooter rider at the M. G. Road intersection. The man didn't file a complaint; I did. I took the stance that no driver can threaten another's life. The union representing the driver pleaded his good record and got his suspension rescinded. That's a good snapshot of India for you. But when I go back to the US or Holland and look out of hotel windows at metal and asphalt, I miss the crowd. People remind me that this – what I see in Bangalore – isn't normal. What can I say? I seem to have gotten used to it.'

We have put the city behind us and Vijay is racing towards the hills. From the passenger seat, I turn to ask Bob my next question. My gaze falls upon the two geared bicycles and I worry about the steep hill that will soon mock my claims to physical fitness...

'Nandi Hills is a great place to unwind,' says Bob. 'But you should know that no Indian has made it to the top the first time.' Great! A challenge. Exactly what I need for motivation. I listen half-heartedly as Bob praises the hill. '...and previously I would ask Vijay to find me a quiet place where I could sip beer in peace after biking. The people always found me though... but I'm no longer the unknown foreigner. Folks know me...'

The curiosity has diminished, so has the fear. I switch to a topic that is tinged with pan-Indian fear – the imminent Chinese threat to Indian IT.

'Two scenarios are possible,' he says. 'One – India loses to China. Is it likely? I dunno. Speaking as a doomsday prophet, increasing salaries might make India incompetent. Yes, India has a decade's head start and the Chinese need to learn management skills. But if Indian infrastructure doesn't keep up, people might say: "I have to go to China anyway for non-IT work. And their IT is getting better. So why put up with India?"

'Now for the second scenario – China won't beat India. Many countries today claim to have IT acumen but don't. Japan, for example. The Chinese are no-bullshit-no-theorising-analysing-please-let's-get-the-job-done people. But IT requires analysis, which the Indians are good at. Their education system is well-tuned to the industry requirements. It drills in the knowledge and ignores the what-you-do-is-what-you-know methodology. Besides, India has the foundations and a stable corporate ecosystem. Bangalore has the momentum. But here's a caveat – to excel, you have to allow people to fail while attempting extraordinary acts. This is against the prevalent ideology in Indian IT. Failure is unacceptable. Leaders want to take safe paths, operate under command-and-control structures. They order; employees listen.'

We reach the foot of the hill and disembark. Bob discovers a puncture in his bicycle's rear tyre. My heart leaps. Perhaps he'll ride the bicycle I'm assigned. Unfortunately, there is a mechanic nearby. So there's nothing to do but wait for the tyre to be mended. I pick up the thread of the conversation again.

'Is that why big companies hardly succeed in offering products?' I ask. 'They seem to be doing the same work as years back but fifty times over.'

'I would look at it differently. Taiwan owns 80% of the computer hardware pie. Despite the hype and hoopla, Indian IT has just 3% of the world IT market share. You're just a dwarf. You need to keep plugging for a 15% share. But yeah, I concur that the product lifecycle – spending money upfront – is not in the Indian culture.'

'And is it right to expect Indian IT to alleviate the country's issues? To initiate rural empowerment, for example.'

'Indian society refuses to be mechanised easily. But I can think of other ways that the IT industry can help. Other industries can learn to stretch their performance like IT. And many business operations can be handled by the young Indian population for ageing countries and IT can enable that. But can it happen with a hapless government? It hurts to see the possibilities of this wonderful city being wrecked by politicians.'

'You have been the most vociferous voice lamenting Bangalore's infrastructure. Is it a conscious decision to be so?'

'Not conscious at all. I do it because I have stakes here. My company is investing $50mn on a new campus close to the Outer Ring Road. What if good roads are never built to the location? Do I lose a part of my workforce that would rather work in a better location? The government has no right to jeopardise capital. I cannot comprehend why Bangalore cannot move along the lines of Delhi or Chennai. Chaos is a part of development, but there are ways of reining it in. S. M. Krishna was fine, but the Dharam Singh government is not sure of itself. Probably because of the fractured mandate from people who have unequivocally said: "Hey, not just IT, we exist too!"'

The tyre is repaired and we mount our bikes. Vijay will follow us in the car.

'Don't let me hold you back,' I say.

Bob needs no more encouragement. He zips away. I try the pedal and find it disagreeable. Vijay asks me to change gears and that provides traction. I ride for the next half hour. The initial flat stretch is easy. But the moment I round the curve up the hill, my eyes turn woozy. I take breaks at each milestone. When I'm six kilometres from the top, I allow Vijay to persuade me to pack up. He reckons Bob must be two kilometres ahead. We speed upwards in the car and find

Bob doggedly pursuing the stationary summit. He is riding the steepest stretch. His sinews are strung tight and his calves bulge like the bulbs his company sells. It is then that it hits me: what a fool I was to agree to bike "along". He is nearly sixty, I'm half that. He has so much more experience. I should have asked for a handicap!

Once at the top, Bob tells me that he has conquered every hill in the vicinity. Either by biking or trekking. As a reward for my terrific debut, he presents me with a copy of his book – *An Exemplary Family in Bangalore*. It is an anecdotal collection packed with strong sarcasm, wry wit and keen observations. Observations of a global citizen?

'Oh, I don't know if a global citizen exists,' he replies. 'Can anyone have that vast a comfort zone? You know, TV channels in the US categorise news as local and international, and there's more focus on the former. That's the manifestation of a society seeking its comfort zone.'

'But what about melting pots like New York? Don't they foster broader perspectives?'

'Yeah, places like NY are helpful. But even that great city breeds a Spanish, or a Jewish or an Armenian neighbourhood. These arise from a need for comfort. That's all. It would be wrong to attribute their presence to stronger emotions like animosity and resentment. It is a simple fact that different peoples will have issues when they come together. In 1975-76, I was in the US. Black-White tension was still palpable and I asked a white man why the hell they don't want to give the blacks equal rights. He answered: "How many foreigners does Holland have? Not many, huh? You'll find the problems arising when their strength touches 10%." And he has a point. At some threshold point, neighbourhoods spring up, a thrust for identity begins and people relearn intolerance. Holland is seeing that today.'

Meanwhile, it is time to head back to the plateau. En route we halt by the "coconut lady" and buy a few minutes underneath the shade. As we sip coconut water, I pursue the same line of reasoning.

'Can't jet-setters like you make a difference?'

'A smidgeon, perhaps.'

'We see cultural intermingling in the corporate milieu, and the issues and reactions are the same as in a park or the road. But companies make it work, don't they? Is it because of having objective goals like profit-making and milestones?'

'Yes, having well-defined motives and work help. Companies also learn to work around unbridgeable differences. They manage them better than nations.'

When we speak next, we are back where we began cycling. The sun is hot, but not unpleasant. We sit under it and I change the topic. The BPO industry.

'Now there's a example of uncontrolled growth,' says Bob. 'They should have built self-sustaining satellite cities to accommodate the BPO industry. Instead of that, BPO firms are coming up at random parts of the city. And so you have thousands and thousands of Sumos carrying employees to and fro, choking every part of the city.'

My next question is sharper.

'Your company has offices all over the world. When you are involved in shifting jobs to India, you know that a real person over there is going to lose his. How do you rationalise the move to him?'

'Shoot. I've faced this at a personal level. My son-in-law lost his job with a global telecom giant and my son works in IT in Holland. And here I am, in a way trying to steal their jobs for India. It's tough. As you said, I cannot explain to the newly unemployed guy that for every job shifted to India, the global economy improves. But logically, it's a costing decision. They'll have to continuously improve to deserve the salaries they demand. Have a look at the farmers here in the fields... you have to agree that to be that guy, it's a prerequisite to be poor. They'll move if they have money. They work in a non-productive setup. Cannot compete with the US farmers. In an open market, they'll lose.

'I used to be a socialist in my younger days. It's sad that the socialist-communist ideas have disappeared and capitalism has survived. But... I had been to Russia during the communist era. The shopkeepers there had the attitude: "Holy shit! A customer!" I realised that controlled society isn't fun. It's better for talented people to make more money.'

It is time to head back. We take our seats. Vijay aims the car at Bangalore and I fire the next question.

'Capitalistic thought is aligned with the human instinct?'

'Yes, that's it. But – don't let the others die. My socialism was rebellion; wanting to be an anti-establishment Flower Power guy, right? But now that I think about it, it wouldn't be bad if India had a revolution one way or the other. A movement to revamp the political system such that it will serve the country. We need that. Mercifully, you have an honest Prime Minister in Manmohan Singh and a great President in Abdul Kalam. I adore that man.'

'You said *we* need that.'

'Yeah. I'm part of the Indianness when I'm here. In Holland, I have a different *we*.'

'So a revolution, huh?'

'Maybe... it's difficult in a world that's put an end to social experiments.'

'And capitalism is the only way forward?'

'Capitalism is seldom implemented in its purest form. Governments lend socialistic colours using public health schemes or social security or whatever. And that combination seems to be it. The only way forward.'

'What about pampered investors? Are they part of the package?'

'Well, I agree that investors are a pampered lot. Some of them are fickle, and companies forget that employees stay longer. Balance is most essential. Because infinite incentives lead to unethical, unwise methods.'

'A CEO has to always display balance and logic. Is he exposed to the danger of losing the human element in the process?'

Bob thinks a split second about this one before answering.

'Yes. You have to account for every cent in a public company... Do you know what's common to companies that outperform the market for fifteen straight years? They have uncharismatic CEOs who don't make sweeping changes and are in touch with the people.'

The traffic is getting thicker, the city closer.

'But let's say you have to fire a bunch of your employees...'

'Is it fair to fire good software engineers in a recession? Maybe not. But it's not about fairness. The question should be whether it's required or not. If it's required, get it done. With dignity.'

Speaking of which, I ask him about being a moving billboard. His watch and his shirt carry his company's logo, as does his car. Is it because he's the CEO?

'Yes, that, and because I have pride in the brand. I really believe we're doing amazing work at our Bangalore office. From 330 people, we've reached 1,500 people now. We make software for DVD players, remote service diagnostics for medical equipment...'

'What did you do in your younger days? Always a Philips guy?'

'Always. Because there were always opportunities. I used to be a research physicist. So I'm trained to observe facts and capture them in a model. And then extrapolate to assess the correctness of the model. That helps me in my job. I can tell a fact from an interpretation.'

Like here's a fact: Bob and his company are getting involved in social work. I ask him to elaborate on that so that I can draw my interpretations.

'One of my regrets,' he says, 'is that I didn't come to India sooner and learn social responsibility. Still, as a CEO I can get more things done than as a grassroots social worker. That's something. But my idea of social service is not doling out free goodies. A commodity that costs nothing has unlimited demand and no supply. Instead, why not create money streams and develop scalable models that work beyond one village? India has to urgently stop the widening income-gap. How many people can you leave behind? I don't understand why it isn't already a problem. Why doesn't that guy living in the slum opposite my house steal my watch when I pass that way? Amazing. But let's do something about his situation now. It's a good thing I'm not a preacher or a priest or an idealist. Be it social work or corporate, I like to have a businessman's perspective of the world.'

And, he adds, he also likes to enjoy life. He is eager to go trekking in the Himalayas before turning sixty. Bob has been an outdoors guy right from boyhood. One of his most vivid memories is of skating on thin ice at the onset of winter, and seeing the sheet ripple like liquid. Sometimes a crack would result and travel the entire lake with a clap of thunder. He also tells me that he had enjoyed going to school and to libraries. But something he has enjoyed a lot will soon come to an end—

'This assignment will be my last. I retire next year. Before then, I want to make a difference to how my company perceives people at the bottom of the ladder. And I want to make Asia-Pacific an equal partner, not just a colonial outpost.'

'What's in your post-retirement wish-list?'
'To travel to New Zealand and the western part of Canada. Maybe, I'll also study molecular diagnostics.'
'Where would all this happen?'
Bob Hoekstra looks at me, smiles and says:
'I'll keep returning to India, but I'll settle in Holland. My daughter feels I haven't taken my grandparenting responsibilities seriously.'

Hope Lives

Meenakshi Koil Street is right around the corner from the glitzy Commercial Street. And it is just as busy during the day. The difference is that the shoppers are less affluent and more fastidious. So they hunt for bargains on the pavement. A small portion of this pavement is occupied by Tibetan vendors and it is to meet them that I become part of the festive spirit of the street.

Sonam Sangmo sits in front of fluffy, colourful sweaters and smiles at me. Even when she understands that I'm not a prospective customer, she retains her warmth. In fact she invites a few more of her ilk to come and share the conversation. All of them speak Hindi and very little English. Sonam tells me that she has been sitting in the same posture at the very spot since the time she arrived in Bangalore as a young girl in 1980. But the Tibetan migration to the city, I'm told, goes back to the sixties. And 52-year-old Norzom came to Bangalore when she was seventeen years old; that dates her arrival to 1969. The man standing beside her, T. Chopel, has a leathery face and beady eyes. He arrived in 1977 or '79, he cannot remember which. Tenzil, the shoe vendor and the youngest in the group, was born in Bangalore. She is just thirty-two and wants her children to have a good education and a better fate.

All of them are fans and followers of the first Tibetan refugee in India – the Dalai Lama. And their presence here can be traced back to China's invasion of Tibet that began in 1950. Nine years later, on 10 March 1959 to be precise, the Tibetan people rose in protest against Chinese repression. The uprising was nipped in the bud and countless Tibetans lost their lives. Just a couple of days back, some of my new friends had participated in a day's hunger strike to mark the forty-sixth anniversary of the uprising. Given Tibet's economic insignificance and military nothingness, this annual protest becomes merely symbolic. And the Tibetans are painfully aware of that.

Mercifully the courage and generosity shown by India, particularly by Jawaharlal Nehru, ensured the Tibetans a ready asylum. And it was a well-placed kindness, going by the number of times Nehru's name figures in their speech. Today, the Indian landscape has a sprinkling of Tibetan settlements. Karnataka has one settlement each in the towns of Kushalnagar, Bylakuppe, Gurupura, Hunsur, Mundgod and Kollegal. Other than providing land, the state and union governments of India helped by feeding the refugees during the initial days. But the Tibetans don't expect heaven to be handed over on a platter. In Kushalnagar, for example, they transformed forest land into a habitable place, then expanded it to accommodate farming tracts, a school and a monastery. A piece of land, however, can only support so many people. That is why new arrivals from Tibet find it almost impossible to get into one of the settlements unless they cite family ties. Governmental procedures have, simultaneously, become more stringent. Till 1979, India used to issue residential permits as a matter of course. That doesn't happen any more.

Meanwhile, people like Sonam annually renew their residential permits in one of these settlements. But Sonam also travels to Mundgod to grow paddy during the monsoon. She and Norzom have an understanding in the matter. If Sonam takes off to farm for a week, Norzam runs her sweater business. The two then reverse their roles. They would prefer to farm the whole time, but they have seen the vagaries of the Indian monsoon.

Sweaters and sneakers will have to do for now. Sweaters, in fact, have provided sustenance since the first Tibetans came to Bangalore and sent word back that the hand-knit ones have a market in this relatively nippy city. Most of the Meenakshi Koil Street regulars rent a small house in Shivaji Nagar and expect the beat constable to show grace. They feel safe and not unwanted in India. Among all the people I have met so far, I cannot think of anyone who has a higher opinion of the country.

'India is nice,' says Chopel. 'According to the Dalai Lama, this is where the Buddha came from. Yeah. Many years ago, people from India came to Tibet to teach us to pray.'

'India supports us,' says the Indian-born Tenzil. She continues in the same breath, 'But if you're quiet, China will invade you too!'

She laughs and I do, too. She is laughing because she feels India is too big and powerful to be invaded by China. I laugh because I realise: *hey, we haven't thought about that for a while, have we?* Sonam punctures our fleeting mirth.

'I want to go back,' she says. 'Tomorrow… if it's possible, I'll go tomorrow. My heart is there. So are people I know who're languishing in Chinese jails.'

Tenzil concurs.

'But you've never seen Tibet. You don't know what it's like,' I protest.

'But it's my land,' she says. 'Besides, my grandparents are there. Do you think... if India will force China... or someone else... do you think Tibet will be a free country again? Do you?'

'Well... I can't say really,' I say. 'I mean, the Chinese will flex their muscles if...' Sonam starts crying. I want to punch the moron between my ears. 'But if you keep fighting, keep believing, I don't see why not.'

'Poor girl! Got reminded of her homeland,' says Chopel. He pats Sonam paternally on her back. Eventually, Sonam stops crying and I take leave of the gentle people. As I walk, I recall reading about Tenzin Delek Rinpoche whose death sentence was commuted after intense international pressure. And I think about the Indian-born Tenzil. She is their strongest hope. If she could identify with her homeland without ever seeing it... if the Tibetans continue to be certain about what home is and are willing to wait and fight for it, there might come a day...

* * *

About a hundred metres from Sonam Sangmo's seat stands the shop of the Chinese shoemaker Yang Tung Hing. An old-fashioned dichromatic board above the entrance reads, C. H. Yong and Co, a reminder that Yang's father established the business he now runs. Yong, the father, came to Bangalore in 1933 after trying his luck in Singapore and Kolkata among other places. Seventeen years later, a teenaged Yang followed suit. It was clear from the first instant that he would also adopt his father's profession, but with an inconsequential difference. During Yang's schooling in China, the Mandarin language had strengthened its influence. As a result, he changed the way his surname was spelt; the pronunciation remained the same.

From that July day in 1950, Yang has lived and plied his trade on Old Poor House Road. And the years have made him popular. Upon ringing the shop's doorbell and getting no response, I look about uncertainly and see Yang arrive. Neighbouring shopkeepers, hoteliers and pedestrians immediately hail him. And he responds to them in clear Tamil or passable Kannada or Hindi. I introduce myself and request an interview. He is neither surprised nor overwhelmed. Several newspapers have featured him as "the shoemaker who is himself an elf" or "the impish shoemaker". There are good reasons to be interested in Yang. He is the oldest Chinese in Bangalore and the only Chinese shoemaker still in action. His diction is clear and... well, un-Chinese. And barring globular puffs of flesh beneath his eyes, there is nothing to suggest his seventy years.

Yang unlocks the tall doors of his shop and invites me inside. Slanted golden rays precede us into the fusty interiors and light up cabinets lined with shoes, raw materials and accessories. The setup has remained unchanged for decades. Neither Yong, who died sometime in the mid-90s, nor Yang believed in renovating and expanding the business.

'I'm a man without tension... free... a freelancer almost,' he says. 'Absence of greed keeps the aging process at bay – look at me!'

'But travelling a long distance in search of Life is usually a sign of ambition,' I say.

Yang disagrees and explains that his family hails from the Guangdong province in Southern China. It is a mountainous land, unsuitable for cultivation. So Hakka people like him have for generations crossed seas and trudged across land to seek their livelihood. It was not love for India or the climate of Bangalore that brought Yong here. The compelling threat of empty plates did. But having come here, he, and then Yang, found the people agreeable, the air pleasant and feet in need of shoes. So they made them. Each one by hand. What, however, makes C. H. Yong & Co. really special is its ability to cater to the handicapped.

That requires practical artistry. And I realise this while poring through long thin notebooks that contain feet imprints of customers. In them, I see feet of every contour, size and deformity. Feet belonging to polio victims, clubfeet, feet mangled by accidents, unformed toes, legs of unequal length... Yang has seen them all and has leather and thread equal to the task. He is understandably proud about catering to a lady who couldn't bend down to tie her shoes. His solution was to create a loop at the back of the shoe threaded with a lace that could be pulled for tightening or loosening the shoe!

The aphorisms stuck on the walls and the tool cabinet now make sense.

My job is to put a soul in your sole.
If you want fast service, go to <name of competitor>.
Shoes are made for your feet, not the showcase.
Minimum charge for any repair is Rs.50/- You can pay me less if you like!

Yang is fanatical about quality control. It is a trait he shares with the IT industry that is changing the world outside his shop. But unlike IT, he has seen his business diminish.. The market is tight-fisted at the strata in which he operates. And he believes that the advent of computers has robbed many tradesmen of their livelihood. Courier services, postal services, even tailors are losing out. Since he isn't dependent on shoemaking any more, it's quite all ·right. His two daughters and son are doing well, and his wants are minimal. He and his wife, Lin Fang, lead a simple life in the inner rooms behind the shop.

I request him to give me a tour of the house. So he leads me past the counter and into a storeroom that has an array of lasts. Beyond this is a bedroom with a rudimentary bed and some basic home appliances. Atop the fridge is a plate of what looks like caterpillars immortalised in gel. Disappointingly, they are merely sausages. From the bedroom, we walk across a nondescript room into a relatively large kitchen. A half-completed crossword is open upon the dining table; a low skylight above it illuminates the surroundings. When it rains, Yang simply slides a corrugated vinyl roofing sheet and shuts the skylight. Yes, it is that kind of a world.

'Nice place,' I say. 'Seems like you enjoy crosswords.'

'I spend roughly three hours on them each day. In my younger days, I used to be a ping-pong player for the state of Mysore and even represented it in the 1969-70 National Games! Nowadays, it's either crosswords or occasional amateur painting...' – he has learnt to dabble with palette and brushes from Manish Dey, who himself was a protégé of Abanindranath Tagore – '... and I read Tamil stories on rare occasions.'

'You can read Tamil?' I ask.

'Yes, although I need to read it one letter at a time.'

'Still...'

'The Cantonment area, you see, has always been a Tamil stronghold. I cannot read or write Kannada.'

Since he has alluded to Bangalore as a city dichotomised by cousin languages, I ask him about another differentiator – nationality.

'We're fools to have and acknowledge geographical boundaries,' he says. 'India and China fought for what? Wasteland. They were disputing boundaries created by the British.'

'Do you know that there are Tibetans around the corner?'
I ask, baiting him.

'Yes, I've seen them. China claims Tibet as its own. And
it says the same about Taiwan. Bush is doing "God's will"
in Iraq. I cannot understand it at all. It's silly to fight. That
pen in your pocket is for writing, that mobile is for staying
in touch with people... what's an atom bomb for? Killing
people! That solves nothing. I remember the Japanese
invading China during World War II. We came to know how
cruel want can be. I wish that we would achieve some serious
success in space exploration. Then nations can colonise
planets. And leave us normal people alone.'

The mosque across the road erupts in prayer. The temple
exactly opposite Yang's shop is throwing open its doors for
the evening darshan. As the zealous capture Old Poor House
Road, I take a quick look at the silent shoes before taking
leave. But a thought strikes me. I turn and say:

'It tickles me that in a city with Chinese cooks, beauticians
and now software professionals, the oldest is still a
shoemaker.'

He replies that it will remain so till his last breath. Proof?
Recently, his daughter in Malaysia invited him and his wife
to relocate permanently.

'I said, yes. Open a shoe shop for me there. I'll come.'

Since that is not feasible, Bangalore can rest assured of
his presence for the time being.

* * *

It is way past Christmas when I meet Sue, the restaurateur,
again. The festive season has taken a toll on her back and
she has cut down her activities. So we decide to meet at her
home. When I reach it, I find her reclining in a chair. She

smiles at me with her eyes. Go on, they seem to say. I know she wants to keep this short, so without prelude, I say:

'Tell me about your past.'

She begins her story. And poignant though it is, she manages to soften it with her light voice and manner.

'I told you the other day that I did my growing up in India, didn't I? It's because I married young and came here in 1978. He was working in Trinidad when I met him through my first boyfriend. My elder daughter was four when we came to India – Coorg to be specific – where he had purchased an estate. Upon reaching there, we discovered that we had been cheated. The man who sold us the estate wasn't the owner. In a flash, I lost my affluent life and hit rock bottom. We lost everything and I mean everything. Even my jewellery had to be sold off. Years later, I realised that I had lost my relationship with my husband as well. He had taken to drink. I tell you, I'd like to write a book about my life one day.'

'Where did you stay if the estate was off limits?' I ask.

'We were still living in the estate along with a set of unwanted legends. The workers believed that a goddess floated around during the night in the form of a headless lady. Not just that, she was supposed to use the well to take a bath. And apparently there existed a cobra with a diamond on its head. It kept the workers from going to certain parts of the estate. You may grin, but we were losing so much cardamom, it wasn't funny. He, my first husband, was twenty-three years older than me so I literally grew up with my daughters. Disillusioned by life, he used us as sandbags to vent his frustration. By that time, I had met Johnny and… it was painful, but I called it quits and walked out. Both my daughters were very supportive. That was seventeen years ago.

'At the same time, Johnny was encountering similar issues. His first wife was dying and he wanted to spare her the knowledge of our relationship. But my first husband told her, and well… the situation aggravated. It was Johnny's turn to lose everything. But he's an intelligent man; he fought back well. And he's been *rock solid* with me all these years. If it weren't for him, I couldn't have dealt with the tough years of fighting for the possession of my daughters…'

I remember the contrasting laughter and calypso wafting inside her restaurant. As if reading my thoughts, she says: 'Today, we lack nothing, I tell you. I have a balanced man for a husband, and would you believe it – he religiously invites my first husband home every Christmas! It's a strange relationship the two share today. That apart, Johnny's so protective of me after all that's happened… he's much older to me too and he's afraid that if he dies tomorrow, the wolves will return. He wants to settle me down in Trinidad before that… he knows I'll not be happy here without him.'

'So it's just a matter of time before you leave India?'

'I don't know. I'm so used to this arrangement. India has given me marvellous learning experiences, and it'll be difficult to separate from Bangalore. I remember wanting to settle here because it was a rare Indian city where people smiled at you… But I adjust well and I guess I'll do that upon going back… I just wish I could turn back the clock and have my husband live with me for a few years in Trinidad…' Before I can respond, Sue shifts from being wistful to pragmatic. 'But that can't happen. When you accept things for what they are, it becomes easier to carry on.'

Latino, Latino

After six months of searching, I'm still miles from locating a Latin American in Bangalore. I have scanned telephone directories online and the old-fashioned way. I have exhausted all my contacts and kept a watchful eye on the roads of Bangalore. I even set alerts on internet search engines. No luck. So I try being a nuisance to strangers.

I call the HAL sports club, the best soccer club in the city although it no longer belongs to the First Division. I'm told that the four Nigerian players in their rolls are being released and the club has no immediate plans of recruiting overseas players. So I'm advised to stop searching for a surrogate Pele.

I then call the Confederation of Indian Industries (CII). The Chilean President Ricardo Lagos had come to Bangalore in January and was followed swiftly by his Venezuelan counterpart, Hugo Chavez. Since the CII hosted the leaders, I expect them to have contacts leading to South Americans working in Chambers of Commerce. But the business delegates apparently enter and depart from Bangalore along with their Presidents. They otherwise seem to have a presence only in New Delhi.

The next call is to the International Energy Initiative. It is a body exploring alternative energy sources, among other things. They have two offices, according to their website. One is in Bangalore and the other in Campinas, Brazil. The kind lady in the Bangalore office informs me that she runs a minimal outfit and no South Americans are visiting at the moment. Such visits are very infrequent and short. I face the same result when I contact the People's Health Movement, yet another NGO with links in South America.

Master Lee raises my hopes when I meet him – yes, he knows a couple of Brazilians. He says they are working in a theological mission on the outskirts of the city, in Kothanur to be precise. But further enquiries reveal that they have left.

On to the Bangalore School of Music then. The School is known to host Latin American musicians frequently. Recently, they had a concert featuring Silvio Lazzo and Paul Grace. But they are closing down for the summer.

And so I call Venugopal of ICCR and he makes another attempt to coax this Guyanese student who has been on our radar for months. But she is either busy with her exams or unsure about meeting strange Indian writers.

Finally, Thomas van Berckel finds me a pretty Latino girl.

* * *

Patricia Ribeiro Pena. Silken straight hair, dark sunglasses, a Western outfit and coffee-coloured nail-polish. Among all those I have met, Patricia has made the longest journey to be at this coffee shop.

'Iceberg, thick but not strong,' she tells the waiter in her undulating accent. The waiter smiles and nods – she is a regular at the joint. When he leaves, she turns to me, smiles and says: 'In India, coffee shops come a close second to *masala dosas*.'

I nod in agreement. Around us are really young people, blowing into designer hookahs, speaking ungrammatical English, wearing skimpy outfits and challenging me with an unwavering look whenever I happen to glance at them. Yes, I decide, coffee shops deserve to be acknowledged for formulating a bold new culture. As I reach this conclusion, she disorients me with her next words.

'If only India could become a bit more open-minded... But then, its conservatism is its forte...' When I coax her to elaborate, she says: 'There's always something about where you come from that you miss. In Brazil, we hug and kiss as a show of warmth, and that's not accepted here. More so if I wear a *salwar* because I then look very Indian. When I was new to Bangalore, my open behaviour sent the wrong signals to Indian boys. Many concluded that I was seeking something different... three years later, I've figured out how to behave.'

I can vouch for that. She has neither hugged, nor kissed me. But I sense that Patricia is not making jovial comparisons between the *namaskar* and the bear hug. Her voice is tinged with sadness. A deep, very personal revelation follows.

'I first came to India to work for an NGO – Atmashakti – and met this guy who ran an NGO himself. We liked each other from the start. We had similar non-materialistic thoughts, even felt mutual admiration which is so important for any good relationship. Ours lasted three years...'

'Family issues?' I ask.

'No. My parents accepted him wholeheartedly, his parents adapted to me. It helped that we're both Catholics. I even used to be a regular visitor at his home. But I guess we took too long to honestly work on our problems. It was the first serious relationship for either of us, so we were learning from each other.'

I request her to give more details.

'After spending a year here,' she says, 'I went back home to complete my education. He visited me there twice. We spent happy times. Here and there. However... finally... we realised that we were culturally alienated from each other. He couldn't understand the difficulties I faced while in India and I expected him to accept me as-is, instead of understanding his reservations. So we couldn't agree on many issues. From trivialities like speech mannerisms to significant questions such as how important is a society's perception of an individual...'

By the time the relationship broke up, Patricia was back in Bangalore, working for an American multinational. The second relocation meant many sacrifices.

'I came to start something new here... with him. And for that, I gave up my life in Brazil – family, friends, work. My parents were naturally apprehensive. Why should their daughter's dreams involve such a faraway place? I had to assuage their fears. You must understand that I've not become a traveller because I cannot be employed in Brazil or because I can't get along with my family. I want to explore the world as a global native – one who becomes an intrinsic part of every place she visits. But having said that, I know that when I eventually go back, things would be a little different.'

In the background, a pair of Indian teenagers are hugging tightly, saying goodbye. Culture, more so Indian culture, defies definition. It is a shapeless, intangible entity. Had I been stung by it, I might have taken the next flight out with bitterness in my heart. But Patricia doesn't speak with malice. In fact, she seems incapable of it. Yes, she is undoubtedly sad. But she also conveys the impression that the lessons she has learnt are important and can be generalised.

'Many Bollywood heroines,' she observes, 'go half-naked on the screen and still stay with their parents. I took a VCD of *Murder* to show my parents. They refused to believe it was an Indian film.'

'They have a puritanical perception of India then?' I ask.

Yes, but she wants to drive home a different point.

'Notice – the *Murder* culture is not welcome into an average Indian home. I don't know if it's hypocritical, but this semi-permeability has an admirable aspect. It's partly the reason grandparents are found in homes and not geriatric wards. Of course, I'm now mature enough to understand that I cannot be part of a joint family... Oh, my God! I wouldn't mind having my mother or mother-in-law on the other side of the street, but as a married woman, I would demand my own space.'

Meanwhile she has created her own space in Bangalore. She lives in the upmarket Defence Colony where roads are strewn with colourful spring flowers and flanked by chowkidars. But more pertinently, the place remains silent during the day, allowing her to sleep well before embarking on night shifts. Patricia's metamorphosis into a corporate employee seems part of a slow, natural progression. To maintain her company's financial accounts for North and South America, she has to be a polyglot. And that is where her past experience comes in. Brought up on a strict regimen of Portuguese, she learnt Spanish during her stint at the Ecuador Cultural Centre at Belgium.

'To be precise, at Ghent, a town close to Brussels,' she says. 'But I also learnt Dutch, which half of Belgium speaks. Otherwise I would have missed the cultural nuances and jokes.'

'And Belgium was obviously different from here.'

'Well, wonderful people, cold country; they don't easily open their homes and kitchens to anyone. But guess what – I've promoted my ex-boss to my second Dad.'

'Okay. That accounts for Portuguese, Spanish and Dutch. But your English is quite good as well.'

'I had English from the fifth grade. But one doesn't learn languages in schools. I became fluent in it only after coming here. So you'll find an Indian flavour in my English. It's something that stumps my American friends.'

I presume that she learnt English during her stint at Atmashakti, Fr. Hank Nunn's world.

'How was it, working with Fr. Nunn?' I ask.

'Hank,' she says, 'is a much respected figure. But we didn't interact with him much because he'd rather spend any free time with the "kids". I mostly worked along with three other foreigners – a Frenchwoman, an Austrian and a German – and well, they became my sisters.'

'You don't seem to believe that family and blood are synonymous,' I say.

'They aren't. I also have two Indian and one Portuguese sister. And I really mean it when I make people part of my family. I'm sprouting relations all over the world. Isn't it a good way of expanding one's family?'

Patricia is also expanding her circle in other ways. Recently, she helped form a Brazilian club in Bangalore. Although she is aware of just one other Brazilian based in the city, the club has grown to twenty members. It includes Indians living in Brazil and even an American in love with her country. The club, however, had its genesis in an untoward incident – the death of Cristiano Junior.

'Cristiano's death brought my own mortality into focus for the first time,' says Patricia. 'And it is so much sadder dying far away from your own people. I and my Brazilian friends around the country rallied as much as we could, urging the Embassy to take affirmative action. I couldn't help wondering if my body would be flown back on time to my parents, were something similar to happen to me... the episode increased my empathy for expatriates... coming elsewhere is a journey in so many ways. The tsunami wouldn't have hit me with the same impact if I had not come to India...'

'How do you find your job?' I ask.

'Oh, it's good. Initially, the brisk pace surprised me. It's so unlike the NGO world. And the standard Indian pace you see outside the workplace. The Indians at work are an aware lot.'

'No problems getting along with them?'

'Well, nobody in my department is trying to poke the other's eye. But I find it much easier to work with North Indians than the Southerners. The Northerners seem to be on the spot, more result oriented. And my bosses let me have my say. So that's not an issue. Except that some people are amazed when I employ the same open mannerism with both subordinates and superiors.'

Indian Sports Falls, Cristiano Rises in Glory

Cristiano Junior, a soccer player from Brasilia, came to Bangalore to play in the finals of the Federation Cup, a premier event in the Indian soccer scene. Kolkata's Mohun Bagan stood between the Cup and his team – the Goa-based Dempo Sports Club. The star all the way, that fateful day at the Kanteerava Stadium, was Cristiano.

Having already scored in the first half, Cristiano was on the verge of repeating the feat in the seventy-eighth minute when Mohun Bagan's goalkeeper Subrata Paul ignored the ball, flailed around and hit him. The ball still bounded into the nets. Cristiano fell to the ground, never to rise again. The doctors and a physiotherapist present on the occasion supposedly took no immediate medical action. Precious minutes passed before he was carried off on a stretcher. Even then, he was not taken to the Mallya Hospital across the street. By the time he was taken to a proper doctor, Cristiano was dead. The official line – that the autopsy revealed a cardiac arrest – found few takers.

'What about the night shift?'

Patricia smiles.

'We get a generous night-shift allowance and timings are flexible. Plus, Bangalore is a safe city. I once had coffee at midnight at this very place and then went for a walk with my friend. There aren't many places in the world where one can do that safely. It can't happen in Brazil.'

'Why not?'

'It's a violent country now. You might say that Brazilians want to *have* instead of just *be*. Acceptance of status quo, of not having, is quite low. People want to get more, using violence if need be. Fights seldom occur because of religion or ideology. Only money counts. In the last fifteen years, the problem has percolated to the countryside from cities like Sao Paulo.'

'That's surprising what you say about ideology,' I say. 'Brazil has a very happening NGO circuit, doesn't it?'

'I know. I come from Porto Alegre.'

As time passes, new insights and theories are surfacing. It is now said that an independent autopsy conducted in Brazil revealed a head injury. It is also alleged that Dempo forced Cristiano to play the finals despite being aware of the head injury that had resulted in a clot. An official of the All India Football Federation also let it slip that Cristiano was dead as soon as he fell, but an announcement was delayed to avert a law and order situation.

Whatever be the truth, there is no doubt that Indian sports let a player down that day. And a guest of the country at that. From all reports, Cristiano was humble, open, highly religious and devoted to his wife Juliana. Being a superstar, it is said, was his teenage dream. And he achieved it the day he died and the score-line read 2-0.

Dempo won the Federation Cup for the first time, thanks to twin strikes by a star that came from afar and shone brighter than the rest.

Facts sourced from Sportstar

Ah! The birthplace of the World Social Forum and home to the poet Mario Quintana. Literally translated, Porto Alegre means Happy Harbour and is situated in the southern part of Brazil. According to Patricia, north Brazil is poorer, and is hence home to humbler, kinder people.

'But Porto Alegre…,' she says, pauses and sips her coffee thoughtfully.

'Yes?'

'I was born there. It's a beautiful, special place. You can experience the four seasons in a single day. You know, it's situated along an estuary, the Rio Guaiba, where you can see the most beautiful sunset in the world.'

'I have a diehard Bangalorean friend who swears that the most beautiful sunset happens at Basavanagudi,' I say.

We laugh. I then ask her about something indisputably beautiful – the Amazon. She replies:

'Hey, I'm a city girl who has always lived in apartments. An only child to boot. I've never been a nature freak. I know that the Amazon is – like – from Bangalore to China…' After a pause, she admits: 'I actually don't know much of Brazil other than a few important cities.'

'But you're still planning to go back, aren't you?'

'Yes. Someday.'

'Why hasn't it happened yet?'

She gets my hint, and responds as openly as is her wont.

'After the relationship ended, I was left confused. I'm still thinking about the next step. It takes time to dismantle a life. Perhaps it's time to move. To a place that'll be easier on me. But I'm not in a hurry. I feel that at some subconscious level, you cannot move till you've absorbed all that a way of life can teach you. So I'm searching the Indian culture to see what I haven't learnt yet. What is it that's holding me back?'

'Any idea where you'll shift to?' I ask.

'Perhaps California,' she replies. 'It's attracting me from far. But will I like it? I don't know. Brazil and India might be corrupt nations, but the people are so nice. I've loved the Indian experience. When I eventually leave, I will miss this place.'

Before I sign off, I thank her for the frank interview.

'It's so personal, this information you've shared with me,' I say.

Patricia smiles yet again.

'I think I'm too open even for a Brazilian. But that's who I am. I don't mind sharing my knowledge. I learn from other people's experiences, so perhaps mine will help someone. That's something I learnt at Atmashakti. As a therapist, you realise that so-called sane people exhibit the same behavioural patterns as the "kids". It's a good eye-opener.'

A Flemish Tale

Among all the foreigners I have met, none have suggested as unusual a setting for a rendezvous as Dr. Daniel Joseph van Cauwenberghe. On a Sunday evening, I head towards the Lalbagh Double Road – the *original* Double Road as old-timers would say – and upon reaching there, I take a side alley that leads me to an unassuming lodging house. It is the kind frequented by those on short-term transfers and/or thin wallets. Or perhaps by Spartan bachelors. As I take four steep stairs to Dr. Daniel's room, I wonder which category he belongs to. I have to wait a while to discover that – his room is locked. So I patrol the high landing and glimpse a very different Bangalore. A couple of tired kites are being flown against a twilight sky. An invisible bird is fighting a tough battle against a concrete mixer for a piece of the soundscape. An old lady – a grandmother perhaps – carries an empty basket above her head while towing a child with her free hand. Uncollected garbage heaps, I learn, look uglier when seen from the top. Far ahead, I see the unlit floodlights of the Chinnaswamy cricket stadium. Before I tire of the scenery, I see a Westerner walk into the lodging house.

A few moments later, Dr. Daniel appears before me. He has silver hair, spectacles dangling from a chain and alert blue eyes that smile. His generous belly protrudes from a T-shirt with horizontal stripes coloured orange, blue and white. We greet each other and proceed to his room. Once inside, he removes his wristwatch and dangles it on a wall-mounted clothes peg. I cast my eyes around the room. There is a washbasin, a small cabinet, a cot, and a computer that sits upon a rudimentary table placed next to a plastic chair. That is all. As for personal belongings, I see a photograph of a young girl, freshly bathed and wrapped in a long Turkish towel.

Dr. Daniel asks me to sit on the cot while he makes himself a stiff drink of cost-effective Indian whisky. He then sits on the plastic chair, keeps a pack of cigarettes (another unglamorous Indian brand) within reach and turns his attention to me.

We are off.

'What am I doing in Bangalore?' he says, 'It's a long story. I used to be a Vice-President of International Finance in a company that's a household name. That meant I was tuned in to forex rates, interest rates, fluctuating political equations... anything that can affect money. I was based in Bahrain when I quit that job in 1993. Why? I guess twenty-five years of intense pressure was enough for me. After I quit, I took a year's sabbatical. And travelled a lot. Hong Kong, Australia, the Philippines, Malaysia, Indonesia... In retrospect, it seems a mistake not to have included India in my travel itinerary. But the news articles that spoke of a poverty-stricken India put me off. Anyway, my intention was to be based in a Far-Eastern country and Philippines appealed to me for two reasons – an English-speaking public and a Catholic majority. I knew I would feel connected. So that's where I went. Back home in Belgium, my first job was that of a teacher in a government school. But after one year of that, I had taken my father's advice to enter the private sector. Now I decided to resume teaching. I got a job in a university in the Philippines and taught finance, economics, advanced econometrics, management and languages.

'I soon became a member of a sort of association of church-goers. We used to meet to express our concerns and exchange ideas about business etc. Melanie Caringas was a member as well. Getting married was never in my scheme of things till that point. But the "superpower" willed it and we got married. I'm very happy for it, really. We now have an adorable daughter – Danielle Carmela. That's her photograph right there.

'But I had other adventures in the Philippines as well. When I was turning fifty, I decided to study for a second doctorate. This time, I chose to do it in philosophy. It took five years to complete. Times had changed since my first thesis. Dissertation skills had to be upgraded. It was tough, but enjoyable and I finished it last year. I like to think my effort inspires my wife – she's a teacher as well – to pursue further studies. And hopefully, my daughter will also want a good education. *Keep the brain alive and you'll live longer.* It's true, isn't it?

'We still haven't gotten to why I'm here. I know. It's like this – full-time teachers in the Philippines get meagre salaries. Say, around ten to twelve thousand Indian rupees. At one point, my wife and I asked ourselves: "Are we going to do this the rest of our lives?" She suggested that we emigrate to the US. I said: "Fine by me." She applied for a job and after protracted negotiation, got an offer to teach in

Maryland. Then she decided that she wanted to study till it was time to go to America. She's now doing her Master's in Special Education so that she can teach children with disabilities. Okay. But – with my earnings alone, it was difficult to support a family. So I searched the internet and stumbled upon an opportunity in Bangalore. Someone wanted a translator and the pay was good. I'm fluent in Dutch, German, French, English and Flemish (that's the primary Belgian language). So I asked my wife: "Should I go to Bangalore?" She said: "By all means, if you can manage it, it would be nice." I came here just before Christmas last year. And learnt that one needs to pay a ten-month rent as advance for leasing a flat. I didn't have that kind of money. But this accommodation is good enough for me... although it's just eight feet by twelve feet. European prison cells are as big.

'So that's how it stands. Soon, my wife will go to the US. If she finds it agreeable, I'll join her there. Else, she'll come to India, or maybe, we'll all go back to the Philippines. That's my story.'

I'm reluctant to break the ensuing silence in the room after his amazing tale. Finally, I ask, rather lamely:

'How do you find Bangalore?'

'I don't much like it,' he replies. 'The traffic and pollution is impossible. I hear Hyderabad has better infrastructure. I'm considering relocating there. I don't want to break my leg while walking on a footpath after dark.'

I think of Thomas and how it isn't necessarily a bad thing to break a leg.

'But,' says Dr. Daniel, 'I like India. The people are nice, friendly and peaceful. One doesn't find violence on the streets. And India is an extremely cheap place. One can survive on a dollar a day. That's special. But it would be a fallacy to term India a country. It's a *continent*! There are so many places to see. And it seems to be teeming with great natural and human resources. India should have been a superpower already.'

He is obviously not referring to the kind of superpower that got him married.

'Why isn't it one then?' I ask.

'Well, uncontrolled population growth seems to keep it down. Although I come from a very big family myself and find it difficult to disagree completely with those who want to have more children... But population, and concepts such as dowry, child-marriages, and polytheism are your millstones.'

'Er... Dr. Daniel, you're a double doctorate holder working as a translator. Is it fulfilling?' I ask.

'No. But one has to remember that the Hiroshima bomb was dropped because of bad translation. "Put on hold" was interpreted as "Don't pay attention". So translation is a significant thing. Companies worldwide know its importance.'

Okay.

'One last question, sir,' I say. 'You preferred coming to Bangalore to going home. Why?'

'I don't like to depend on charity,' he replies. 'At fifty-four, I'm still strong enough to work and provide for my family.'

I say goodbye and let myself out. Outside, the kites and birds are fast asleep.

The Palestinian Emperor

Majed A. A. Sabha was born in the village of Kufferellabad in Palestine towards the end of the winter of 1960. The second son of what would develop into a large family of ten siblings, Majed spent his formative years scampering around date and olive trees. But when he turned thirteen, events took a drastic turn. His agriculturist father died, leaving behind children in various stages of maturity.

Majed's elder brother shifted to Saudi Arabia to support the family. Majed, in turn, borrowed from his brother's experience as a mason and took up odd jobs during the school vacations. By laying tiles and creating mosaics, he not only earned enough for his upkeep but also contributed something to the family. Six years later, he passed his intermediate examinations, and like many Palestinians, went to Jordan to seek admission in an engineering college. Unfortunately, his marks weren't sufficient to get him a seat there. He had to look elsewhere for opportunities. But where? For some reason, he told himself:

'I'll try my luck in the Indian sub-continent.'

So in the November of 1979, Majed Sabha landed in Pakistan and obtained a tourist visa on arrival. For two weeks, he roamed Karachi and Lahore in vain – the universities in both cities were closed for the winter. Hoping for a better reception in India, he secured a three-month tourist visa, travelled by train to the border and then by bus to Delhi. While there, he slept in churches, mosques and bazaars by night and sought admission into colleges by day. On a visit to the city's Jordanian Embassy, he came to know of colleges in Bangalore that admitted students who were prepared to pay a donation; it was an option many of his fellow nationals were taking. Without a second thought, he travelled south to Bangalore and with some ado obtained admission in a private college by paying about $4,000 for an engineering seat.

But Majed Sabha wasn't satisfied. He immediately took off for the holy town of Benares. Reason? In his unbelievable naivety, he nurtured hopes of admission into the renowned Benaras Hindu University. During the forty days he camped there, all he managed to gain were sixteen (!) kilos in body weight. Sigh! So it was back to Bangalore... What followed was a year of academic misery. He failed in seven out of eleven papers and it was only after the students staged a *dharna* that he and others in his situation got promoted to the second year.

From then on, due to extra effort and a scientific study methodology, his marks improved. Majed went on to become a studious as well as an active student who often stuck his neck out for others. In 1981, he made front-page news by taking his university to court for allegedly tampering with his marks. In the truest sense, Majed Sabha had arrived in India when he won the case.

The courage the young student showed in confronting powerful forces took him far. After he completed his engineering and then his MBA, Majed launched himself as a businessman. This was 1987. Bangalore, with more trees and fewer vehicles, was decidedly colder than it is today. So he decided to sell a product with a future – solar water heaters. The product was genuine; it even had a stamp of approval from the Bureau of Indian Standards. Yet convincing people of the merits and necessity of solar heaters was an uphill task. It took door-to-door canvassing, networking and marketing. Testing times, which he describes as: '...overcoming the hurdles...sweating...with determination; come what may; finally to succeed in the venture.'

After six successful years in the business, he was in the mood to move back to the college campus. So he created one. Today, as Founding Trustee of the Brindavan College, Majed Sabha runs an institute that fulfils diverse needs.

When I visit his office, it is immediately evident that he is on top of every happening. Wearing a suit, a bristly moustache and square spectacles, he sits on a high chair, and receives and despatches employees as if he is an Eastern potentate dealing with minor petitioners. The placement of the chairs for visitors strengthens these notions of royalty. They don't face him. Rather, they are placed like courtier seats in Mughal courts. Or, perhaps, the arrangement is in keeping with Palestinian custom.

When he sees me, Majed Sabha says that he is having a packed day as usual. Then he grants me an hour for a chat and begins by asking in a deep, slow voice:

'What do you want to know?'

Soon he is narrating his life story. As I listen, it strikes me that there is hardly anything spectacular about this gentleman's life. It is all about old-school grit and confidence.

And he doesn't come across as one who refers to management books to resolve issues. Instead, he relies on the instincts he developed as a youth.

'To manage anything in life, one should have self-confidence,' he says. 'You ask me how I manage diversity in the college. And I reply: by ensuring that students follow norms. Be it a governmental law, a university procedure or a college rule, it has to be followed. No mobile in the classroom and no smoking in the campus means *no*. We keep the students close to us. But at the same time, we extend maximum support to make them feel protected. I believe that I own their problems and I try to solve their issues from that level of seriousness.'

'Don't clashes occur between students of different nationalities?' I ask.

'Not as often as you might think. If a misconduct occurs, we go by the first explanation of the student. No updates to that are entertained. That way, we train the students to be on the right always.'

'Is it always a homogenous approach?'

'When we began, I was not aware of how diverse the world is. Now I know. So I've learnt to use a somewhat heterogeneous approach. And I've learnt that geographical proximity doesn't make two nations similar. A Maldivian and a Sri Lankan are not alike. Why, even a Sri Lankan Tamil is nothing like a Tamil from Tamil Nadu. So we study the culture of each nationality and treat each as required. With some peoples, one has to be soft. With others, one needs to take stern measures.

'You must understand,' he continues, 'that our unique environment is in itself an auxiliary education, a golden opportunity. I remember this wonderful pair of students, Rami, a Palestinian Christian and Lavin, a Sri Lankan. After the completion of college, Rami went and stayed for a month with Lavin in Sri Lanka. In a place like this, it is possible to forge those kind of bridges.'

'The bridges seem to be Afro-Asian at the moment,' I say. 'Is it at all possible for students from Western countries to come to India and extend the outsourcing rainbow?'

'Oh, the rules and regulations of the Government of India need revamping if we have to expand,' he replies. 'I have one student of German origin and one Japanese. If I can have one, I can have ten. If I can have ten, I can have a hundred. It's just that the government needs to take specific interest.'

'If and when that happens, the rents in Bhoopasandra would hit the proverbial roof,' I say.

He nods.

'The residents of Bhoopasandra are getting urbanised,' he says, 'and they're getting to see Mauritius and Uganda right here. It's been a huge jump for them.'

'And for you.'

'Yes,' he says and turns slightly nostalgic. 'I have taken a few leaps of faith myself. Come to think of it, I've been a Bangalorean since the time there were just two traffic lights all the way from Rajajinagar to the airport. Yeah. My entire mature life has been spent in India. And I intend to spend the rest of my life here, in the land that has accepted me… that's why I took Indian citizenship. This way, I can contribute to society and be surefooted.'

'What's next in life?' I ask.

Majed Sabha smiles. He says he can interact with the foot soldier outside his door and the Chief Minister of Karnataka with equal ease. He concludes:

'What has been achieved is significant. Whatever is left to achieve will happen soon, given my self-confidence and loyal staff.'

I take leave of the Emperor and the next subject is ushered in.

Que Sera Sera

O n a pleasant Sunday, Thomas drops by as planned and we head towards a pub to celebrate the sunset. On the way, our scooter is hailed by a clump of wayside smokers. They are Thomas' workplace friends, having a get-together. We join the assembly out of politeness. But upon entering the host's house, a cold mug and the gathered guests easily keep me engrossed.

There is Sylvia, a loud and friendly Spaniard who came to Mumbai a few months back on a blind date. She didn't like the guy but fell in love with the country and decided to stay on. A Finn girl with an unobtrusive charm is inseparably linked with a shy, dark-skinned Indian. And then there's the soft-spoken host of Chinese descent, Waikam, who is married to Somana, a Coorgi Indian. Somana matches Sylvia in loudness and tells jokes that are a generation outdated. But he delivers them with contagious relish and a faith that is almost childlike. It works; he has his audience in splits.

As the beer is unusually good, Thomas and I decide it is imported, only to be given a lesson in prejudice by a lesser-known Indian label. Someone points to a gramophone and requests a song. Somana summons an all-time favourite and plays it. "Que Sera Sera" croons a lethargic, yet raunchy, male voice. Somana transfers the record to a functional electronic gramophone and this time the lady's voice fills the room as expected. Sylvia accompanies the singer, and those unfamiliar with the lyrics hum along.

I look around the room, which is a wonderful amalgamation of two ancient civilisations. Chinese fans of different sizes are staggered on a pale yellow wall. A mango-wood sculpture of a buxom Indian goddess stands underneath. Mirroring the inanimate are Waikam Somana's two unusually tall sons – Siddharth and Sudarshan.

Thomas and I leave once the song ends. But not before I secure Waikam's consent to be interviewed.

* * *

A few days later, I'm back at Waikam's house to meet her and Somana. Shrek, their brown-and-black dachshund, sends out a fusillade of barks to greet me before Waikam opens the door. While Somana leaves to prepare tea, Waikam offers me a seat and tells her story. She is now an Indian citizen, she says, to make sure I understand that she is technically not a foreigner.

'Leaving China must have been difficult,' I say.

'I've never even been to China,' she replies in her earnest underplaying manner.

Her parents fled Guangdong in southern China to escape the Communists and rebuilt their lives as restaurateurs in the Malaysian city of Ipoh. Waikam was born in 1950 and became part of a strong contingent of immigrant Chinese who proudly retained their culture. She even went to a Chinese school where, ironically, she was taught to be a good Malay national. Sometime during her school days, the city saw riots break out between the Malays and Chinese. 'During such times, you always side with your own people, don't you?' she asks. Mercifully, it was a one-off incident and easily controlled. Waikam completed her schooling without much ado. And later, probably because she inherited the itinerant gene, came to India in 1974.

'And I got enrolled in the Mysore University to pursue a post-graduate degree in Indology,' she says.

Soon after entering the campus, she met Somana, a naval officer. He was at that time in charge of the National Cadet Corps unit in the campus.

Let's see if I get this right:

Waikam travelled thousands of miles to an unknown country. There she chose a university located a couple of hundred miles inland from the sea. There she met the naval officer she would marry.

Que Sera Sera!

In two years, Waikam had completed her Master's and Somana the formality of seeking Presidential approval to marry a foreigner. One of his friends, the then Bishop of Mysore, adopted Waikam as his daughter and gave her off in matrimony. As a dutiful wife, Waikam followed Somana wherever he was posted. Cochin, Mumbai, Vishakapatnam, Coimbatore and even the Andamans. But she found the Kannadiga to be the friendliest and most hospitable among Indians. Needless to say, she was very happy when the family settled down in Bangalore once Somana quit the navy.

The time had come for her to acquire a profession. For ten years beginning in 1980, Waikam ran a garments' export firm by simultaneously playing the roles of a seamstress and a designer of clothes. Labour issues and the needs of growing children put an end to that phase of her life. Her present incarnation had to wait till her sons grew up. Today, she is a language and culture specialist catering to the Bangalore IT industry. Meanwhile, her sons are embarking on their own missions.

When Siddharth and Sudarshan began schooling, their classmates nicknamed them Chang. Both of them. Siddharth became Chang, the best All-India NCC cadet. Sudarshan became Chang, the captain of the Karnataka under-18 basketball team. He now plans to become an English language instructor and head off to Beijing.

'With the Olympics approaching, they'll have a shortage of English speakers,' he predicts. When I prod him further, he admits that the reason is partly atavistic. That is why he is learning Mandarin from Waikam and plans to stay in China for at least three years.

* * *

Now here is an interesting aside: it takes me three meetings with the family to get this much material. The first couple of times, I return dissatisfied that I haven't gathered interesting anecdotes. After all, the family represents the union of two of the oldest and richest civilisations in the world. So it troubles me that Siddharth and Sudarshan find their parents to be no different from others, or that they don't have a bank of funny school incidents... Shouldn't they be flaunting their uniqueness like a medal? Also, both Somana and Waikam are completely casual about their differing ethnicity. Each member of the family offers a reason for this.

'Perhaps because I'm a Coorgi,' suggests Somana, 'and my community is known to have a Western outlook.'

'Maybe because my father is secular and my mother an open-minded Buddhist,' says Sudarshan. 'Or maybe because we speak English at home!'

'Perhaps,' says Waikam, 'the Chinese match the Coorgis when it comes to tolerance.'

I have a theory as well. I think the family expertly irons out differences and concentrates on the straightforward task of leading a full life. It is a family no different from any other because that is exactly how it wants to be. And I think I know an appropriate song to describe them. How does it run now? Oh, yes:

"Que Sera Sera..."

Good as Gay

Tall buildings on either side of Cunningham Road create a tunnel effect as I ride into it. Not many roads in Bangalore offer that. Plus, Cunningham Road has a distinct metropolitan air. Busy offices coexist with roadside eateries and the ones where customers are allowed to linger. So for most of the day, the road remains gay and active. That means parking is a minor challenge. When I finally find a spot, park and walk into the charming new tea shop, I find Jack waiting. We greet each other and take a window seat from where we can watch the traffic rushing past.

When Jack is convinced about the project, I make my opening gambit. He must remain anonymous in the narrative. Not because I disapprove. But others do. And since there are few homosexual foreigners in town, it is better not to talk about his profession, or any other giveaway topics. He agrees, albeit for a different reason. Many gays, he says, are "out" in the open in other circles, but not necessarily in the professional arena.

'I fear discrimination,' he continues in his deep voice. 'Professionals I would like to work with may avoid me simply because they feel uncomfortable with my sexuality.'

Otherwise he couldn't care less if people knew. That doesn't mean he is insensitive. In fact, he gives ample evidence of his sensitivity by taking his time before talking about his partner Shantanu (name changed).

'Do you have strong inclinations that dictate your choice of a partner?' I ask.

'Preferences tend to be strong among gay men,' he says, using the easy slang that NGOs shy away from. 'One may be attracted to skinny men or fat, older men or younger. Some white men find Indians attractive or vice versa.'

Racist?

'Not at all. It's a matter of preference. I never felt attracted to Indian men back home. Only after living in Bangalore for a few months did I find a diversity of Indian men attractive.'

'What was your initial experience in Bangalore?'

'Oh, many guys hit on me merely because of my foreign appearance. It took a while to be accepted as just another gay man. Personally, I've never specifically sought men of a particular race... although in the past, I was largely attracted to white men. I guess I have changed. I've matured since discovering my sexual preference as a fourteen-year-old. I've met a lot more people and find a greater spectrum of people attractive, depending of course, on their character and personality.'

That doesn't mean Jack is planning to be unfaithful to Shantanu.

'Shantanu and I have been in a relationship for the last four years,' he says. 'In between I have travelled back to my country for long periods of time, even a year or more. So we've had to periodically redefine our relationship. It's exclusive right now, but it's a challenge to be committed when one is apart. If I'm gone for years together in the future, neither I nor he can be expected to live without a relationship. So we don't make explicit promises although we feel strongly about each other. We'll have to deal with the distance when the time comes. See, even now, we don't live together. Both of us lead full lives and most often get together only on Saturdays. I stay with a straight roommate who has a girlfriend. And he's cool about my sexuality. I met him through a gay friend, in fact.'

'How does it feel to share an apartment with a straight guy?' I ask.

'It's interesting. Like, when his parents come visiting, we hide his girlfriend's shampoo in my room! And his straight friends bring their girlfriends to our apartment for the occasional rendezvous and use my key to get in.'

'And is there anything different about having an Indian boyfriend?' I ask.

'Well, every relationship is unique,' says Jack. 'It needs work. A lot of it. Adjustment knows no racial tones. The relationship I was in before was a bit... traditional, if you please. We spent all our time together. That can get quite intense. And also collapse when it acquires a habitual or dependent overtone. But Shantanu and I function independently, and yet make decisions about ourselves and the future together. We have very different occupations. That helps. And he's anti-conventional-marriage, so we've not had to talk about that.'

Especially in India, the gay man marrying heterosexually is a looming issue. Those who step out of the closet often face massive parental pressure. Parents may even accept the situation so long as their gay son or daughter marries to provide an outward sign of stability! This pseudo conservatism leads to bigger issues. By unwittingly accepting a gay husband, a heterosexual woman gets trapped in a sexless, loveless marriage. Unfortunately, the bulk of the Indian gay community lead their life through marriages of such one-sided convenience. In two episodes of *We, the People*, Barkha Dutt of NDTV boldly confronted the staunch conservatives about such pitfalls, and the gay community for allowing such a pitfall to exist.

The still fledgling gay community in India has few answers at the moment. Jack estimates that there are 300-500 openly gay men in Bangalore, but popular internet gay forums have thousands of members. This is still the tip of the iceberg. Many gay and bisexual men anonymously scan websites in search of partners. Amongst this group are opportunists who try to offer lifts to unsuspecting "prospects", or try to find fleeting pleasure in crowded buses and trains. It is quite likely that the same people would also be callous husbands in heterosexual marriages. Perhaps their callousness is a survival tactic?

'Being gay does not automatically translate into being non-discriminatory,' says Jack. 'We have our share of misogynists. It's disillusioning to see gay men get married. We discuss the issue in *Good as You*. It's the only official forum in Bangalore for gay men, where I incidentally met Shantanu. We're just around twenty men who meet regularly every Thursday and share a space where we can be totally free with our thoughts. When it comes to this particular topic, the opinion is split. While some don't see it as an issue, I personally feel that no amount of familial pressure is sufficient to rationalise it. Even IT professionals who earn well indulge in matrimony, though they can afford to move out of a rigid family. But the fact is: those who marry are seldom openly gay. So they've not been questioned about their stance.'

'Would you grill a guy doing this?' I ask.

'Oh, no. Never in a frontal attack on an individual,' he says, alarmed at my impertinence. 'But we do discuss it, especially with regard to the spouse's health risks and emotional upheaval.'

'Is it the legendary gay sensitivity on display?' I ask.

Again, Jack disagrees.

'You see,' he says, 'we look at a married man as one in a transition phase. Not having an official stance is not a sign of lenience. Nor does it have anything to do with the harsh judgements passed against the gay community. The basic premise upon which *Good as You* operates is openness, which the man has initiated by coming to the forum. It's that simple. Is it any wonder then that I have immense respect for Indian men who resist marriage and its concomitant conservatism? Observe the gay Indian artist – he may be a dramatist, or a writer, or a musician. He is in a profession that's more receptive to alternative sexualities. Yet he finds it difficult to be open about his preference. He fears, rightly, that his work would be seen as a manifestation of his sexuality. Who wants to answer the same awkward questions to the media all the time? Indian media might have woken up to the gay phenomenon, but it lacks sufficient skills to project the social complexities behind the movement. Do they see the group as one under threat, one whose rights are being violated? What the media mainly tags is the government line that this group is a high-risk HIV transmitter.'

Recently a national daily carried a photograph of a high-profile fashion designer kissing a man. Surely, that kind of sensational coverage is unwarranted?

'Yes, it was sensationalist,' agrees Jack. 'But even that is welcome. Because the topic at least gets spoken about *and* a man has gone public about his sexuality.'

That does seem to be a big deal. Most individuals are "open" only amongst the LGBT (Lesbian Gay Bisexual Transsexual) communities. In Bangalore, these communities form a parallel universe hitherto unexplored by heterosexuals. It is a world where lesbians, married or single, are forced to have their surreptitious meetings during the daytime, before social curfew kicks in. Gay men, meanwhile, prefer the evenings to socialise. That is one of the reasons the two groups meet less often than is desirable. In fact, says Jack, the entire sexual minority movement in America has been illogically estranged from other movements like the feminist movement or the civil rights movement. Bonds between these communities were much stronger when all of them were inchoate movements during the 1960s and 70s. Seen in that light, the situation is less divisive in India. Jack informs me that prominent Dalit and women's rights activist Ruth Manorama recently lamented the overwhelming existence of a "hetero-normative" space in the country.

But then, can India ever relinquish its diversity? The answer is no, considering the diverse, and in some ways divisive, classifications that exist within alternative sexualities. Lesbians, gays and bisexuals are dichotomised into masculine and feminine essences. (Some masculine gay men even ridicule the effeminate gay man by asking: *Who's that Queen?*) Outside these communities stand the fringe – though not mute – groups. Highly voluble among them are the *hijras*. Born biologically male or "inter-sexed", they eventually opt for castration. *Kothis*, on the other hand, can be loosely defined as transvestites. They are mainly homosexual or bisexual men who prefer a feminine expression and in that sense, are akin to "Queen" gays. Many *kothis* become sex workers for want of options. If you remove the urge for feminine expression from a *kothi*, he becomes a "double decker". And of course, transgenderists are those who choose surgery or hormonal treatment to undergo a sex change.

Barring the transgenderists, an overwhelming majority of the fringe groups hail from poor backgrounds. This isolates them from the lesbian, gay and bisexual communities. Jack believes that there is partial truth in the claim made by some *hijra* groups that the gay community is elitist. At the same time, one finds myriad linkages between the groups. Some *hijras* prefer to date lesbians; some gay men prefer *hijras*. With the core idea being exploration and peaceful coexistence of alternative sexual preferences, all combinations are welcome. But, adds Jack, class intermingling is rare. Even support mechanisms seem to be mutually exclusive. Bangalore NGOs such as Sangama, for example, provide space to the lower-class Kannadiga and Tamilian homosexuals in addition to other groups. In such spaces, the struggle for expression is more poignant.

The *Hijra Habba*

On 18 June 2004, a 21-year-old *hijra* named Kokila was gang-raped in Bangalore by a group of hooligans. Upon seeing a couple of policemen approaching, the hooligans vaporised. The cops took Kokila to a suburban police station and tortured and raped her themselves. The *hijras* rose in protest.

Sexual minorities in the city have been asserting themselves since December 2002. That was when they formed a consortium named Vividha (meaning Diverse) and organised the first ever *Hijra Habba*. Sports, cultural events and demands for political rights mark the festival. The demands include the repeal of Section 377 of the Indian Penal Code which sees homosexuality as a crime, legal recognition of sex change, and employment opportunities. Politicians and celebrities attending the event give it widespread social sanction. In 2003, the event was even moved to the Town Hall. On a more continuous basis, an NGO named Swabhava has been operating a helpline for sexual minorities since 2000.

Indeed, Bangalore is taking small steps towards becoming a truly diverse city.

'It's a myth,' says Jack, 'that lower-class people have less to lose than elite, professional, English-speaking, strongly-identifiable gay communities. They can lose access to society, nothing less. Their financial vulnerability is an added dimension of woe. Even law and order mechanisms pay heed to class. In prominent Bangalore parks, a cop is likely to let go of a gay middle- or upper-class couple if caught in the moment. But a lower-class pair is bound to be harassed or arrested or both.'

'Still,' continues Jack, 'it's a tribute to India that we discuss class issues in *Good as You*. In a supposedly progressive country like America, it's not discussed at all, although the gay movement is much older and has gone through many transformations.'

It is interesting to observe that homophobia is increasingly conspicuous in America even as societal acceptance is on the rise. Public acceptance is increasing in Bangalore as well. It has now become possible to conduct festivals like the *Hijra Habba*. Additionally, people may not realise it, but they frequently share recreational spots with the gay community. For example: following a specific timetable, gay men visit a very popular Bangalore park and intermingle with the wider society. Outside the internet, parks act as primary spaces (others spaces include malls, public toilets and transportation) for fostering gay relationships. And the relationship building happens chiefly through a process called cruising. It is something every youth, gay or straight, indulges in. If your roving eye makes contact with another eyeball, you are cruising. The difference is that habitual gay cruisers usually convert a positive cruise into a conversation. And the act is not always a precursor to sex; it could just be a building block for a gay person's society. Other than that, the Bangalorean gay man attends parties to widen his circle. They don't occur often. Once every three to five months according to Jack. It may be in a well-known discotheque or pub, or in a private residence. The handful of straight women who are invited to similar parties in Mumbai find them irresistible – they are sure to be spared the ogling and the fondling.

That opens a new train of thought – what many think of as perverse actually offers options for asexual encounters. Straight men attending lesbian lunches, straight women thronging gay parties, gay men attending potluck with local housewives... we haven't reached that level of acceptance yet. For that, we need to see these communities for what they are... Or, at the very least, place the concept of alternative sexuality in the proper context. As Jack says:

'I'm a self-confessed gay man. But I wish people would realise that my sexuality is only a part of my personality.'

Queens of Clubs

Five months after my first attempts to contact the Overseas Women's Club (OWC), I clinch an appointment with its secretary Ava Kramer. I feel particularly happy this sunny morning as I ride towards Ava's house on the city's outskirts. I recall the emails that sunk into black holes and phone calls that, at best, resulted in polite refusals to be interviewed. And in the same five months, I have run into hordes of detractors of OWC. They are usually former members, or those who declined membership after a look-in, or those with memories of a perceived slight. One such detractor went to the extent of saying: .

'I thought you're writing a sensible book. Why do you want to meet overseas women who congregate simply to lament the dishonesty and inefficiency of Indian housemaids?'

Even the softest critic accuses the OWC of being impenetrable to outsiders. My own experiences seem to confirm this opinion, but it would be premature to take a harsh view. Perhaps the OWC members are just comfortable being on their own. Immigrants are natural seekers of that elusive sensation – comfort. So unprepared to consider elitism a sin, I arrive at Ava's home with anticipation. And encouraged by her congenial presence, I ask her why it is so difficult for OWC members to grant an audience.

'You must understand that plenty of people approach us with their own agenda,' she replies. 'Quite often they are businesspeople who want to push their wares. And the club doesn't exist to fulfil their aims. We have some very high-profile executives as members, and therefore an obligation to protect their privacy and interests. We cannot, for example, share the OWC phonebook with outsiders.'

She has a point. The club underwent a revival of sorts last year with membership rising from 200 to 455. Given that, even a conservative estimate puts the combined expendable income of the club members at around a million dollars per annum. That phonebook would undoubtedly be a best-seller in the telemarketing industry.

'Still,' continues Ava, 'it's surprising that you've had to struggle so. Perhaps office-bearers were relocating back home around the time your emails came in... members keep pouring in and out of Bangalore all the time... I'm sorry for what happened.'

'It's quite all right. Members are wary, that's all. Tell me about your club.'

She begins with the genesis of OWC. Back in the early 1960s, the American Women's Club of Bangalore was formed along the lines of existing clubs in Madras (now Chennai) and Delhi. Only in the early 1980s was the membership extended to overseas women of all countries (and to Non-Resident Indians who have spent at least ten continuous years abroad). Needless to say, the club was also rechristened with its present name. Today the OWC has members from thirty-four countries. But as one might expect, the US, Europe and Australia bring in stronger contingents. The club's primary goal is to help newcomers settle in Bangalore. It achieves this by providing them a ready social network and by sharing accumulated wisdom. Ava shows me an in-house book titled *In and Out of Bangalore*. It suggests dos and don'ts while in the city and also informs the members which shops, schools, hospitals, etc. are time-tested. Since the advertisements featured in the book have covered the publishing cost, the proceeds from book sales are channelled into charity work.

'We promote social welfare without regard to caste or creed, either with funds or personal involvement or both,' says Ava.

'What other means do you use to raise funds?' I ask.

'For any activity, say a chilli cookout, we charge participating members a premium over the basic operating cost and funnel the profits of the evening to a charity. Sometimes a corporate house sponsors our activities.'

All this sounds exceptional, but the OWC is not the only club of its kind in the city. The Community Services of Bangalore (CSB) has similar aims. A few weeks back I had met two members of CSB – Judith Mohr, a Canadian, and Kiran Chainani, an Indian. Formed in 1998, the CSB membership varies between 80 and 130. Eleven countries were represented in the club last year. The marked difference vis-à-vis the OWC is that CSB's membership is open to all Bangalore women.

'Ask any CSB member and she'll tell you that the diversity of women involved makes it a great club,' says Kiran. 'It helps the club become a learning-teaching centre where fresh ideas are exchanged; we also learn about new cultures and crafts. Each member can share what she does best. But for the CSB, our paths may never have crossed. Now I have forged many great friendships with both Indians and expatriates.'

'CSB's primary function,' says Judith, 'is to raise money for local charities but it is also a great forum for fellowship. It helps newcomers acclimatise to Bangalore and become a part of the community.'

'Are the foreigners better at raising funds?' I ask.

'I think the foreigners and locals make a great combination. Certainly, at times, being an expatriate may open a door – some business establishments that'll refuse the locals point blank may donate to foreigners. But with Bangalore becoming increasingly cosmopolitan, being an expatriate will soon lose its allure.' Evidently, the allure is already absent in CSB. 'The locals in CSB, in addition to fund-raising skills, also bring knowledge of the milieu. So as a combined force, we can accomplish almost anything. But it's not our fund-raising abilities, but the camaraderie, that I value the most. I always try to grab any opportunity to experience the local culture of the places I visit... it's nice to learn, share and understand different viewpoints.'

There are occasions when differing viewpoints lead to humorous chaos. For instance, while preparing for the annual fund-raising Christmas bazaar, the members have to decide upon the price of the commodities on sale.

'Someone will hold up an item and ask others to suggest a price,' says Judith smiling. 'Inevitably the locals would price it really low. This will prompt the foreigners to protest that it's a great item and, after all, it's for charity. And they'll go on to quote a much higher price! But my point is: our perspectives may occasionally differ, but our goals are the same.'

The shared goals can be broadly divided into two categories. One: self-development and two: development of society. Achieving the latter requires a few processes. Both the OWC and CSB scrutinise the records and credentials of local charitable organisations before donating funds. And the two clubs have learnt to synergise. The OWC's greatest strength is its ability to mobilise funds to an extent that the CSB cannot imitate due to its smaller size. There are occasions when the CSB does a needs-assessment and finds itself unable to fulfil the entire need. At that point, it contacts the OWC, and whenever possible the latter supplies the deficit.

'We don't want to replicate each other's efforts,' says Ava.

'With proper coordination, we can avoid that and also complement each other wonderfully,' says Judith.

Interestingly, Ava and Judith are members of both clubs and nurture positive feelings about both. Each club has its distinct identity. The CSB, for example, frequently invites guest speakers to conduct *Know India* programmes.

'Because,' says Judith, 'irrespective of how long one has lived in a place, there's always something new to learn about it.'

The OWC, on the other hand, organises a monthly cocktail hour to which spouses are invited, and has a book club that meets every month. It also organises playgroups for their children. And when it meets every Thursday in a plush coffee bar to chat, unemployed husbands of working expatriate wives are allowed to attend. They are, however, discouraged from attending the regular meetings.

'I don't think they'd be terribly interested in skincare and jewellery,' explains Ava.

Product of the Times

Although Bob Hoekstra has pointed out the logic behind the Indian IT industry's focus on the software services sector, I'm not wholly convinced. Agreed, the industry has cultivated a few strengths while focusing on services. Its onsite-offshore model is wonderfully geared to execute specific customer solutions. It has learnt to control the quality and cost of a project better than the competition. And it has continuously and successfully scaled up its operations (and in the process provided massive employment opportunities). None of these achievements can be overstated. No wonder, then, that the world has taken note.

Perhaps it is now time for the industry to attempt bigger challenges – creating products and intellectual property. And why is that important? Because that is where the *real* money is. Product-makers revolutionise the world; service-providers ride upon the revolution to create localised pockets of satisfaction.

Does this mean that an application software (created by a services company) and a product software are totally unlike each other? Not really. At the lowest level, both are made up of lines of code. They may even use the same technology and architecture. Why, then, haven't the big Indian companies made a serious dent in the products sector? Why don't their limited product lines generate a turnover as befits their stature? Well, for one thing, it is much safer to play the services game. The service-provider supplies the human resources and the client assures his payment even before the effort begins. Once the effort materialises, the client enjoys the business benefits derived from it.

Creating products, on the contrary, is inherently risky. The product-making company has to offer a widely applicable solution. So, not only should it fully understand the business domain in which it operates, but it should also have the vision to predict the future needs of the market. It should be willing to invest large sums upfront, hire highly talented and motivated teams, create the software and then market it aggressively. Then it has to persevere. Even if the company has got it right, it might take years for the returns to pour in. Meanwhile, it cannot take the organic route to growth – that is to say, it cannot simply add 20% to the workforce in a year and see a proportional growth in turnover. All in all, it is more challenging to build a product.

Does it mean that the Indian workforce cannot deliver one? Not at all. Large multinational product companies employ Indians in Bangalore and other cities to further their progress. So if anything is holding the big Indian companies back from making revolutionary products, it is "conservative capitalism". Conservative capitalists tend to invest in models that have low risks and provide good returns. They shy away from mid- to high-risk, exemplary-returns models. This attitude may not impact the industry immediately. But what happens when Indian salaries lead to an escalation in the cost of operations, and competition from other developing countries intensifies? It is a point worth thinking about....

Having spun my theories thus, I decide to seek a success story set in Bangalore. A story that would encourage the small and mid-sized Indian companies involved in product development. Eventually, I find one that goes back a few eras in IT-time, and also promises endurance. It is the story of Texas Instruments (TI) in India.

Some media reports mention TI as the first IT company in Bangalore. The truth, however, is that TI was the first IT multinational to set up operations in the city in 1985, by which time companies such as TCS, Wipro and Infosys were already in existence. Leading TI India's Software Division today is Sham Banerji, a British national who has worked with the company's research teams in Europe, America and Asia for the past twenty-five years.

'I was in the US when TI opened the Bangalore office,' says Sham. 'And I later saw this picture of a satellite dish being unloaded from a bullock cart. The image has stayed with me because it depicts the zeal with which work was accomplished despite limitations. And it also shows the leap of faith that TI as a company took with India when it was undergoing great political change.'

The private sector had just begun participating in the silicon industry, hitherto monopolised by the governmental departments of Electronics, Space, etc. So the prevalent rules and regulations were being revamped to accommodate the private sector, and temporary solutions were employed in the interim. For example, the Official Secrecy Act prohibited unmonitored uplink of data by private enterprises, although there were no restrictions on downloads. The stopgap arrangement was to post a government official within private enterprises to monitor all outgoing communication.

Similarly, customs procedures were not equipped to handle electronically transmitted software exports. So the solution was to copy software deliverables onto tapes and physically ship them to overseas customers.

India has come a long way since then. Twenty years later, American citizens are getting *Bangalored*. It has been a marathon as well as a sprint for the city. While the service industry has sprinted, research-based outfits like TI have run the marathon – researchers need stamina. And funds. I ask Sham if cost considerations were responsible for bringing TI to Bangalore.

'Capital always flows to the low-cost, talent-rich economies,' he replies. 'In the case of TI, cost wasn't the primary consideration. More pertinent was the availability of quality engineers. The Bangalore office initially worked in the area of Electronic Design Automation. And projects were specifically chosen to leverage the high literacy of electronics engineers in topics such as layout and logic synthesis. It was a success right from the beginning. Our teams innovated with passion and laid the foundation for what we are today. According to a recent Dataquest report, TI India had registered the highest number of patents compared to any other private development centre in India. So to answer your question, cost is always a factor in any business, but creativity and technological excellence are most important in the long run. You observe, don't you, that this contrasts sharply with the "safe" strategies that a lot of companies get trapped in. We do otherwise and are proud of our effort.'

'That TI India was purely a cost centre and still delivered?'

'Yes, that too. Initially, we did not have the distraction of a local market. That can be a blessing because an emerging market can confuse and divert attention. But with a constant global perspective, we don't lose focus. We started as a place of innovation and we remain so... in fact, once TI India became a successful R&D model, it wasn't long before various TI business divisions began operating key projects in India.'

'What does the Indian researcher offer as value-add?' I ask.

'It would have to be his humility and appetite... an almost naïve appetite.'

'Did you say naïve?'

'Yes. Let me explain. The US and the UK have better established R&D cultures and a history of achievements. In India, at least as of today, one senses a younger and hungrier environment. People are unencumbered by a legacy of factors that define a task as impossible. That kind of naivety is great for the organisation.'

'And great for outsourcing?'

'I always say that TI has an "in-sourcing" culture. It has never considered India as a place to send uninteresting or simply scalable work. The work is both interesting and strategic for TI. That's why we do not worry unduly about the outsourcing scare; we are part of a worldwide unit and we have been here for twenty-odd years to everyone's benefit.'

'What's your focus area as head of the software division?' I ask.

I have touched a special spot in the professional's heart. He opens a presentation on his laptop and launches into his perspective on Indian IT.

'Let's first talk about the good news in Indian IT – \$21.5bn of annual revenue, servicing more than 50% of Fortune 500 companies, a fertile higher-education system that helps a 25-30% year-to-year growth... we all know this. Now for the bad news: the revenue of the largest software company in the world is 1.8 times that of the Indian IT, ITES and hardware industry put together...'

Real money.

'... revenue per employee begs to be improved. Precious few products are launched. And significantly, R&D consumes just 3-5% of the revenue for most Indian companies. The industry-wide strategy so far has been to provide high quality at attractive cost. For India to get really cracking, it has to become a hub of world-class and innovative products. That means we need a multifold improvement in productivity and a massive increase in research spending – and *that* will lead to a multifold increase in revenues.'

I tell him it sounds simplistic and sanguine. Undeterred, he unfolds his plan and premise. India, he says, has started making a mark in embedded software. This is software that is plugged into mobile phones, videophones, earplugs for music, wireless computing tools, organisers, and many other gadgets. According to a 2004 survey conducted by Forward Concepts, six out of the top ten companies in the field – Ittiam, Wipro, Sasken, Emuzed, FedTech and Hellosoft – were Indian. Interestingly, most of these companies generate a sizeable portion of their revenue through services.

'So the idea of Indians making products isn't as farfetched as you think,' says Sham. 'The turnover isn't high yet, but this is where the future is. And the model taking us forward will have Independent Software Vendors (ISVs) creating original software and partnering with ODMs/OEMs who will provide the hardware. That's our plan in TI. To partner with creative companies and the top universities. After all, SUN Microsystems started as the Stanford University Network.... As of now, we have around 300 Digital Signal Processing (DSP) labs around the country; a few of them are located in the IITs. We believe that one has to contribute to the ecosystem, not just draw from it. Only then will universities breed start-ups for the industry.'

'And how does that benefit you?' I ask.

'TI alone cannot possibly be the source for all product concepts and innovations,' he points out. 'We need creative ideas to grow. So we network with students and academics who will research and build product ideas on our platforms. If I equate TI to a printing press, then it would be foolish of us to write *all* the novels we could print. That doesn't mean we stop writing a few best-sellers. But partnering is the need of the hour. We can provide the highest processing power per rupee on a piece of silicon. They can help us to develop killer applications and killer products... It's like being co-authors.'

The idea seems intrinsically sound – to build a world full of friends with the magical capability of multiplying one's own creativity. Other companies in Bangalore are also taking the same route.

'We need to merge the left and right portions of our brain,' continues Sham. 'Creativity should go with logic. I'll give

---

Not as Bleak

- According to NASSCOM, India's share in the global software products market is 0.2%. In comparison, India's share in the global services market is 1.5%.

- In 2002-03, Indian software products registered a 29.4% year-to-year growth to generate US $1.4bn in export revenues. This made up 14.3% of the total export revenue generated by the industry.

- Approximately 300 Indian companies occupy the product development space today.

- Leading product development companies from around the world have initiated a new wave of outsourcing – offshore product development. By sending portions of their work to India, they can not only cut costs, but also reduce the gestation period.˙

- An estimated 60% of the top global independent software vendors are leveraging India for maintenance of their existing product lines and development of new products.

Source: * - *the* Hindu Business Line. *All other details sourced from* NASSCOM.

you an example: when we commissioned the noted sculptor Balan Nambiar to create a piece of art, we wanted it to reflect our base technology and friendly work environment. And he responded with a perfect creation.'

Upon my prodding, he gives me the story of Balan Nambiar's stainless steel sculpture. As a pioneer of Digital Signal Processing in the country, TI India briefed Balan Nambiar about sculpting an image that would conceptualise the rise and ebb of signals. Balan Nambiar chose the motif of a rare conch called the *valampiri shankha*. Unlike common conches, the *valampiri shankha* has a clockwise spiral when its siphonal notch is at the top. The sound it produces equates to the *Omkara* – the perfect pronunciation of *Om* (with its three root sounds of *a*, *u* and *m*). Moreover, two identical conches have never been found in nature, but each undamaged, fully-evolved *valampiri shankha* has the same width-to-height ratio (1:1.618). This, of course, is the golden proportion (or golden section or golden mean) made famous by Dan Brown in the *Da Vinci Code*. Greek architects, and later European renaissance painters, sculptors and architects believed this to be the perfect proportion because it is found abundantly in nature. Even the human body exhibits the golden proportion.

Having thus chosen his theme, Balan Nambiar first designed the sculpture on the computer – after all, any depiction of DSP deserved modern technology. Stainless steel was chosen as the medium because it adapted most easily to the idea. The steel was then machined using precision laser beams to produce the component parts of the sculpture. All that remained from that point was a little welding and assembly.

What happened next was eerie. Or perhaps it was logical. Sham, out of curiosity, uttered the *Omkara* (*a*, *u* and *m*) into a mike and studied the resultant spectrogram on his computer screen. When he now speaks, his voice is controlled. It seems to me that he is suppressing his excitement.

'The pattern produced – yes – was a golden mean and had the shape of a *valampiri shankha*.'

I say goodbye to Sham Banerji and walk away in a daze. I take the coming together of signal processing, the golden mean, the *valampiri shankha* and *Omkara* as a sign of hidden possibilities. And I wonder: how many hidden possibilities is the Indian IT industry leaving unexplored?

No to School

Rain threatens yet another evening as I hit the by now familiar Outer Ring Road. I am wearing my rain jacket in preparation of the imminent downpour as I follow the heavy, lethargic trucks. The traffic seems thicker than it was the last time. So I'm glad when I take the turning into Hennur Main Road and leave the Ring Road behind. I have not been to Hennur before, but I know what to expect. It is one of those fringe suburbs that have outgrown the blueprint. The road, therefore, seems narrower than it is. Still, I manage to reach the Reddy residence without incident. Samuel Reddy greets me at his doorstep and invites me inside.

The Reddy family relocated from South Africa to India for many reasons. One of them is atavism. Showing me records attested by the Kwazulu-Natal government, Samuel says:

'This is my grandmother's immigration record. The other one is my grandfather's. Not only do they tell us which ships brought them to South Africa, they also mention their origins. Right down to the *taluk* and village in the district of Vishakapatnam.'

I note the date in one of them. 1889. Roughly four years before the Mahatma made the same journey. Interestingly, the document has a column indicating the caste of the immigrant.

'What do you intend to do next?' I ask.

'I have initiated enquiries. I hope to meet a few of our relatives soon. I know we won't have much in common, but we should be aware of our heritage and they should know that we exist.'

'We're very excited about it,' adds his wife, Devi, whose ancestry can be traced back to Tamil Nadu.

'Another reason why we came here,' says Samuel, 'is to give back to India. My wife and I came visiting in the 90s to try our hand in business. To buy commodities here and sell there – Indian saris sell for four times the price in Natal. But we did not have the knack for it. So the visit achieved a totally different purpose. It made us see the sufferings in India. We decided to come back later to do our bit. Now that we are here, I'm trying to help out on primary health issues because both my wife and I studied to be Community Health Workers in South Africa.'

'And I believe there was a third reason?'

'Yes. We want our children to benefit from the education system in India. The quality of the South African education is comparable to India's, but higher education is quite expensive. India seems to offer more options.'

So the Reddy family – except the eldest son and his wife – came to India. Their second son is getting trained as an IT technician, another is studying in college. But the one who, perhaps, underwent the steepest transition was the youngest member of the family. Indeed, fourteen-year-old Rosetta

Reddy did not take a cheerful view of the relocation. She landed in Chennai, was immediately assaulted by a "smell" and decided to clam up. She didn't speak a word during the train journey to Bangalore. What is more, she didn't utter a word throughout the next week. She missed Durban, and more specifically, the predominantly Indian community living in the suburb of Phoenix.

'Although we had told the children what to expect,' says Devi. 'no preparation is adequate to face the chaos of India. She is a very independent girl, but she slept in our room that first week.'

Rosetta eventually emerged from her shell and found her father in the process of getting her admitted into a school.

'We first tried the International schools that have sprung up,' says Samuel, 'because they don't enforce an Indian language upon students. But they were unaffordable. So after a lot of attempts, Rosetta got admission in a school nearby. She attended classes for a week.'

'And you opted to drop out?' I ask turning to the girl. 'Why?'

'I was having trouble learning Hindi. I learnt the basics of the language in South Africa. But it was an optional course in school and didn't require me to take an exam. The bigger reason, however, was my isolation.'

'They boycotted you?' I ask.

'No, the girls were quite friendly. It was the language barrier... I couldn't understand anything being said during the recess, for example. I had to keep asking: "What did she say?" It was frustrating.'

'How was school in South Africa?'

'It was nice. I had Indian as well as black classmates.'

'No whites?'

'None.'

'How were your relations with the black kids?'

'Good. But Indians mostly grouped with Indians. The Africans did the same.'

'Why do you think that happened?'

'They're different from us... They prefer to speak Zulu outside the classroom. Indians use English at all times... some of the Africans used to swear at Indians in Zulu. The girls mostly got along fine. But the boys slugged it out.'

'There's history behind the bitterness,' says Samuel. 'In recent times, it can be traced back to the Group Areas Act introduced in 1950. It mandated different residential and business areas for different races; people were efficiently segregated. My wife and I went to a school that enrolled only Indian students. The former Indian Prime Minister Lal Bahadur Shastri was instrumental in providing aid to these schools and as a result, Indians had a better schooling system. Rosetta was just three when apartheid ended and she has always been part of a mixed classroom. Things are changing, but very slowly.'

'Tell me Rosetta, at what age do you think you became aware of your Indian identity.'

After a number of supplementary questions on my side and introspection on hers, she arrives at the answer:

'I guess I have been aware of it even as early as kindergarten.'

Hmm. I return to the present.

'So what was the next step after dropping out of the school?'

'I enrolled in the National Institute of Open Schooling,' she says.

I learn that it is a distance-learning programme run by the Indian government. It doesn't impose Hindi, Kannada, Sanskrit or any other Indian language on the student, is cost-effective and seems to be working for Rosetta. She has to attend around thirty classes a year and take her exams at specified locations. Otherwise, she is a stay-at-home self-learner.

'I occasionally miss school. But it's fine,' she says.

'Distance learning has its advantages,' says Samuel. 'I know expatriate children in Bangalore who find it difficult to cope with mainstream schooling. The hours are longer, and travelling back and forth is strenuous. So many more are taking the Open Schooling route.'

'Speaking of coping, do you find any subjects to be particularly tough?' I ask Rosetta.

'Yes. Mathematics is of a slightly higher standard. And social studies involves Indian names and events I cannot easily remember.'

'Given the choice between the Indian and South African schooling, which would you choose?'

'The South African,' she says without hesitation. 'I find the system easier. Less homework pressure.'

'Would you prefer to continue your higher education over there?'

'Yes. I hope we return by then,' she says, looking doubtfully at her father.

'Hasn't anyone told you that India offers more opportunities at the moment?' I ask.

At first, I think Rosetta hasn't understood the query, but she replies:

'Then why do some of my friends enrolled in Open Schooling want to go abroad at the first available opportunity?'

'I don't know,' I say, smile and take leave of the Reddys. Not a drop of rain has fallen the whole evening. I stuff my rain jacket into the bag and return home.

Unpatentable

"**P**atents Bill to be tabled in Parliament": the moment my eyes fall on the front-page headline, I know I won't be meeting Sameer (name changed) tomorrow as planned. I call and he confirms my hunch. From the UN-sponsored HIV/AIDS conference in Mumbai, he has gone straight to New Delhi to lobby politicians to incorporate safeguards in the Bill. I wish him luck, hang up and think about our first meeting. Dressed in a tight T-shirt that accentuated his well-toned body, Sameer had looked quite unlike a crusader. In fact, he still looked like a lawyer protecting the intellectual property rights of huge corporations.

'Who were your clients?' I had asked. In reply, he rattled off a list of global giants that included an apparel-making firm, a liquor-making giant, a credit card company and a merchant banker. His job was to create intellectual property (IP) out of thin air and guard it with feverish zeal. For example, a client named Vaster Card could ask him to prevent any firm, not just a competitor, from using the word "vaster" on its product lines. Another day, he would help the "Complet Beer" manufacturers successfully sue a firm having a bikini line named Complete Beach (it didn't matter that their brand had an extra "e"). Almost the only thing he was not expected to do was to sue the Oxford University Press for mentioning the word in the dictionary. That is why basmati, neem, naan, turmeric and hundreds of other natural or cultural products from the Orient are coming under the gavel in the West. In many ways, the concept of Intellectual Property seems like an auction in which only one bid is entertained per item. All that is required to obtain a monopoly is being the first in line.

'I was fed up,' said Sameer, 'with the way corporations abuse patents, copyrights and trademarks. And with the global politics of intellectual property. Around the same time, the aftermath of 9/11 changed my worldview. Big pay was my only bond with my big law firm, and money lost its charm for me in the new scheme of things. I began seeing law as a tool used by the powerful against the weak. From then on, it felt as if that office space was choking me. I was having huge arguments with my boss anyway. Since I wasn't prepared to fight a case without legal merit, I was termed a "legal idealist". That made it easier to decide. I knew I would soon quit.'

Passionate he might be, but Sameer is not impulsive. He put the idea of reinventing himself in cold storage for two years. And used the time to come to terms with his new self. He had to consider the practical implications of the decision. Like his marriage.

'I got married when I was just twenty-five. Sometime after that, I briefly relocated to Belgium while my wife completed her Ph.D in our home country. She then joined an NGO and went to work in Ghana. Over time, we could feel our personalities and outlook change... After I resolved to quit my job, I told her that I was planning to join her in Ghana. She suggested that I don't because the marriage was not working... Don't you feel that relationships are a matter of timing? The situation has reversed today. She's still in Ghana, but now works for the European Commission on development issues and funding. Perhaps her ideals have changed since she went there. And here I am. Sold my flat, all my possessions... and without hassles tying me down, here I am.'

Yes, here he is. But...

'Why India in particular?' I asked.

'At first, I thought I'd go to Geneva where the World Intellectual Property Organisation is based. But their policies are pro-IP. I couldn't be of use there. I needed to go to a country that is aligning its IP laws with the West... a place where I could use the experience gained from sitting on the other side of the table. And it would be like having a ten-year head start; I could anticipate the next change and the next and do my best to counter the emerging system. India offered a couple of advantages. It has a legal system similar to home. And this Bangalore NGO I now work with offered me the opportunity...'

'So you're here as a crusader?'

'Well, I'll not put it so strongly. It's not possible to determine the right from the wrong till you experience both sides of the issue. I change every day and so do some of my views... that's part of the experiment. No permanent allegiance to a concept, or perhaps even a person, without complete comprehension and belief.'

'Do you think you'll go back to your old life?'

'I think it's unlikely, although I won't discard the option. At this moment, I feel that my work here is important. And my views seem solid. Let's see...'

We had ended the interview on that ambiguous note. And he is now offering his expertise to anybody opposing the Bill. Although the BJP had drafted the Bill when it led the previous coalition government, it is now opposing it. The Left parties, allies of the present Congress-led government, are opposing it as well; they are looking for concessions that would go down well with their electorate. And in the midst of this legislative turmoil, Sameer is working to make the amendment as equitable as possible.

* * *

Two weeks later, Sameer, Komala and I are seated in a Keralite restaurant that is popular with foreigners. Soft Carnatic music plays in the background. The waiters lend authenticity to the setting by wearing the traditional *mundu* and speaking with rich accents.

'What happened in the capital?' I ask Sameer.

'Well, you might have noticed that most of the Indian media just went to sleep over the issue. All they did was relay statements made by Kamal Nath, the Minister of Commerce and Industry. Only the international press covered the NGO perspective. So in addition to lobbying the Left, Congress and BJP MPs, we were holding hurried press conferences. Meanwhile, the government consulted all stakeholders and finally released the text of the amended Bill around midnight, just hours before it would be voted upon by the House. Even lawyers find it challenging to understand the nuances of legal clauses in a few hours, so you can well imagine the plight of MPs. So we were calling them up late into the night, and briefing them about the draft. And I was pleasantly surprised to find them picking up their phones at that late hour.'

I compare Sameer's narrative with the eyewitness account given by another activist. Apparently representatives of giant pharmaceutical companies had been camping in the capital for the past four months to prod the Bill through. So when a delegation of activists finally got an audience with senior Congress leaders, they were supposedly asked: 'Where has the health movement been all this time? *Where are the voices of the Indian people*?!' The Minister of Health then asked the delegation to convey its reservations on the Bill, and further commented that the scientific community had not spoken on the matter at all. It is another matter that the Minister of Health as well as the Minister of Science and Technology had minimal involvement with the Bill. Significantly, the Bill was championed by the Minister of Commerce and Industry. Perhaps the government saw patents as a purely commercial issue?

'One got the feeling,' says Sameer, 'that with a looming deadline in mind, the government was determined to pass the Bill with minimum fuss and – as one MP put it – amend it later. The text of the Bill was cloaked in secrecy till the last moment.'

As I listen to him, I get the feeling that Sameer didn't let the political machinery fluster him. He has concentrated on his small sphere of influence and in the process gained good experience.

'Seems like you had a busy time,' I say.

'Oh, it was buzzing the whole time we were there. It was nice being part of a dedicated team. Since we were all from different NGOs, we had differences of opinion. But we handled them well.'

That is saying a lot. Asking a typical NGO activist to compromise on ideology is like asking a corporate house to sideline the balance sheet. That is the reason it is quite difficult for NGOs to form cohesive consortiums. In this case,

Sameer takes what he terms a realistic view of the patents issue. According to him, IP laws in India and elsewhere will become more stringent with time and one should try to make them equitable instead of trying to do away with them altogether. Others of his ilk consider the idea of monopoly over a particular thought appalling.

But there is much more to the patents debate...

* * *

Taking seriously the Health Minister's observation that the scientific community appears unconcerned about the changing IP scenario, a group of NGOs organised a seminar at the Indian Institute of Science. Along with a sparse sprinkling of students and faculty members, I attended the meet with a twofold agenda – to understand the topic and hear Sameer speak on the occasion. And this is what I learnt:

In the year 1952, an American study concluded that medicines sold in India were amongst the most expensive in the world. Clearly, the patent regulations carried over from colonial times weren't working. The change came with the 1970 Patents Act. The Act abolished monopolies for drugs and agro-chemicals, and built safeguards to prevent abuse of patents by other sectors. "Compulsory licensing" was introduced to allow competing companies to manufacture new drugs in exchange for a licensing fee. The measures gave the desired result. Competition within the Indian pharmaceutical industry drove the cost down, although innovation was minimal. India's approach to patents became a benchmark for developing countries. At the same time, India began exporting drugs all over the developing world. A 2005 estimate suggests that 60% of HIV/AIDS drugs consumed by the world come from India. Seen in this context, any change in the Indian Patents Act becomes a global issue. Without generic Indian drugs, some African countries would have to spend more than their GNP on HIV/AIDS treatments (the annual cost of antiretroviral treatment, which allows an AIDS victim to lead a near normal existence, is down from $15,000 per patient a decade ago to about $200 now).

Even back in 1986, when the AIDS epidemic had not acquired its current proportions, Indian generic drugs mattered to the world. In that year, the Uruguay round of GATT negotiations saw the introduction of Trade Related Intellectual Property Rights (TRIPS) as part of the Dunkel Draft (some detractors claim that lawyers belonging to the corporate world drafted the TRIPS laws). Naturally, India was expected to lead the fight against it along with Brazil, Argentina, Thailand (and later South Africa which was still under apartheid). The strongest arguments against TRIPS were that patenting was a non-trade issue and each country had to determine its way forward according to the particular economic condition it found itself in.

So it surprised many when in 1989-90 India caved in and agreed to include TRIPS under the GATT umbrella. TRIPS thereby gained a new lease of life. In 1995, the TRIPS agreement was signed under the WTO insignia and countries like India were given ten years to revamp their laws as per the stipulations. Since then, India amended its Patents Act twice – once in 1999 and then in 2002 – before the latest amendments were made in 2005.

Meanwhile, resistance to the TRIPS laws has forced changes in them. During the WTO ministerial conference in Doha in November 2001, it was clarified that countries have the right to safeguard public health at the cost of patenting. In other words, a country can declare a state of emergency and cancel the patent on a drug it desperately needs. India's burgeoning AIDS problem – even Indian army personnel posted in the North East are being stricken down by the disease in alarming numbers – has till date not encouraged it to declare such an emergency. On the other hand, the United States threatened to cancel Bayer's patent during the 2001 anthrax scare if the company did not cut its price.

Overall, successive Indian governments appear to adopt sterner postures than even the TRIPS laws decree. Many of the safeguards that TRIPS allows have been ignored in the latest Bill. For example, inventions that are of purely economic significance could potentially be patented (they need not be technical advancements). The Bill also retains ambiguities with respect to "evergreening", a trick used to create minor molecular variations of the same drug thereby making it eligible for a fresh 20-year patent. And going forward, if a particular drug is not meeting the demands of the market or is priced high, generic drug makers can apply to copy a patented drug three years after the patent has come into force. But the patent owner can challenge the application or demand a high royalty since this amount remains unstipulated. Moreover, drugs tend to become obsolete in three to five years. This is especially true for specialised therapies dealing with diseases such as HIV/ AIDS. As the body of a victim gathers immunity to the drug, he has to move on to newer drugs. If these happen to be prohibitively expensive, the issue becomes one of human rights.

The other side of the story is that companies investing millions on research deserve to get back their due. It is estimated that India's loose patenting laws cost US pharmaceutical companies $1.7bn annually. Where is the incentive for innovation if copycats lurk around every corner, easily devouring years of hard research? One activist I met answered this question thus:

'The so-called free traders are simply afraid of competition. And they will go to any lengths to create their exclusive fiefdoms. Although we have managed to include nine safeguards in the latest Bill, everybody will soon realise that the common man has still lost out.'

* * *

My thoughts come back to Sameer and the mysterious smile playing on his lips.

'India seems to be shifting,' he says. 'It doesn't want to be a spearhead of hope for other developing countries any more.'

'I hope some other nation will step in then,' I say thinking of those who have to look elsewhere for drugs. *But where from?* is a bleak question. According to one of the speakers in the seminar, East Timor and a small island nation he couldn't recall the name of were the only two nations that did not have the concept of patents.

'I'm planning to go to Sri Lanka,' says Sameer veering off the chosen track.

'What for?' I ask.

'To shoot pictures,' he says. 'If it doesn't matter financially, I would like to see the world from behind a lens eye. Of course, whether I could make a living out of it would depend on how good I am. But India is a good place for a guy on a shoestring budget. All I need money for is to get from there to there to there.'

It turns out that Sameer took a fancy to photography during a visit to Mount Kilimanjaro. After that, he went on a different kind of trip to Palestine.

'It was when my frustrations with the global situation were coming out,' he says. 'I got involved in the Stop the

War movement and the International Solidarity Movement. I went with a camera as an observer-activist and stayed in refugee camps in Tulkarm and Nablus. I was witness to curfews, gun battles, tank incursions and fearful threats. A father was worried about his house being demolished because his son was suspected of being a resistance fighter. One day, I saw a farmer being taken away by Israeli soldiers. Palestinian children are so afflicted by the world around them... Young boys play with guns dispensing plastic pellets; schoolgirls create pictures of tanks in their drawing classes... The Palestinian agony is that they have little to fight back with; I felt for them. But strangely, the Israelis fear the Palestinians more. I also feared for my life while walking in the Jewish quarter of Jerusalem; I could so easily have been bumped off by a suicide bomber.'

I pause looking for appropriate words.

'Seeing Palestine,' he continues, 'put my career change fears in perspective. I realised that we humans are more adaptive than we think.'

I nod. He continues:

'Palestinian kids don't know any English other than the phrases used by visiting foreigners. So in most places, kids greet a stranger by asking: "Hello, what's your name?" But in the Gaza strip, they say: "Oh my God! *Oh, my God!*" That's how the foreigners react when they see the place.'

There is no way I can provide a rejoinder for that. So Sameer concludes:

'Everything in this world is interconnected. One has to take responsibility and stop doing something one no longer believes in. But it's a tough choice to try and live without reverting to our devilish ways...'

Carry on Jones

As soon as I began this book, I made a verbal agreement with a waiter of a pub frequented by foreigners. In return for a small sum, he promised to put me in touch with a foreigner who perennially badmouths India.

Months later, I get a call from him on a Friday evening.

'I found you one. But he won't talk for free,' he says.

'What does he want?'

'Beer.'

I reach the pub exactly an hour later and find my friend, the waiter.

'That guy at the corner table,' he says escorting me. 'He's going through his third pitcher.'

Jones (name changed) gives me a quizzical look and nods. I silently take a seat opposite him and wonder if his story will be worth the expense.

'In the one month I was back home,' says Jones, 'the traffic has worsened. Although I don't know how that's possible.'

It is my turn to nod and study the man. Jones is heavy-set with a generous belly and a face so closely shaven that not even a hint of stubble remains. He could have been thirty-five or fifty-five. At the end of the evening, I realise that he didn't smile once; and I never got to see his upper set of teeth.

'I'm told you're prepared to hear nasty,' he says.

'As nasty as it gets,' I answer.

'I will remain anonymous.'

'No problem.'

'If it comes to that, I never said anything,' he says.

I nod again, wondering if I myself should exit this scene from a two-penny novel. I feel an excitement that comes from not knowing if one is the hunter or the hunted. A part of my mind registers his accent and hence his nationality. I wait for him to break the silence.

'So why are you writing this book?' he asks finally.

As I explain my reasons, I'm unsure whether he is really listening to me. He eventually focuses a piercing look upon me and asks what kind of people I have met so far.

'Oh, different kinds,' I reply casually. 'Those who like India, those who hate it and...'

'How many of the latter?'

'Quite a few,' I lie.

'Well, it's your business why you want to write a book about this rat hole. Ask. What do you want to know?'

'Why are you here?'

'Why are you?' he asks in return. 'Do people really control their destiny? I mean, wouldn't you rather be elsewhere yourself? Been outside India? Well, if you had, you'll know what I mean.'

'But in your specific case...'

'A bitch of a girlfriend I idolised.'

With that, Jones begins a disjointed narrative that takes him half an hour and a whole pitcher. The story revolves around Donna, his high-school sweetheart who drifted away and later re-entered his life once he had divorced his wife. At one point, he contradicts himself in part by saying that one should never marry high-school sweethearts because that is what his wife was and see where she had led him. At any rate, it appears that Donna gave him hope when all was lost. They were ideally suited for each other; both shared the same interests except one. She loved to travel and his one brief overseas trip during his younger days had convinced him that there was no place like home. Still, one made concessions for Donna. Jones endured a Caribbean vacation and a fortnight in Mexico. But he somehow talked her out of going on an African safari... One day, he foolishly told her about an office memorandum that announced incentives for those agreeing to relocate to Bangalore for two years. She saw perfect sense in packing their bags. It was not like they had children or anything to think of. Good money, new place, better job security in these uncertain times... what else could one ask for? Jones directed her attention to the pitfalls but to no avail. Had she not dared him, not accused him of being a softie with no adaptability, he would still be working in the town he grew up in. But she wore him down, and he signed his way into Bangalore.

'Four months back,' continues Jones, 'Donna broke up with me and left.' I search his face for telltale signs of loss, but he shrugs it off. 'Ha! What the f___. Good riddance.'

'Maybe you can go back,' I suggest.

'Don't think that's difficult,' he says. 'I just have to get a position that's equal to me. In my younger days I was a fox in AS/400. None better. Today I'm the best manager in town. But I don't want to accept a lower position just because I'm desperate to leave Bangalore. There's a lot of fun things to do here. See that girl in the red pullover by the bar? I screwed her last week. It's so easy for me to pick up any woman I want.'

'Because you're white?' I ask.

He answers that obliquely as he pours from his pitcher. 'They're so easy. They have small coteries in these places. They always sit on the barstools and discourage any new Indians from breaking into their fold. But a guy like me is welcome... Frankly, I would rather have a voluptuous white woman. Well, you cannot blame these girls for trying. They at least acknowledge that one of you wrote the *Kamasutra*. You people are either prudish or sluttish. See that bitch.' He points to the girl in red again and goes into graphic details of his encounter with her. In the middle of his description, Jones gives the first indication of being drunk. He stops midway and demands of me:

'So tell me – how does the IT thing work? Huh? Somebody else does all the innovation. *We* innovate and *we* carry the world forward. Then you guys come and say: "Thanks, now we'll do our pitiful little coding using these magnificent tools and since we live in a rotten place, we won't mind accepting less money. Let us know when the next big thing comes along. We're ready!" Is that – what's the word...'

'Honourable?'

'That's the thing! Your IT guys have no honour. My first day at the Bangalore office, they had a reception committee for me like I was the Pope or the President. And I'm just an overseas employee of the same firm, not even a client. It took a week for the fanfare to end. Is this honour?'

Jones stares at me in cold anger. He takes a large swig of his beer and remains silent for a long time. When he speaks, the words are distorted and unconnected, but with patience I'm able to understand what he wants to say.

'Indians have no sense of ownership,' he says tapping his temple. 'Up here. I haven't come across a guy who is concerned about the big picture. If I were an Indian, I would want a clean city and good government as much as a good car. But… if I were an Indian, I wouldn't have been brought up to care for those things. You people just aspire to live in an apartment with power-backup. Then when it threatens to rain and the city blacks out, you sit in your balcony, sip beer and feel happy that you're not part of the inky darkness below. No honour. Small world. No room for honour.'

I see the girl in red give Jones a hostile stare on her way out. She is escorted by an Indian, making me wonder how much of Jones' monologue is a figment of the imagination. Meanwhile, he empties his pitcher and gets ready to leave.

'No honour,' he says. 'Indians. No honour.'

I pay the bill and the waiter, and head home. Jones has ensured that I'm completely sober in more ways than one.

The Other Side

I f only the sun shone all the time… the crops would wither and we would have many more insomniacs, although solar-powered cars would get a boost and tube-lights would become optional. The point, blasé though it may be, is that any phenomenon has both pros and cons. The same goes for the presence of expatriates in Bangalore.

Imagine this – a desk editor of a city daily is walking down M. G. Road. It is 6:30 p.m., so the road is packed. Out of nowhere, an African student walks up to her and asks for a date. He seems quite harmless and friendly. He just wants to *know* the nice lady. Like a much-licked lollipop, the situation gets sticky only when the pleading turns incessant. Alarmed, the lady quickly whips out her only protection and dials a friend. That finally makes him merge into the madding crowd. Phew! A few days later, she experiences another sticky episode featuring *two* African students. The difference, this time, is that the guys are looking for someone to "pick up". Of course, it is already 9 p.m. Which is perhaps past the time when one would want to *know* the other. To get out of the tangle, the lady creates a scene and alerts a nearby cop.

Such incidents seem to occur regularly. A male colleague of our lady friend has been made a similar offer by an African girl. There are two ways of looking at such incidents – harmless cultural differences or dangerous desperation. And one might say that only the extent of pressure exerted determines whether it is a cultural or criminal phenomenon.

Raveena (name changed) carries the argument forward when I meet her. She leads a life that regularly brings her in touch with foreigners. In fact, she had once opened her house to two Australian girls.

'They stayed for two and a half months,' she says. 'It was a memorable experience. They never kicked a fuss, made my dinner if I was late from work and never tempted fate and Romeos by dressing provocatively. It was easy for us to find common ground. Perhaps good human beings from anywhere would find common values, ideas... And the differences can be hilarious. For example, as far as I'm concerned, the pressure cooker is just a tool to cook rice in. The two girls saw it as an exotic Indian vessel they wanted to take back home. Of course, they didn't. Because the neighbours would have definitely complained about eerie noises! But my point is about beautiful possibilities.

'Foreigners add cultural depth to any society. I know of many who come here to conduct workshops for underprivileged children, or marry Indians and have great children. Unfortunately, there are those who expect royal treatment from Indians. Once, a German rang our office at closing time to request a meeting. He was surprised when we suggested that we meet the next day. Have you been to Germany? You could be snubbed for hinting at an after-hours meeting. How do the rules change after they disembark from the plane?

'And I've seen foreigners who want privileges but don't want to accept their responsibilities. Like this American family that lived in my neighbourhood. Mindless of the comfort of neighbours, they used to loudly celebrate Saturday nights in their apartment. If they try that back home, somebody's going to dial 911 sooner than you can say tequila.'

Paresh, a project manager in a software company, has observed a foreigner exhibit the same disregard for rules. He says:

'The moment the cop sees a fair-skinned foreigner commit a traffic violation, he's mentally multiplying his bribe amount. The simple-minded outsiders might pay the bribe and grumble about Indian corruption, or opt to pay the fine. But I've seen a 6-foot-zillion-inches European kick up a fuss. He knew he was guilty, but he also knew that he was untouchable. If a guy like that shows up at a traffic police station, the inspector is probably going to scoot. Or, at the very least, let the matter drop. The law and order machinery isn't geared to tackle foreigners. This guy I'm referring to actually threatened to call up his embassy for support... If this attitude isn't a colonial hangover, then what is? In New York, by the way, you can be certain that the exact opposite would happen. An Irish American would be let off with a slap on the wrist for a minor offence. An Asian on the other hand... well, he better pray that it isn't a cold night because a strip search cannot be discounted. In India, we are biased against our own kind. If a foreigner brings in dollars and wants to start a school or a college where people who look and talk like him will come and study, well, the government jumps and helps him get land. But how many Indians can afford that college? Has the government done enough to promote even primary education for children? No. We and our politicians always take the easy way out.'

I concede Paresh's point and keep my eyes and ears open for more such stories. My vigil is rewarded when Antara (name changed) narrates a terrible tale that centres on a tall, macho Arab. She says:

'He is a frequent visitor at the expensive cafés in M. G. Road, wears a black scarf over his head and has big tattoos all over his body. He is HIV positive and I've been told that his parents sent him to India just so that he can stay clear of the stringent law and order machinery back home. This guy once visited a dentist who checked his health records and politely told him that he wasn't equipped to treat him. But he would surely refer him to a good hospital that had the proper facilities for a HIV patient like him. The Arab blew his top and beat up the dentist... he physically, brutally beat him up. The dentist's daughter – she's my friend – called the police. They didn't even register a case. My friend didn't protest. She just wanted the incident to end. But till date, she gets threatening phone calls... if you're looking for a Rich Man's Spoilt Kid stereotype, go to M. G. Road and look for that goddamn Arab.'

* * *

Antara's story reminds me of another youth I came across at the Tanzanian Independence day bash. The party hadn't begun yet and I was chatting with a few Tanzanians when he staggered towards us. He greeted us with a trembling hand that loosely held a joint. The other hand carried a half-empty bottle of very cheap whisky. He blabbered inaudibly and evoked a mixture of disgust and sympathy from his audience. Few of his fellow students had seen him sober in the preceding months. I was told that he hailed from the Ivory Coast and was offloaded in India by parents who "wanted him out of their sight". The Tanzanians felt that the ICCR was quite decent in giving such fellows multiple chances to mend their ways. When I brought up the boy's case during my next meeting with Venugopal, he informed me that he was being deported.

Unfortunately, not all student problems are as easy to solve. One incident is so disturbing that it still haunts me although months have passed since that fateful day...

* * *

I'm woken up early one morning by an SMS from Patrick Ojwando. An African student had died in an accident the previous night. Since I'm on friendly terms with the brother of the deceased, I reach the post-mortem section of the Victoria Hospital within an hour. It seems as if I'm the first to arrive, but after the guard lets me into a courtyard behind the morgue, I see a small group of Indians gathered around an African. He informs me that the body had arrived a few minutes ago and the perennially broke students were probably making their way to the hospital in buses and auto-rickshaws. The brother has gone to the police station to complete the formalities.

The African resumes the entertainment of his admiring audience.

'I consume one kilo of beef a day. And at least a few Kingfisher bottles,' he brags while twisting a cap around his head. Then he ambitiously begins speaking in Kannada. He exhausts his vocabulary in ten seconds, turns to me and asks: 'Do you have a cigarette?'

When I come up empty, he nonchalantly rustles up a stick from his pocket and lights it without an apology. Traffic thunders past on the flyover just above us. People gaze at the small courtyard as they would at a shop or a temple. Death seems far away. But it is here. Right here, behind the stone wall I'm leaning against.

Soon, Patrick and the victim's friends start pouring in and give me an account of what transpired. The boy was returning from a party that broke up only around dawn. He was not alone. He had a girl on the pillion. And she is right now in the ICU at the Manipal Hospital.

We wait.

Someone leaves to bring the necessary documents like passport, residential permit and photographs. I see Patrick making enquiries over the phone. When he hangs up, he tells me that a businessman who knows the drill is on his way. He will take care of the coffin, travel, customs clearances, bureaucratic greasing... everything. A package deal. A cop approaches us and asks for the victim's home address. *Will they be sending Christmas cards*? He then informs us that two Indians are required to identify the body. That is nearly impossible.

'Can foreign students know even one Indian who won't mind getting entangled in a police enquiry?' asks Patrick.

He is losing his cool. But there is more to come. The "package dealer" arrives and soon tells us that the photographer's charges are 250 rupees. What photographer? He points to the man standing in the company of two policemen. Moments later, the photographer informs us that his charges are actually 500.

'Very reasonable,' he beams.

Will you make sure the snaps are good? Will you ask him to say cheese? Will you? I'm beginning to lose my own cool.

'There's a photo in his passport. Why won't that do?' asks Patrick.

'It's for your own good,' says the senior-most cop. 'So that you'll not have issues at the airport and other places. I don't benefit.'

We resume the endless wait. I ask Patrick if he is experiencing all this for the first time. He gives me a wry smile and starts listing the precedents...

A Sri Lankan died three years ago.

In '97, three Kenyans had a bad smash. One lost a leg, one got lifelong facial scars and the third died one prolonged year after the accident.

After that, three Ugandans went into coma and miraculously recovered.

In 2002, a boy named Amos was comatose for fifteen days and eventually lost his mental balance.

Then two Bangladeshis...

* * *

I stop listening to the list once I understand that the number of accidents is disproportionate to the student population. Finally, Patrick summarises—

'And these are cases that I know of. The actual numbers must be much higher.'

'Late-night parties have to stop,' I suggest. Patrick shakes his head sagely.

'The students will be careful for a couple of days; some may even decide to give up riding. But the resolutions will soon be broken. The fact is we can't control the bikes like Indians can. We just can't. That's what causes most accidents.'

Weaving through the Indian traffic is apparently a genetic gift.

'All the more reason for folks to avoid drunken driving,' I say.

Patrick's mobile rings. He answers it and almost immediately hangs up with a:

'Shit!'

'Now what?'

'The girl's dead.'

I can think of nothing to say. I can only wish that every foreign student in the city learns from this tragic tale. So does the senior cop I meet later.

'See what these boys are up to!' he tells me. 'Who's to blame for what happened? Is this the impression they want to make? And to think that either the Indian government or theirs is sponsoring the bloody mess! Tell this story in your book. Maybe that will help.'

I'm inclined to agree with his sentiments. But at the same time, I feel that the true poignancy of the situation lies elsewhere. That a 24-year young man and an even younger girl should meet such an ignominious end so far away from home... without dignity, without purpose. Just anonymity and trouble to usher them out. What a complete waste of youth and life.

* * *

All this happens despite the appreciable efforts of ICCR. Venugopal gives a sad shrug when I chat with him about the accident later. During the talk, I get to know of another issue.

'Many ICCR scholars,' says Venugopal, 'seem to be unhappy about their financial state of affairs. If their stipend cheque is delayed by a week, I get a million frantic calls.'

'How much is the cheque for?' I ask.

'Six thousand six hundred rupees,' he replies. 'It is meant to cover rent, food and study material.'

What the students don't realise is that many Indian families in Bangalore survive on that amount. To them, the amount is meagre. It cannot possibly take care of mobile bills, booze bills, inflation in petrol prices, new clothes and funky CDs. I cannot help thinking that a lot of good government money is being wasted on those students who are neither interested in their books, nor in the Indian environment. In the last few months, I have found them easy to identify. Two minutes after getting introduced, they will begin cribbing about the infinite miseries associated with life in India. Mercifully, I have also met quite a few students who count their blessings.

Raveena, however, isn't prepared to be as benign in her summing up.

'It's quite clear,' she says, 'that some students left home without the intention of graduating. They're simply cutting their sexual teeth, or experimenting with grass. Each one lives in his own private illusion... being in a place that's culturally so alien doesn't help matters when the hormones are peaking. Some just find respite in violence. Or in milder instances, in rudeness. You'll be surprised to know that no landlord in my locality will rent his house to Africans. They come in droves asking for accommodation, even offer higher rent... but they're unbelievably rude.'

'But isn't it also true that landlords demand a higher rent from them?'

'That's true,' she concedes. 'Landlords hike their rents. And funnily enough, other Indians crib that the foreigners are impacting their cost of living.'

I laugh.

'Come now, shouldn't the IT industry be blamed for that?' I ask.

* * *

Ever since my interview with Jones, I cannot stop thinking of the alleged barstool coterie. So one day I revisit the same watering hole where I met Jones and occupy a stool. The space around soon fills up with Indians and foreigners who exhibit backslapping intimacy. I could be sitting in a pub named Salamander Hatter or something of that sort, in a small Irish village. Everybody knows everybody else. Well, not quite. Seated next to me is an Indian in his early thirties and he is just as lonely as I am. Our eyes meet and I strike up a conversation. Now and then, he looks around ruefully. And once, when he catches the gaze of a middle-aged woman, he winks at her.

'What's going on?' I ask him.

He sizes me up and decides to include me in his secret.

'She,' he says pointing towards the middle-aged woman, 'is a very important person over here. If any new patron is worthy of her attention, she'll get introduced to him and then network him with the other regulars. The rest will be cold-shouldered.'

'Er… I suppose you haven't been networked.'

He takes a sip of his beer and carefully keeps his mug down.

'It costs a lot of money to frequent this place,' he says. 'I've been coming daily for three weeks.'

So the answer is no.

'What about foreigners?' I ask.

'Foreigners are always welcome.'

'They aren't scrutinised like you are?'

'No.'

'And skin colour doesn't seem to matter much.'

'Doesn't matter at all. White, black, yellow… all get the same treatment.'

'Well, that's an improvement,' I say as I choke my laughter. Our talk moves into other channels. When a new song begins, my new friend immediately whips out his mobile, calls, and *does not utter a word into it.* He disconnects the call when the song ends.

'That's my favourite song,' he explains upon seeing my quizzical expression. 'I call my wife whenever it is played. It doesn't matter what part of the world I am in or what time it is.'

It gets curioser because a moment later, a dainty girl walks in. My friend gives her a hug and she takes the adjacent stool. We exchange first names.

'He was just speaking about you,' I tell her.

'Who do you think she is?' he asks.

'Your wife?'

He laughs uproariously and the lady joins him.

'Man, do you need a lesson in social etiquette,' he says turning away from me. He puts an arm around her and whispers something which makes her laugh again. I understand. And keep my peace. I interrupt them only when I'm ready to leave.

'What is your opinion of this barstool coterie?' I ask him.

'It sucks. I haven't faced this in New York, man. Or Jakarta or Shanghai. I'm a great project manager, mind you. I've been to most places in the world and the ones I've not visited are not worth spitting upon. I've *always* broken into the circle. But in Bangalore, I need to undergo plastic surgery before I'm accepted. It sucks, man, it sucks.'

Whatever his flaws as a husband, he has a point.

The Flag-bearers

Although I have been exploring the various facets of nationalism in every interview, it occurs to me that the intensity one associates with it has been missing. I ask myself: where can I find it? Answer: in a war, a parade, a riot or a game. I choose to go to a game. *The* game. Today, India is playing Pakistan in the third test at the Chinnaswamy stadium. It is the fifth and final day of the match. India needs to score 383 runs or play through the day to win the series it leads 1-0. Before the day begins, Pakistan appears to be slight favourites, but it has to run through the famed Indian batting line-up to triumph.

A scary spectacle awaits me when I reach the stadium. Fifty thousand people are straining against the gates, impatient to get in. I'm not the only jobless guy in this city after all. I walk around in an attempt to locate Pakistani supporters. There aren't any to be found. So I procure a cheap ticket and enter the gallery stands. The papers have already informed me that I won't find any Pakistani supporters here either. They have been allocated seats in the better-provided G7-G10 enclosures on the other side. The authorities have even arranged for special vendors selling *halal* meat dishes exclusively to the Pakistanis. The government obviously doesn't want the Indian and Pakistani fans intermingling. Why create frustrations that might lead to a nuclear holocaust?

So the whole day, I try to get closer to the Pakistanis; but the G7-G10 stands are always a galaxy away. During the lunch break, I try a couple of popular *biryani* joints hoping to bump against them. Zilch. I have no choice but to sit through a humiliating Indian defeat before hurrying around the stadium. As I wait for the Pakistanis to come out, I reflect that Mohammad Ilyas' prediction has come true. Both India and Pakistan have scored one victory each in the test series. The honours will be shared.

A few minutes later, I see a man emerging from the stands. He might be from Pakistan, or he might live a kilometre away. But this is not the time to be politically correct. My take is – you look Muslim enough, wear a *salwar* and speak a tongue that tangs of Punjabi, I'm going for you. So I stop him. He happens to be a Kashmiri. Close enough.

'Why are you looking for a Pakistani?' he asks.

'To interview him,' I say.

The reply assuages his suspicions.

'I'm a Pakistani supporter myself,' he beams.

I congratulate him on the victory. And although I understand why some Kashmiris would be Pakistani supporters, I cannot stop myself.

'Why?' I ask. 'Why are you a Pakistani supporter?'

He looks at me quizzically, then decides there is no harm in stating the simple, profound truth.

'*Aise hi hai* (Because that's how it is).'

Fair enough. The next guy I stop is much younger and wears the right kind of clothes to be my candidate.

'No, I'm not from Pakistan. I'm from Shivaji Nagar,' he says.

The guy from one-kilometre away.

'Sorry,' I say lest he feels offended.

'Oh no, I'm a Pakistani supporter,' he replies.

This time, the question inadvertently springs out.

'Why?'

The lad – he must have been nineteen – skips away in mild alarm. He just about manages to give a vague, almost inaudible explanation about his uncles being Pakistanis. Before I can say 'But…' he has vanished. I stand still and theorise. What made me radically Indian by that age had made a Pakistani out of him. His loyalty towards Pakistan is dangerous – but only for him. He has to conceal it well. At the same time, I cannot help wondering if he is the manifestation of India's inability to handle heterogeneity.

My brown study makes me miss the first wave of Pakistani supporters exiting the stadium. It takes me five more minutes to meet someone who is willing to give an interview. He provides me a hotel name and room number and asks me to meet him there. I run towards my bike. Another spectacle, however, makes me halt in my tracks. Two jean-clad blondes are walking ahead of me. Both are carrying Indian flags and are undoubtedly coming after a day at Chinnaswamy. I have to record this.

'Excuse me,' I say, prompting them to turn around and reveal Indian flags painted on their cheeks. 'Don't call for the police. I'm a writer.'

Sheesh! That is almost as bad as: 'FBI! Come out with your hands up in the air.' The ploy, however, works. Barbara Tonachio and Mandy McLaughlin, both Americans, introduce themselves. Barbara volunteers with the Global Cultural Exchange as part of her studentship whereas Mandy is learning photography and *kathak* in Bangalore. Wow!

'I have one question for you,' I say. 'Why were you supporting India?'

'Because we've been here for a year and a half,' they say in unison. 'So we will root for India in a cricket match. We took the day off to be here.'

At this point, a sweeper working the street wipes his brow and approaches us to ask for the score. Mandy doesn't know how to reply to that, but she says: 'Our team lost.'

Loyalty? Towards what? Decency? In what sense? I don't know. I really don't know. I can think of just one explanation. Sports in America tend to be parochial. Americans are used to cheering their city, state and college teams. They seldom associate sports with nationalism. Moreover, one might say that Barbara and Mandy are doing nothing more than imitating Indian H1-B engineers who take a fancy to, say, the Milwaukee Bucks or the New York Knicks. Still, the two ladies have made me happy. Perhaps we can hope for the demise of nationalism some day. I thank the duo and ride towards the Pakistanis.

I find Rana Usman, Hasan Malik and Usman Ghani in their room. Although an auto-rickshaw driver refused to ferry them because India lost, they have reached the hotel without being assaulted. They are thrilled, of course, with their team's victory.

'Pakistan had to win,' they tell me. 'After all, we undertook a long journey from Lahore. You must come to Lahore. *Zinda dilaan log* (Lively people). *Jinne Lahore nahin vekhya oh jamyahi nahin* (He who hasn't seen Lahore hasn't really been born yet).'

I make a mental note about sojourning for a mid-life rebirth and then ask them about their day.

'Oh, we may have been in the minority, but we gave you Indians a great lung-fight. When the gallery shouted Pakistan *hai hai*, we started abusing them in Punjabi. With each wicket, the crowd went silent as a snakebite victim.'

Yeah. Rub it in.

I notice that Hasan speaks without mincing words. So I ask him if the special *halal* kitchen was good.

'No,' he replies. 'The food in India carries a weird stink. We came via Delhi. The food stank there as well.'

Thankfully, he has a good opinion about Indian liquor. Bottles of whisky and beer are taken out of the cabinet and there is no question of me refusing their Lahori hospitality. I shall have a couple of rounds unless I'm a Paki-hater or a Muslim-baiter in general. I agree to prove my secular credentials and clink a glass with them. We talk about various things, and a peg later, I'm declared to be a fine man. I hope the effect is induced only partially by alcohol.

They are preparing to visit a discotheque once they get rid of me. For the time being, I sit, sip and listen. They sound just like Indian teenagers. Perhaps a bit outspoken, a little spoilt, but quite decent. Mingled with their words, I can hear the roar of the Chinnaswamy stadium.

India! India!

Pakistan! Pakistan!

Nobody was shouting:

The world! The world!

If the initial idea was that each nation would act as an autonomous department and keep itself beautiful and peaceful, it certainly isn't working. The concept of the nation-state has grown stronger and failed at the same time. Americans in Bangalore have no option but to be answerable for George W. Bush, a Saudi Arabian is a potential Osama, a Brit has a colonising past, a Spaniard has the heart of a conquistador, all Germans are potential Nazis, the Chinese are intent on making the rest of the world unemployed... nationalism has seeped into our thought processes. The nation-state has become a cage that jealously guards ignorance and pettiness.

The stadium roars into my eardrums again... I wish nationalism could be a cloak that one wears to a stadium. The cloak would make one rage furiously in support of one's team. After the match, one comes back home and discards the cloak. Perhaps such a thing will be possible when we realise that we are all similar in ways we haven't even begun fathoming. With that will come another realisation: our differences always fall in the realm of things we do not understand.

Expatriates in Bangalore
–A Brief History

The Early Years

Legend has it that a thirteenth century Hoysala king named Veera Ballala Raya II once lost his way and eventually reached the village of Kodagahalli, in the outskirts of present-day Bangalore. The king was hungry and a kind old village woman fed him a sparse dish of cold boiled beans. This prompted the king to call the place Bendakaalu ooru (in Kannada "benda kaalu" means boiled beans and "ooru" means village) and this eventually became Bengalooru. Some historians, however, dispute this story by pointing out inscriptions found in the village of Begoor, about fifteen kilometres south of Bangalore. The inscriptions, which date back to AD 900, have the name "Bengaluru" occurring in them.

With the advent of the British, Bengaluru became Anglicised to Bangalore. That, however, happened much later. Between the naming and the Anglicisation, the city changed hands numerous times and thus became an important witness to the medieval history of South India.

One might say that it all began with the illustrious Yelahanka *prabhu* (chieftain) Kempe Gowda I, the man who founded Bangalore under the aegis of Achyutadeva Raya, the ruler of the Vijayanagara empire. Kempe Gowda I began by building a mud fort in 1537, then went on to build temples, tanks, and planned residential layouts. His administrative skills transformed a cluster of villages into a small and pleasant town. Simultaneously, his annexation of the villages of Domlur, Halasoor and other places made the expansion of the city possible. Unfortunately, he was falsely accused of exceeding his authority and sent to prison. After five years of incarceration, he convinced the Vijayanagara king to pardon him in return for a huge sum of money. He returned to Bangalore and ruled it till his death in 1569.

Kempe Gowda II, who succeeded his father, carried forward the good work. He built watch towers for keeping guard over the city, vastly improved the irrigation facilities and made improvements to the existing temples. He enjoyed a long stint at the helm till trouble marched in from the north – sometime in the late 1630s, a massive army from Bijapur attacked the city and defeated him. Kempe Gowda II signed a treaty that, among other things, required him to relocate to Magadi.

The treaty was negotiated by Shahji Rao Bhonsle, the Maratha warrior who held a key position in the Bijapur army. In recognition of the crucial role he played in various battles, including the one against Kempe Gowda II, Bangalore was given to Shahji as his personal *jagir*. The city thus became the birthplace of what would become the powerful Maratha empire.

Shahji was an ambitious ruler who valued military might. He strengthened the city's fortress, maintained an agile army and made small expansions by grabbing surrounding areas such as Tumkur, Kolar, Doddaballapur and Sira. His presence also curbed the expansion plans of the Wodeyars of Mysore. Bijapur had every reason to celebrate its arrangement with Shahji. He had made improvements to the revenue collection system and was prompt in sending part of the money to Bijapur while utilising the rest to maintain his state.

In 1640, Shahji called his son, Shivaji, and his first wife, Jijabai, to Bangalore. Shivaji stayed in the city for the next two years and married Saibai in the interim. This short stay would have an impact on the city's history later on. Meanwhile, it was time for the Bijapur-Shahji honeymoon to end. The trigger for this was Shahji's growing stature and independence, which no doubt alarmed the Sultan of Bijapur. The Sultan took action when Shahji and a Bijapuri military leader named Mustafa Khan were laying siege to the fortress at Gingee in Tamil Nadu. Shahji was seized and an army sent to attack Bangalore. The aggression, however, did not work and the Bijapur army suffered heavy losses. It was again time to negotiate. This time, Shahji was bargaining for his freedom. And he obtained it by ordering his sons Sambhaji and Shivaji to surrender Bangalore and Sinhagad (in Maharashtra). He also reaffirmed his loyalty to the Bijapur throne. Surprisingly, that was sufficient. The Sultan, apparently moved by the gesture, restored Shahji to his former position. But Shahji, instead of returning to Bangalore immediately, decided to operate from Kanakagiri while two of his sons – Sambhaji and Ekoji – ruled Bangalore. Shahji eventually returned to Bangalore in 1658 and remained there till his death in 1664. Ekoji inherited Bangalore.

Ekoji's stepbrother Shivaji, who was preoccupied with combating the Mughals through innovative guerrilla tactics, initially stayed away from Bangalore. In 1677, he wrote to

Ekoji asking for his share of Karnataka. Ekoji preferred to meet Shivaji in the battlefield. Shivaji won and was magnanimous in his victory. He transferred Bangalore and the adjoining areas to Ekoji's wife Deepabai and allowed Ekoji to retain Thanjavur in Tamil Nadu. Ekoji soon moved to Thanjavur to concentrate on the issues surfacing there. Without a proper ruler, Bangalore became easy pickings. It fell in 1687 to the Mughal commander Khasim Khan. The Maratha hold over the city had come to an end.

In 1690, Khasim Khan is said to have leased the city to the reigning Wodeyar, Chikkadeva Raya, with the understanding that the Wodeyars would lend an army to the Mughals when the need arose. The Mughals moved to the nearby town of Sira to keep an eye on the Wodeyar administration. It was now time for Chikkadeva Raya to realise his long-pending ambitions. He set about expanding his kingdom by capturing Hoskote, Banavar, Tumkur, Chikmagalur and Magadi. He also built a new fort in Bangalore and introduced an efficient postal system.

Chikkadeva Raya's death in 1704 left a vacuum in Bangalore and adjoining areas. This was compounded by the splintering of the Mughal empire in 1712. In the ensuing turmoil that lasted for decades, a dark horse named Hyder Ali emerged the undisputed ruler of the Deccan.

And it was under Hyder's rule that Bangalore experienced its first substantial expatriate influx.

Under Hyder and Tipu

Hyder Ali's journey from obscurity to immortality is one of bravery, military genius, cunning, foresight and many wars. It is also a story that demands its own canvas. But it needs to be said that Hyder was a willing learner who welcomed innovativeness from all quarters. That is why he recruited Portuguese and French soldiers in his army and achieved better results at warfare with their help.

Hyder's admiration for the French military can be traced back to one of his war campaigns in 1755, a little before he was gifted the city of Bangalore as a *jagir*. He saw that the

---

Veni, Vedi and Nothing More

Possibly the first Dominican to arrive in India was Niccolo of Pistoia in 1291. He spent his lifetime in Mylapore in present-day Chennai, the same place where many claim St. Thomas, the Apostle, stayed. The Dominicans later became the earliest Christian evangelists (and hence some of the first expatriates) to enter the state of Mysore. Anthony Simo in his book *History*

French soldiers were highly disciplined and had the ability to execute simple yet effective strategies. And he resolved to make use of them.

Years later, when he brought Frenchmen to Bangalore (and also Srirangapattana, Chitradurga and Nagara), warmongering became the first industry in the city to employ foreigners. Skilled Frenchmen were hired to supervise stockpiles of sophisticated military equipment. Great quantities of gunpowder, cannon balls and arms were manufactured daily; blacksmiths and foundries were kept busy making swords and brass guns respectively. French munitions experts helped Hyder manufacture his famous rockets, which played a major role in his victories. It is estimated that Hyder had 1,200 rocketeers and 180 Europeans, mainly mercenaries, in his employ.

With a technologically superior and disciplined force under his command, Hyder was more than a match for the British. Realising the British threat, Hyder even took the initiative of building alliances with the Nizam of Hyderabad and the Marathas. Had it not been for the diplomatic warfare employed by the British Governor-General, Warren Hastings, Britain would have completely lost its hold on South India. Still, Hyder proved to be Britain's nemesis during his lifetime. And this was partly due to his ability to recruit diverse people with rare skills.

Sidi Hilal, an African commander in his army, is a case in point. In the Battle of Pollilur in 1780, Sidi Hilal blew up the artillery wagons of Colonel Baillie's army and forced

---

of the Archdiocese of Bangalore refers to a tombstone in the town of Anekal that dates back to the fourteenth century. It is estimated that a sizeable Christian population (around 900) existed in Anekal by the sixteenth century. By this time, Portuguese Dominicans had arrived in Goa in large numbers. But neither are there reports of Dominicans in Mysore resorting to ruthless tactics, nor did they enjoy the same success as in Goa.

the British to surrender. Perhaps it was Sidi Hilal's prowess that prompted Tipu Sultan, much later, to request the French to send him "free Negroes" for the army he was trying to build to fight the British.

Meanwhile, Hyder Ali received a special guest towards the end of his reign. Pierre-André de Suffren, one of the finest Admirals France has produced, met him to convey the good wishes of his monarch Louis XVI. The visit was an acknowledgment that Hyder had been the only Indian leader to provide onshore assistance to de Suffren during his two years of naval warfare against the British.

Hyder's military escapades eclipse his achievements in other spheres. So the fact that foreigners came to his territory for reasons other than warfare may be easily overlooked. For example, an Arab mason named Hazrat Tawakkal settled down in Bangalore during his reign. Today, a *dargah* carrying his name can be found in the Cottonpet locality of the city.

Hyder also created the beautiful Lalbagh garden in the city of Bangalore. Lalbagh imitated the design of Emperor Shah Jehan's gardens in North India. Shah Jehan, in turn, had based his design on gardens in various parts of the Islamic world, notably Syria and Persia. Lalbagh was later stocked with flora from Kabul, Persia, Mauritius, Pakistan and Turkey. Over the years, many foreigners became its caretakers. The list includes Dr. Cleghorn, William New, John Cameron and a German named Krumbeigal. Each enhanced the beauty of the garden and furthered Hyder Ali's wish to add variety to it. In short, ideas, nature and people from around the world contributed to the making of Lalbagh. Hyder's plan seems to have worked.

Hyder Ali died on 7 December 1782. By that time, he had sown the seeds of globalisation in Bangalore.

* * *

Tipu Sultan, the son of Hyder Ali, inherited not just his father's kingdom, but also his penchant for utilising foreigners to ameliorate the condition of his land and its people. It is believed that as a young man, Tipu was instructed in military tactics by French officers employed by his father. It is not surprising then that he retained Hyder's faith in French mercenaries and weaponry. When Louis XVI sent him a retinue of engineers, artisans and skilled labourers, Tipu found employment for them in various fields.

There were ample opportunities for them because the kingdom of Mysore was undergoing rapid industrialisation. Factories in Chennapatna were producing high-quality glassware and sugar. Silkworms were imported from Bengal, Muscat and China to enhance silk production. Fine cotton cloth was being woven in Sarjapura. Gunny was being manufactured in and around Bangalore. Tanneries and oil presses were also operating in full swing. Hour-glasses, watches and cutlery were being rolled out elsewhere. A paper mill was opened in Srirangapattana, Tipu's capital.

Dr. Francis Buchanan, the man commissioned by the Governor-General, Marquess Wellesley, to survey the state of Mysore after Tipu's fall, however, opined that Bangalore had become an important trading centre due to the "judicious government of Hyder". But, he added, Tipu ruined the picture by enforcing strict measures such as prohibition of trade with the states of Hyderabad and Arcot.

Popular opinion does not agree with Dr. Buchanan's conclusions. Historians today say that the condition of the state improved under Tipu. He certainly established strong trade links with many countries like France, China, Turkey, Iran, Egypt and Arabia. He even owned factories in places such as Muscat, Jeddah, Basra and Aden. Under his rule, Bangalore became one of the important cities of the East. And this happened despite Bangalore not being a port city.

* * *

In the month of March 1797, an insignificant Frenchman named Francois Ripaud arrived at the court of Tipu Sultan in Srirangapattana and kicked off a series of darkly farcical events. But in order to put the visit in context, one needs to understand the history of the preceding two decades.

Tipu Sultan, like his father Hyder Ali, realised the danger posed by the British, very early in his career. And he spent his entire lifetime in striving to banish them from the country. Put together, father and son fought four battles with the British. The first Anglo-Mysore War (1767-70) took place soon after the British established themselves as the dominant European power in India. Hyder Ali was equal to the challenge; he ably commanded his forces and managed to crush the British. The Second Anglo-Mysore War was longer (1780-85), and saw a mid-action change of guard due to Hyder's death. Tipu replicated his father's feat, and once again British aspirations in South India were put on hold. The tide changed in the Third Anglo-Mysore War (1789-94). Tipu was defeated despite putting up a brilliant military performance against the powerful alliance of the British, the Marathas, and the Nizam of Hyderabad. Lord Charles Cornwallis negotiated a peace treaty which cost Tipu Rs.33mn, half his territory and the humiliation of handing over his two sons as hostages. Additionally, Bangalore suffered under the plundering of Cornwallis in 1791 before Tipu retook the city.

Hyder had formed an alliance with the French during the Second War, and this was carried over to the Third. But at a crucial juncture during the Third War, the French worked out a compromise with the British. As a result of this, the French army under the command of de Cossigny received an order from de Bussy to abandon Tipu. Moreover, even a certain de Lally, who was directly employed by Tipu, was ordered to leave along with his troops. Even this explicit desertion does not seem to have changed Tipu's opinion about the French. He only saw the French as a countervailing force to the British and preserved his faith in them till the end.

As early as 1787, even before the Third War began, Tipu had despatched three ambassadors to the court of Louis XVI. In the summer of the following year, Paris seems to have amused itself with these exotic Oriental men. They were well received, entertained and made to wait an interminable time. When they eventually met Louis XVI, they conveyed Tipu's wish to have a grand alliance with the French, beginning with the despatch of 6,000 troops who would be well taken care of. The request was refused, and the ambassadors sent off with an array of gifts for the Sultan. The reason for the refusal was the fluctuating relationship between the French and the British. The two nations had signed a peace treaty in 1763. But in 1776, the French gave all-out assistance to America's fight for independence. That was swiftly followed by the Treaty of Versailles in 1783. Times were such that it would have been impossible to predict how the two imperial powers would treat each other in the subsequent months. They might have been engaged in battle in one colonial outpost, and were perhaps shaking hands elsewhere. Even after Louis XVI's royal neck came under the guillotine, the French remained an unreliable ally. While Napoleon gave continuity to French conquests, Tipu Sultan made political updates to his character. He began experimenting with Republicanism, and on occasion called himself *citoyen* Tipu (to be fair to him, Tipu placed great emphasis on public welfare, craved peace and was not at all the church-burning religious bigot the British made him out to be). Napoleon was engaged somewhere in the Mediterranean when Ripaud arrived in Srirangapattana in 1797.

By this time, the writing was on the wall for Tipu. He knew that he would soon have to fight not only the British, but also the Nizam of Hyderabad and the Marathas. So it is little wonder that the beleaguered Sultan received Ripaud warmly. In fact, he actually pretended that Ripaud's arrival was a sign of renewal of ties with the French. Ripaud informed Tipu that he had been involved in an "engagement" in the Arabian Sea and his ship had almost foundered. He also told him that a considerable French force was posted in Ille de France (Mauritius). This set the Sultan thinking. He sent word to his *sardars* (department heads) that he intended to retain Ripaud as a *wakil* (ambassador) on a generous salary. But since he was operating under a treaty with the British, the ostensible purpose of retaining him would be to purchase his ship, load it with black pepper and other articles of merchandise, and despatch it to Mauritius with two of his own confidants on board. That way, he could resume negotiations for an alliance with the French. Ripaud had agreed to this proposal, and Tipu now asked his *sardars* what they thought of it and how he should proceed in the matter.

Almost to a man, the *sardars* distrusted Ripaud. They called him a scoundrel, a trickster, a deceitful and lowly creature and an "unreliable compound of air and water" who was unworthy of this high mission. Suggestions included testing his authenticity and influence with the higher authorities. It was even ascertained that Ripaud had left his home in Bourbon along with a French ship captain named Aubaine. Their mission apparently was to waylay and plunder British ships, which perhaps explains the engagement in which he had participated in the Arabian Sea.

But Tipu was desperate. He was already making parallel ambassadorial attempts through a delegation headed by a certain Pierre Moneron. He decided to try out Ripaud as well. A treaty was drafted, and Husain Ali Khan and Muhammad Ibrahim were selected as ambassadors. As the treaty was read in the court before their departure, Francois Ripaud is reported to have stood up and taken an oath of loyalty upon the insignia of his nation. The team set off for Mangalore from where they embarked on their voyage. The only thing that went according to plan was that Tipu acquired the clove and nutmeg trees he had asked for. According to the account of one of the ambassadors, the journey, which began only in December 1797, was quite unpleasant. After travelling five miles off the Indian coast, Ripaud confronted the ambassadors, snatched from them the envelopes carrying the treaty and letters, and almost opened the *kharitas* (tissue or silk cases normally used to carry such documents) before they successfully invoked the fear of retribution. The next day, he threatened to abandon the mission if the ambassadors did not immediately part with the money he was promised. After forty-four torturous days of rationed water and unfit accommodation, the ambassadors and the ship reached Mauritius. Ripaud immediately disembarked and returned late in the night claiming to have represented everything to General Malarctic.

But the next day, the General did not even entertain the idea of including Ripaud in the meeting because he was not a *wakil*. He was a lowly second officer of a ship whereas the ambassadors had come from the Sultan, the Shadow of God. Along with General Malarctic, the other side of the table included the likes of General de Cossigny, M. Descomber, etc. The ambassadors were informed that they had been duped by Ripaud. Apparently the French in Mauritius had received only a single battalion since the commencement of the Napoleonic War. That, too, had been promptly redirected to Batavia to assist the Dutch. (This was a quid pro quo for material assistance received from them). The General added that it was highly inconvenient at the moment for France to send an expedition to India; the plan was to maintain peace with the British in the near future.

This sentiment contradicts a letter written by Napoleon himself. Although the letter was intercepted before it reached Tipu Sultan, it clearly indicated his ambition to march into India. It further inquired about Tipu's political situation and asked if it was at all possible to despatch a trusted lieutenant for talks!

But what mattered was the mood on Mauritian soil. The French could only promise the despatch of "interested freelance volunteers" who would have the liberty of leaving the Sultan once the contract expired. Furthermore, General Malarctic broached no argument regarding the pay-scale. It would be 600 rupees per mensem, or four times the rate compared to a decade back. (It cannot be said with authority, though, that the Republic bred inflation!) General Malarctic made one concession – were the Sultan desirous of punishing Ripaud, he would take him into custody and ship him across. He further added that the Sultan should not send such people as *wakils*.

Meanwhile, the innovative Ripaud was hatching other plans. In a comparatively irreverent letter written to Tipu Sultan in May 1797, he revealed an intriguing scheme for nailing Dampars Raymond, the commander of the European troops in the army of the Nizam of Hyderabad. The letter alludes to Raymond having contacted Tipu for an alliance. Reminding Tipu that Raymond was a dubious Republican on enemy rolls, Ripaud proposed to lead Raymond on till "he falls on the very track that will answer your purposes".

It is unclear whether Francois Ripaud went back to Srirangapattana. But for certain, two Frenchmen – Chapuy and Dubuc, commandant of land and marine forces respectively – were sent back with the ambassadors along with a motley crew of officers, ship-builders, linguists, and European soldiers as well as soldiers of mixed parentage. Ninety-nine people in all... presumably to take on the might of the British. The indefatigable Tipu promoted Dubuc to the post of (yet another) ambassador and despatched him to Paris. Dubuc spent or lost all of his advance money before reaching the Danish fort of Tranquebar, which is situated on the Tamil Nadu coastline. He then lost his ship to the British and requested a year's advance pay to cover the expenses of his family. Dubuc finally left for Paris on 7 February 1799. Too late.

Tipu's overtures to the French provided sufficient grounds for the Governor-General, Marquess Wellesley (then Lord Mornington), to declare war on him. The Sultan made a feeble attempt to postpone the inevitable by writing to the Governor-General that he had enjoyed hearing about the triumphs of the English over the French in Egypt, that the French were "crooked, faithless and enemies of mankind". It did not work.

History was standing at a juncture of inevitability. Even if a resolute Frenchman had appeared on the scene, it was most unlikely that he would have persuaded his seniors to ally themselves with the Sultan. But with someone of Ripaud's character initiating the negotiations, it was doomed before it began. British officer David Baird led the attack on Srirangapattana. Fifteen years back, Baird had been one of the officers imprisoned by Hyder during the Battle of Pollilur. Tipu, perhaps India's first true freedom fighter, died after a valiant fight. When he fell on the battleground, sword still in hand, the glorious days of Srirangapattana came to an end. Upon getting the news of his death, the Governor-General, Marquess Wellesley, is said to have made an impromptu address to his dinner gathering. Tipsy with whisky and wine, he rose on his unsteady feet and said:

'Ladies and gentlemen, I drink to the corpse of India.'

Thus ends one of the most important chapters in South Indian history. Only a footnote remains: most of the foreigners who interacted with Tipu during his last days were probably unfamiliar with the nearby city of Bangalore. But they had all worked together in a manner that changed the city's destiny. As Srirangapattana fell by the wayside, Bangalore acquired a halo and entered a new age of significance.

The Wodeyar Years

Jean-Antoine Dubois, better known as Abbé Dubois, is believed to have arrived in India as a twenty-seven year old in 1792, the year the French Revolution broke out in his homeland. Some believe that the flight from the fusillades of the French Revolution brought the abbé to India. The man himself has substantiated this claim by saying:

'It is quite true that I fled the horrors of the Revolution and had I remained I should in all probability have fallen a victim as did so many of my friends who held the same religious and political opinions as myself; but the truth is I embarked for India some two years before the fusillades referred to took place.'

Whatever the circumstances leading to the journey, Abbé Dubois made India his home for the next thirty-one years and brought to his job, well, a missionary zeal. In 1803, after noting that around a thousand (mostly European) Catholics resided in Bangalore, he set about attempting to boost this number. His headquarters, so to speak, was the St. Mary's chapel situated in the Shivaji Nagar area of the city. (Contrary to popular belief, he was not the founder of the chapel.)

The history of the St. Mary's chapel stretches back a century before the abbé's Indian sojourn. It was built in the beginning of the eighteenth century by two Jesuit priests, Rev. Fr. Boulet and Rev. Fr. Manduit, who supposedly came to Bangalore from Vellore. It had a thatched roof and a deity that was "christened" *Kannikai Matha* or *Arogya Matha*, and was called a *kovil* or temple. The reverends were understandably trying to ease the populace into Christianity with inspired nomenclature. *Arogya* means health in Tamil, the language predominant in the area, and with nonexistent healthcare facilities, a goddess that bolstered the immune system made sense. Representing the Foreign Mission Society of Paris, Abbé Dubois became associated with the chapel immediately after the fall of Tipu Sultan in 1799. He replaced the thatched roof with black tiles in 1811 and built a residence for priests. In 1832, communal riots literally shook the chapel to its very foundations and the parish priest barely escaped with his life. The British, who had taken over the direct administration of the state of Mysore the previous year, mobilised troops to guard the chapel. In 1882, a certain Fr. Kleiner expanded and beautified the edifice. The next change in the chapel was superficial. Stained glass windows installed by Fr. Kleiner were removed during World War II and were reinstalled only in 1947. The crowning glory for St. Mary's came in 1973 when the Vatican consecrated it as a minor basilica. Such is the history of the chapel. The abbé's is no less interesting.

More than two centuries have elapsed since the abbé came to Bangalore, but his fame and influence have only increased in the interim. And he owes it mainly to his seminal book on Hindu life titled *Description of the Character, Manners and Customs of the people of India, and of their institutions, religious and civil*. To write the book, the abbé studied "books held in highest estimation amongst the people of India" and "scattered records as fell by chance" into his hands. He also incorporated into it his own first-hand observations. The good abbé is reported to have dressed as a *sadhu* and moved among the local people to understand their psyche and gain their confidence. This unconventional method sometimes led to sticky situations. Accompanied by a retinue of servants, the abbé was once travelling in South Mysore on horseback. He stopped by a village at dusk and solicited the village chieftain's hospitality. The chieftain, a Brahmin, agreed to play host provided he got the assurance that the servants were of a higher caste. This was done, and as was their practice, the servants also slapped in a few lies about the abbé's meat-abstaining, teetotalling ways. The chieftain nevertheless posted one spy with the abbé and another with the servants. When the second one reported that one of the servants did not perform ablutions after a call of nature, all hell broke loose. The team had to move to a cowshed, and finally flee the village since the matter showed no signs of abating.

Such episodes, however, were rare. Abbé Dubois mostly experienced cordial receptions wherever he went. And despite his strong Catholic convictions, his book is objective and intellectual *for the most part*. It is divided into three sections – the first provides his perception of the social order, the second details the four stages of Brahminical life, and the third describes rituals and deities as well as prevalent military and administrative structures. Using this format, Abbé Dubois has debated upon the merits and demerits of the caste system, portrayed the role of Indian women in society, described Hindu rituals in detail, and even observed the procedure used by *sadhus* to render their penises impotent.

Upon completion of the first draft of the book in 1806, the abbé sent it to Major Mark Wilks for his opinion. Major Wilks was not just the British Resident of the state of Mysore, but also a passionate historian. In a year's time, he had discerned the quality of the manuscript and warmly recommended it to the government at Fort St. George (Madras). His opinion was endorsed by James Macintosh and W. Erskine. All this led Lord William Bentinck to purchase the manuscript on behalf of the British East India Company for 2,000 star pagodas. The abbé invested the money in government bonds and used the interest to meet his expenses. Meanwhile, the manuscript was sent to London, translated into English and published in 1816. But a year before that, a Superintendent of the local Board of Examiners happened to lay his hands on a copy. Thereafter, he contacted Abbé Dubois and suggested a revision. The abbé himself had learnt a lot more in the interim, and concurred that the book could do with improvements. When he finished his second draft, it barely resembled the first, other than in structure. By then the original translation was out, and that was the version Europe read till Henry Beauchamp's translation appeared in 1897!

That apart, the book was applauded not just in the West, but also in India. Noting its sharp incisive observations, the social reformer Raja Ram Mohun Roy has said:

'The European who knew the Indian best and described her most truthfully, was the Abbé Dubois.'

The book must have been a good ally to the Raja who spent his lifetime battling the caste system. By giving the centre-stage to the Brahmin, the abbé made the book a commentary on social injustice. He saw Brahmins as hoarders of knowledge and prejudiced preservers of the status quo. He felt that they had distorted an originally rational scheme. Inequality was their official doctrine. Using his angst against the Brahmin, he goes on to make a somewhat obtuse connection:

'Under the supremacy of the Brahmin,' he said, 'the people of India hated their government, while they cherished and respected their rulers; under the supremacy of Europeans, they hate and despise their rulers from the bottom of their hearts, while they cherish and respect their government.'

The quote betrays his approval of British presence in India. In fact, the abbé was convinced that the British, so beneficent and humane at home, could not compromise their nobility and impartiality elsewhere. Continuing along the same lines, he lamented that it might not be possible to ameliorate the condition of Indians because they "neither possess the desire to be happy, nor are anxious to cooperate to this end".

Perhaps the abbé, at some level, was guilty of the same failing he abhorred: *Brahminical prejudice*, although of a different variety. In describing the "hypocritical ways" of the sanyasi, he drew a comparison with the "pure motives" of John, the Baptist. By making such generalisations and by not recognising his blind spots, the abbé failed to rise to the level of a true humanitarian. But it cannot be forgotten that this book was one of the first documents on Indian culture by a Westerner. And it no doubt inspired other writers to study India. The achievement is all the more startling considering that it was written during the abbé's leisure hours. And there couldn't have been much leisure in his life because he interested himself in many diverse activities.

For example, he was the Superior for the St. Joseph's College and Schools in Bangalore. He was also instrumental in getting Indians vaccinated against the small-pox virus. One account estimates the number of vaccinations made at his behest at 25,432 in the year 1803-04 alone. This effort earned him the title of Doddaswamiayavaru (Great Lord or Big Master). He also made similar pragmatic attempts to eradicate poverty. Understanding the agrarian basis of life in India, he founded agricultural colonies in many places. And although he modestly disclaimed dexterity with the pen, he also wrote another book titled *The Exploits of Guru Paramarta* in addition to translating the *Panchatantra*.

When Abbé Dubois left India in 1823, the British East India Company gave him a generous pension. But despite his numerous achievements, he was by then a disillusioned man.

'To make a new race of the Hindus,' he observed, 'one would have to begin by undermining the very foundations of their civilization, religion, and polity, and by turning them into atheists and barbarians... During the long period I lived in India, in the capacity of a missionary, I have made, with the assistance of a native missionary, in all between two and three hundred converts of both sexes. Of this number two-thirds were Pariahs or beggars, and the rest were composed of Sudras, vagrants, and outcasts of several tribes, who, being without resources, turned Christians in order to form new connections, chiefly for the purpose of marriage, or with some other interested motive. Among them are also to be found some who believed themselves to be possessed with the devil, and who turned Christians after having been assured that on receiving baptism the unclean spirits would leave them and never return; and I will declare it with shame and confusion that I do not remember any one who may be said to have embraced Christianity from conviction and from quite disinterested motives. Among these newcomers many apostatized and relapsed into paganism, finding that the Christian religion did not afford them the temporal advantages they had looked for in embracing it; and I am very much ashamed that the resolution I have taken to tell the whole truth on this subject forces me to make the humiliating avowal that those who continued Christians are the very worst among my flock.'

Immediately upon reaching Paris, Abbé Dubois became the Director and later Superior of his Mission. He died in 1848 at the age of eighty-three.

* * *

The same year that Abbe Dubois finished the first draft of his book, an Englishman named John Richardson brought out the first *authoritative* Persian-English dictionary. Richardson had been commissioned by the Board of Directors of the British East India Company because it was felt that any Westerner working in India should know more than a smattering of Persian. Looking at Indian history, one feels obliged to agree that both the language and the people deserve that significance. Persian gifts to India include *ghazals*, poetry, prose, calligraphy, carpets and horticulture. But there is more. Says a Bangalorean who is an expert in all matters Persian:

'Indo-Iranian people interaction precedes British India. If bilateral possibilities have dwindled today, it is due to the popularity of the English language and the formation of the separate state of Pakistan.'

It is not surprising, therefore, to know that Persians made a profound impact on Bangalore. One family that traces its ancestry back to the town of Shiraz, in particular, contributed immensely to the development of the city. The progenitor of the Shirazi clan was Aga Ali Asker Shirazi.

Ali Asker was escorted into Bangalore in 1824 by his two elder brothers when he was just sixteen years old. And the only reason they towed him along was to ensure that he did not get into mischief back home. According to some reports, the three brothers were accompanied by an entire retinue of horsemen, scribes, cooks, barbers, a mullah and even a goldsmith. The barber and the goldsmith are definite exaggerations according to a member of the family, but the fact remains that it was a well-planned trip. And it was made with the intent of selling horses to the British.

After successfully transacting their business, the brothers returned to Iran in high spirits. The plan was to make another trip at the soonest to fulfil Bangalore's huge demand for good Arabian horses. But once back in Shiraz, they learnt that their father had died in the interim. So the eldest brother stayed back to take care of the family and estate while the younger two set forth on their second voyage to Bangalore. The trip proved fatal for the second brother – he drowned in the Cauvery while travelling from Mysore to Bangalore. Ali Asker suddenly found himself the boss of the establishment. He took charge of the few stable-boys, the horses and trade negotiations. One can only speculate how he would have fared had his brothers been around, but in their absence, Ali Asker rose to the occasion.

In no time at all, his stables earned a reputation for selling excellent horses. In addition to the British, Ali Asker sold the horses to the Maharaja of Mysore. Business ties with the Maharaja, in fact, led to a close friendship. It is said that women of Ali Asker's family had access to the Maharani's chambers and vice-versa. Ali Asker gave proof of the intimacy between the families after the death of the Maharaja. He is said to have petitioned Sir John Lawrence, the then Viceroy, to express sorrow that the Maharaja's adopted son could inherit his property, but not his kingdom. Mark Cubbon, the Commissioner of Mysore who also happened to be Ali Asker's friend, was supposedly a fellow petitioner.

The petition, of course, was rejected and Ali Asker experienced a rare failure. He, however, flourished in other areas despite lacking formal schooling and being handicapped by his unfamiliarity with English and Hindustani. One of the reasons for his success was the fact that his horses regularly won prizes on the turf. Once the business was well established, he was ready to settle in Bangalore and start a family. His first wife was Kadu Bibi, a lady belonging to an affluent Muslim family from Chennapatna. After her death, he married Shehr Bano, a lady who, some say, came directly from Persia (others claim that she hailed from Lucknow). The two women helped him raise a large family.

Meanwhile, Ali Asker began diversifying his interests; he became a builder of many fine houses in Bangalore. But the strongest edifice he built in his lifetime was his family. It was upon the foundations of this family that Ali Asker's grandson Sir Mirza Ismail built his illustrious career. As the Dewan of Mysore between 1926 and 1941, Sir Mirza proved to be an able, secular and wise administrator. Today, his descendants love repeating a particular story that highlights his capabilities. Apparently, Gandhiji once came to Bangalore to determine for himself how the state of Mysore was faring. Upon seeing Sir Mirza's work, he immediately packed his bags.

'Mysore is being taken care of. My work lies elsewhere,' he is reported to have said.

Ali Asker, buried in a nearby cemetery along Hosur Road, must have smiled in approval.

* * *

Ali Asker was a man of rare character and nothing illustrates this better than the following story:

Ali Asker had a thick friend in Aga Khan, a personage of royal blood based in Bombay. During a visit to his friend's house, Ali Asker discovered that he was not the only guest. Two aristocratic women who had been exiled from his homeland were enjoying Aga Khan's hospitality as well. The reasons leading to their exile are now lost in time, but it is certain that they were a queen mother and her beautiful daughter named Kawkab, which in Persian means planet or star. Seeing Kawkab, Ali Asker had no hesitation in proposing the marriage of his son Mohammad Bakar with her. Outraged by the commoner's impertinence, the mother funnelled her anger at Aga Khan, who in turn coolly decided that the matter didn't concern him.

So the mother came up with a ploy to snub Ali Asker and maintain decorum at the same time. She demanded an exhaustive list of items as dowry or *jahaz*. It was excessive even by princely standards. But Ali Asker shocked her by accepting the demands. It is said that the lady rushed back to Aga Khan for help. He gave her none.

'Why did you underestimate him?' he asked. 'Now you have no option but to keep your word.'

Kawkab's groom Mohammad Bakar was a handsome lad and a fine horseman to boot. Soon after the wedding, Ali Asker despatched him to Madras to participate in a steeplechase. Bakar was in the habit of winning huge sums for his father and there was every reason to believe that he would continue to do so. As fate would have it, Bakar suffered a tragic accident during the race and died soon after.

Ali Asker was distraught at losing his son. But was he to lose a brand-new daughter-in-law as well? It is said that when Kawkab took leave of his family and sat in her palanquin, she heard a heart-rending shriek from her father-in-law's room. She ran in with the others to investigate.

'You cannot leave,' said Ali Asker. 'You came here as a bride, and you will not leave my house as a widow. You will marry my son Abdul Hussain.'

Since that was Bakar's deathbed wish as well, Kawkab acquiesced. But on the wedding night, she spoke to her new husband of her desire to convert Bakar's wealth into a benevolent trust. Abdul Hussain reported the matter to his father in the morning and in reply, Ali Asker sat down and wrote his will. Sometime ago, he had purchased a property in Sankey Road and had used it to build the Bedford House. He now renamed the area Bakarabad, created the Bakarabad Trust and entrusted it to his four living sons. Today, the exclusive Windsor Manor hotel stands at this location. This piece of land later became the centrepiece of a long-drawn legal battle.

* * *

Ali Asker proved that it was possible for a foreigner to be assimilated into Bangalorean society. That too, on his own terms. It should be noted that he lived through exciting times in the history of Bangalore. Change was in the air. The administration of the city would flip back and forth between the British and the Wodeyars during the next century or so, but the city grew rapidly, irrespective of who was at the helm. And as it grew, its appetite for newcomers increased. Many of the newcomers were expatriates with ambitious projects in mind.

And they helped Bangalore attain the next level of maturity.

After the British Takeover

The British took over the direct administration of the state of Mysore from the Wodeyars in 1831. While a lesser-known junior Commissioner named Lushington was responsible for shifting the capital and the Secretariat from Mysore to Bangalore, it was the first solo Commissioner of the state of Mysore, Sir Mark Cubbon, who er... made his mark. Born in 1785 in the Isle of Man, Sir Mark was a relative of Mark Wilks, the gentleman who forwarded Abbé Dubois' manuscript to the British East India Company, and he assumed office in 1834 after an illustrious career in the 2nd Madras Battalion.

Right from the outset, Sir Mark proved to be an able administrator who laid specific emphasis upon improving Bangalore's infrastructure. His tenure saw the state add 1,597 miles of new roads and 309 bridges. He also introduced telegraph lines in Bangalore in 1853. By 1864, a railway link was completed between Bangalore and Jolarpettai. This added a new dimension of importance to Bangalore. Bankers and merchants belonging to various cultures – the Banias, Marwaris and Katiawaris from India, as well as Pathans from Multan (now in Pakistan) – began thronging the city. Bangalore's population was now second only to that of Madras (now Chennai) in South India. Sir Mark's stress on infrastructure was, therefore, not misplaced.

Meanwhile, Sir Mark had replaced pagodas with silver rupees in 1854. Prior to that, in 1834 to be precise, he had abolished the practice of publicly auctioning women charged with adultery (*samayachara*). These are his better known contributions. There are a few unsung ones as well. The establishment of the government press for example.

The idea originated in 1840 from Rev. J. Garett who was managing a small printing press for the Wesleyan Mission Society in Bangalore. Rev. Garett persuaded Sir Mark to have a dedicated press to cater to the government's printing requirements. A manually operated press was set up in 1866 – after Sir Mark left office – and Rev. Garett became its first Superintendent.

Another distinctive feature of Sir Mark's personality was his love for civilian solutions despite his military background. During the height of the Uprising of 1857, Sir Mark argued the advantages of establishing a civil, rather than military, authority in the city. Clearly, the prevalent mood was against him – the Civil and Military (C & M) station (known more popularly as the Cantonment area) was soon created, dividing the city into two parts. Ironically, Cubbon Park became the point of demarcation between the city and the Cantonment till the two sections were merged in 1949.

A description of Sir Mark is available thanks to Charlotte Canning, the wife of the Governor-General Lord Canning. She has said:

'[He is] the most *grand seigneur* old man I ever saw. The old general is most remarkable. He has the most perfect manners and is a very fine looking man and yet he has been 58 years in India. He has a store of most interesting recollections and can give information in the most agreeable manner and is as alive to all that goes on in Europe as if he had but just left it.'

Sir Mark Cubbon resigned from his position in 1861 and made way for Lewin Bowring.

* * *

The next expatriate to add to Bangalore's history was Dr. Charles Irving Smith. Dr. Smith is believed to have been Sir Mark Cubbon's personal physician, but his claim to fame lies in the establishment of a mental health care institution at a time when a general hospital of repute did not exist in the city. In fact, it was a time when the Garrison Hospital that treated European and Indian soldiers was considered the best in the region. But Bangalore's medical fraternity was about to undergo exciting changes. Having taken over the direct administration of the state, the British were in the process of building civilian health care facilities and introducing western medicine to the general public. Such were the circumstances in 1838 when Dr. Smith obtained Sir Mark's go-ahead to open a ward in the *pettah* (city) hospital for mentally ill native men and expanded its scope to admit women a year later.

Dr. Smith's interest in mental health care stemmed from the fact that a high proportion of cases resulted in death. Convinced that more focused care would make a difference, he used the available resources and knowledge to treat cases of depression, dementia and various other psychoses. Since the facility proved to be popular, a separate asylum was built some years later. Dr. Smith admitted patients depending on "the need for the protection of the community, of the patient himself, and of his property, or the cure or alleviation (or failing both) the retarding of his disease". In 1850, this asylum could house 260 patients. The inmates were a mix of Indians from all parts of the country, as well as Armenians, European Catholics, Italians, Irish and English. In the "simple, but airy" buildings, inmates were kept busy with chores such as gardening, rope weaving and domestic work. A large number of paupers were also admitted to the asylum for humane reasons.

Dr. Smith eventually returned to England and died in 1871. The techniques he used to treat the mentally ill outlived him in Bangalore till at least the end of the century.

According to Dr. Sanjeev Jain of NIMHANS, membership rolls in England had inducted the first Indian psychiatrist by the 1890s. But the asylum itself lacked formally trained Indian psychiatrists. A process of reforms was therefore initiated in the 1910s. Francis Noronha was sent to England for training, and upon his return he became the first qualified in-house Indian psychiatrist. From then on, the asylum kept track of the progress made in the field. Measures followed in the West were quickly replicated. This eventually led to the institution itself participating in novel research and rehabilitation projects.

Meanwhile, a growing city was placing increasing demands on the asylum. So for decades, it continued expanding and relocating. The Maharaja of Mysore provided much-needed stability by allocating suitable land in Bangalore to the institution (the administration of the state had reverted to the Maharaja by then). Construction of a sprawling campus was completed on this land by 1934. The

Lunatic Asylum moved into the premises and adopted a more sensitive nomenclature. It was now called the Mysore Mental Hospital.

The second Indian head of the hospital, Dr. M. V. Govindswamy, took it to the next level of proficiency and awareness. During a visit to London, he made a lasting acquaintance with a German doctor named Wilhelm Mayer-Gross who, after escaping Hitler's ethnic cleansing, had become an important staff member of the Bethlem Royal Hospital. In 1951-52, Dr. Mayer-Gross was deputed to the Bangalore institution as a consultant to the World Health Organisation. His primary responsibility was to suggest mental health reforms in India.

By this time, the institution was part of the All India Institute of Mental Health (it was named NIMHANS only in 1974). And it was best suited to host India's first postgraduation training facility in psychiatry. That explains Dr. Mayer-Gross' deputation to Bangalore. He spent two years in the campus (1951-52 and 1956-57) to plan the post-graduation course material and to give lectures to the staff. By the end of his stay, he realised that the visit had benefited him as well. His experiences with patients in Bangalore forced him to alter many of his ideas, and helped him in writing his path-breaking book titled *Textbook of Psychiatry*.

'The book introduced classic German psychiatry to the English-speaking world,' says Dr. Sanjeev Jain. 'Its theories are in complete contrast with Freud's ideas. It says: one does not understand how the human mind works. One ought to look for physical reasons instead. It made a huge impact in psychiatry.'

* * *

Sir Charles Wood's Despatch of 1854 ushered in systematic modern education in the state of Mysore. By then, British missionary institutions – the London Mission and the Wesleyan Mission in particular – had already created a sound base for a new education system in Bangalore.

The London Mission began its education programmes in the city in 1820. Rev. W. Campbell, and, after him, Rev. B. Rice, guided the programmes during the initial years. In 1840, a Mrs. Sewell established the first Kannada day school for girls. Two years later, Mrs. Jane Rice, the wife of Rev. Rice, founded the London Mission Girls' Boarding School. After her death in 1864, the next generation of the family took charge of this and other schools in the city. The students were taught to read and write in English and Kannada, elementary geography, arithmetic, the Bible, knitting, crocheting, spinning, cooking and to take care of children! In 1902, the Mission opened what was the only High School for Indian girls. The Mission also ran a Collegiate High School for Boys.

Meanwhile, the Wesleyan had begun its operations in the same year as the London Mission, and a certain Joshua Hudson started an English school in the Cantonment area in 1834.

Interestingly, most of the Europeans and Anglo-Indians attended separate aided schools. In fact, fourteen such exclusive schools had come into existence by 1879, thirteen of which were located in the Cantonment area alone (one was located in the city of Mysore).

By 1860, three to four high schools had been established in the Bangalore district. One of them was the Baldwin Boys' High School which was founded by Bishop Oldham. Three years later, the city had produced its first candidate for the Madras Matriculation Examination. Two more years elapsed before the establishment of the renowned Bishop Cotton Boys' and Girls' School.

Kindergarten classes were introduced in Bangalore in 1906 by Miss L. R. Latter, the Assistant Superintendent of the London School Board. Due to her sudden death in 1907, a certain Miss A. Williams took over the process; she was aided in her efforts by Miss Z. R. Hart.

* * *

In the year 1854, even as Sir Charles was initiating reforms in the education system, the Congregation of Good Shepherd Sisters sent a few committed souls on a long and hazardous journey from Europe to Bangalore. Some of them hailed from Germany, others from France and Ireland; all of them were aged between eighteen and twenty-six. For the congregation they represented, such missions were routine and meant a lifelong commitment. In this particular case, the Sisters were answering Bishop Charbonneaux's plea for assistance in educating girls in Bangalore. Upon arriving in Bangalore, the Sisters set up their headquarters in what had been a dark and dreary prison on Museum Road. The location soon boasted not just a school, but also an orphanage and a teenage shelter.

The Sisters might have maintained a serene and worthy status quo had not events challenged them to rise even higher. Between 1876 and 1878, the state of Mysore reeled under a terrible famine and an outbreak of plague. Thousands of people migrated to Bangalore from rural areas, further aggravating the fragile infrastructure of the city. Countless children died on the streets. The government began laying a railway line to Mysore to provide relief employment (although historians have recently found data that suggest that the policies formulated by Viceroy Lytton during this time were anything but humane). Talented craftsmen rushed in to work on the project; many never returned to their hereditary professions. Although the situation improved by 1880, Bangalore struggled with sanitation issues for the next two decades. The situation was especially worrisome in areas like Blackpalli (now Shivaji Nagar). Hence the second and more serious outbreak of plague in 1898-99 would not have come as a huge shock to the administration. The impact, however, was calamitous. One estimate put the casualty figures at a million people in the entire state. And it would have been a little higher without the Good Shepherd Sisters.

As soon as the first plague broke out, the Good Shepherd Sisters threw open their premises to treat the ailing. Seeing cholera and starvation claim umpteen lives, one Sister in particular decided that it was time to do more. She was Fanny Leusch, known in her circles as Sr. Mary of the Visitation. Born in the German town of Eupen, Sr. Mary's background provided a stark contrast to the impoverished surroundings she made her own. Her father was a wealthy Prussian banker and her mother hailed from a respectable French family. But Fanny Leusch relinquished her comforts and joined the Congregation in Angers, France. And from the very beginning, she felt as if India was calling out to her. So when 24-year old Sr. Mary was assigned to work in Bangalore in 1862, she did something typical. She leapt with joy. Literally. Clothed in a starched white habit, she jumped over a bench that lay in her path, totally unmindful of what her watching superiors might think. Many looked at her relocation as a "bad investment"; such a frail creature of the Lord couldn't survive three months in India. They were off by thirty-odd years. Sr. Mary used those years to make a profound impression. As a Superior, she preferred to issue requests instead of commands. But even as she livened up her workplace with her gift of humour, she knew how to exercise her authority when required. Additionally, she was a Latin scholar, adept at astronomy, a passionate gardener and knew something about architecture. Not surprisingly then, one observes a Gothic sturdiness in the buildings she built. The one she was inspired to build in 1877 was a hospital.

There were hurdles, both within the congregation and without, and they seemed insuperable. Some Superiors felt that medical work was not the primary objective of the congregation, and wanted to remain faithful to the mission that brought them to Bangalore. At the same time, government officials were sceptical about the feasibility of the idea. A single, untrained woman running a hospital, even with a congregation backing her, seemed farfetched. But she soon found hope. His name was Rev. Fr. Bonnetraine of the Missionaries Entrangers de Paris.

Francois Bonnetraine was born in France in 1843 and came to Bangalore in 1867. His work required him to travel through the state of Mysore and the Madras Presidency, and he used the opportunity to learn the local languages and customs. He mooted novel ideas for evangelisation and was known to analyse everything. And he shared with Sr. Mary a love for ambitious and humane projects. Just as he had convinced his Bishop of the necessity of a Catholic hospital in Bangalore, he fell ill and had to go home for treatment. Coming back in 1877, he landed right in the middle of the plague epidemic. With the government's help, he acquired some land in Siluvepura outside Bangalore and set up a farm-cum-orphanage. And all the while, he dreamt about doing more. The opportunity came with his appointment as the chaplain of the Good Shepherd Sisters in 1880.

It took Sr. Mary (who later became Mother Mary) and Rev. Bonnetraine four years to convince all parties to give their consent for the hospital. The Maharaja of Mysore donated twenty acres of land, Sr. Mary dipped into the Leusch family wealth, the people of Bangalore contributed according to their means and St. Martha's eventually opened in 1886. Standing inside the fully functional hospital, Mother Mary said to Fr. Bonnetraine (neither of them were young anymore):

'There is your hospital, Father.'

'No, it is yours, Mother,' he replied.

'Well then,' she conceded, 'let us call it *our* hospital.'

The hospital saw many challenges – funding issues, administrative hassles, experimental coalitions with other medical bodies in the city, and even a brief period of leadership that wanted it closed. Somehow, it survived. Work took Fr. Bonnetraine away from St. Martha's for long periods of time, but Mother Mary carried on. When she passed away, others equally capable took her place. The first among them was a midget-sized Swiss of peasant stock named Sr. M. Hyacinth Gonnet. Appointed in 1895 as the first Superior of the hospital, Sr. Hyacinth displayed remarkable administrative abilities. During the day, she rallied the Mysore administration for different kinds of support (funds, medical expertise, etc.). But she always spent her evenings in taking care of the patients. Perhaps her indomitable strength came from having experienced sorrow at a personal level – her elder sister and parents had died by the time she was seven. At any rate, she was adept at handling suffering. When she arrived in Bangalore in 1869, she was first assigned to a silk farm in Kengeri, which employed orphaned children and young women. She fought tuberculosis and malaria during her stay there. Later, when she was assigned to a small school and dispensary in Vellore, she struggled against malaria and blackwater fever. In the two plague epidemics that struck Bangalore, she continued her exemplary work. And she never ceased to smile. The depth of her personality was revealed in 1917 when she was forced to take rest – twenty-five abscesses were discovered all over her body. Hyacinth Gonnet died in 1920. By then, St. Martha's already had a glorious past behind it.

In the interim, Rev. Bonnetraine had once again become associated with the hospital. This time, in addition to reassuming his position as the chaplain, the founder was also a patient. He had turned deaf but that did not prevent him from planning new projects. He wanted to open a home for the aged and the poor. At his behest, priests' quarters were built inside St. Martha's so that missionaries could recuperate or wait for the day of reckoning. In 1913, Fr. Bonnetraine was at last allowed to retire at the age of seventy. It didn't last long. Due to the very real threat of the First World War, France recalled several young missionaries. So at the age of seventy-two, he became a seminary rector! A more permanent retirement came upon his death on 31 March 1917.

Meanwhile, St. Martha's continued to attract humane Christians from all over the world. As late as 1965, an Irish-English woman named Mother Mary Aloysius ran the hospital after having served in Burma and Sri Lanka. Even today, three Irish Sisters are leading a retired life in the St. Martha's campus.

* * *

Bangalore was certainly coming into prominence as the nineteenth century drew to a close; irrefutable proof of this came eleven years after the end of the first outbreak of plague. In 1889, Prince Albert Victor Christian Edward of Wales, the son of Queen Victoria, paid a visit to Bangalore. A wonderful eyewitness account of the royal visit is available, thanks to the Kannada writer D. V. Gundappa.

According to Gundappa, the royal party got down at the City Railway Station and proceeded towards the city in horse-drawn carriages. At the Totadappa Choultry Corner, the Dharmambudhi Tank – which was later drained to house the city bus terminus – hosted a sight to behold. On a sheet of clear water, a gently gliding *theppa* (float) carried a party of Bharata Natyam dancers in colourful attire. Traditional musicians lined along the way, playing *nadaswarams* and other Indian instruments. Later in the afternoon, a huge reception was held for the prince in Lalbagh at the newly constructed Glass House. Years later, Queen Elizabeth II also visited Bangalore and the Lalbagh Glass House.

Meanwhile, it was time for another British personality – one who was destined for greatness – to make his appearance in Bangalore.

Turn of the Century

In 1896, a subaltern named Winston Churchill honoured Bangalore with his presence. Undoubtedly a central figure of the next century, Churchill spent a humdrum year or so in the city. However, he did leave behind an unpaid bill of thirteen rupees at the Bangalore Club, and thereby, a legend of Churchillian proportions. One feels that Churchill must have found the club to his liking. It was an exclusive haunt for the elite, quite apt for one who felt "the keenest realisation of the great work which England was doing in India and of her high mission to rule these primitive but agreeable races for their welfare and our own".

To understand what Churchill thought of Bangalore, one doesn't need to look beyond *My Early Life*, the first volume of his autobiography. In it, Churchill notes the following: the climate of Bangalore is excellent, the roses of Europe attain the highest perfection of fragrance and colour, snipe (and snakes) abound in the marshes, brilliant butterflies dance in the sunshine and nautch-girls by the light of the moon. It is a wonder that he managed such vivid observations, considering that he busily promoted the imperial cause by... er... playing polo. One could easily buy a pony by approaching fat, urbane, quite honest, agreeable and mercilessly rapacious native moneylenders who charged 2% interest a month. That made it easier for him and his buddies in the IV Hussars to concentrate their energies on the Golconda Cup. Their focus paid off. Their regiment won the Cup within fifty days of arrival, a record hitherto unbroken, and will presumably remain so, given the shocking lack of desire on the part of Indians to see another British cavalry regiment patrol their land.

Life seems to have been a lark for the great man. Each morning, he would be woken up by a "dusky figure with a clammy hand adroitly lifting one's chin and applying a gleaming razor to a lathered and *defenceless* throat" (italics mine). This would be followed by ninety minutes of drills and manoeuvres, bath and breakfast. At nine, he would leave for the stables and orderly room and stay there till half past ten. Long before eleven, all white men were happily under their bungalow roofs. Unfortunately, Churchill had to skip across in the blistering heat for luncheon in the mess, after which terrible task, he could sleep till five. It was then time for polo, the thing that made everything else bearable! Evenings were meant for dinner, the strains of a regimental band and the clinking of ice in well-filled glasses. The day ended with an hour or so of "smoking in the moonlight". As he has himself said, it was not such a bad day.

By the winter of 1896, another keen realisation seems to have dawned upon 22-year old Churchill. He felt himself "wanting in even the vaguest knowledge about the many large spheres of thought". To bridge the gap, he began delving into topics such as ethics, Socratic philosophy, history and religion. Perhaps – just perhaps – the intellectual capacity he exhibited later on was due to the system of self-study he adopted in Bangalore.

Yes, when it comes to brass tacks, Indians will somehow find a way to take credit.

With people like Churchill gracing the city, it becomes easy to ignore the unsung. But when unsung people of any particular kind achieve critical mass, they merit a little thought. A case in point is that of the British womenfolk in India. Theirs is a Raj story that remained unchanged even as it spanned centuries.

From the beginning of the nineteenth century till the time of Indian independence, unmarried British women came to India to hear their own wedding bells. Of course, few dared the dangers during the initial days of British domination. And since the East India Company offered perks to officers who married without journeying to Britain, many married Indian women. The Anglo-Indian girls born of such marriages provided a ready supply of brides to the succeeding generation. At the same time, the "Fishing Fleet" from Southampton increased in numbers. To maintain propriety, they were either accompanied by a relative during the journey, or had one waiting to pick them up when they disembarked. With fierce competition from Anglo-Indians and peers, many went back single and were callously labelled "Returned Empties".

The successful stayed back. Since the groom's brigade was not averse to footing the expenses, they had a good wedding one way or the other. It was then time to settle down and tackle the challenges. Their husbands usually gave them charge of a bungalow full of native servants – a cook, a bearer and ayahs were absolutely necessary, but sweepers, water-carriers, gardeners, grasscutters, washermen and scullion were kept part-time. The higher-ranking officers also hired grooms and coach-drivers. Dealing with the servants, all natives in fact, required tact – the wives could neither be too sympathetic nor too imperious.

In addition to keeping the house in order, they were expected to host countless dinners. The supply of drink and food had to be abundant and appetising. Help was at hand. Bangalore had a Spencer's outlet as early as the 1880s and it was stocked with almost everything that a homesick Englishman could ask for. Of course, Spencer's couldn't help them with social etiquette. That was learnt on the job. Soon, they became mindful of their husband's rank and the resultant pecking order. It was a serious business. One couldn't be too individualistic, and many found life to be an endless drag. It wasn't everybody's cup of English tea.

As early as 1885, a lady named Flora Annie Steel wrote a handy book titled *The Complete Indian Housekeeper and Cook*. She dedicated it to "The English Girls whom fate may assign the task of being house-mothers in our Eastern Empire." Each anxiety-ridden girl probably slept with a copy of the book on her bosom.

One wonders if she felt commoditised. Or perhaps *outsourced*?

* * *

In 1896, around the time Churchill was planning polo campaigns, the father of the Indian industrial movement Jamsetji Nusserwanji Tata was thinking of setting up a world-class research facility that would push the frontiers of science and engineering. That, he was convinced, was the path to progress and he wanted his nation to walk it. In his own words:

'What advances a nation or community is not so much to prop up its weakest and the most helpless members, as to lift the best and most gifted so as to make them of the greatest service to the country. I prefer this constructive philanthropy which seeks to educate and develop the faculties of the best of our young men.'

With this noble intention, he roped in an educationist named Burjorji Padshah and took his help in forming a Provisional Committee to take the vision forward. As a first step, the team approached the government of India with a proposal for establishing a research institute. What followed was a decade of nitpicking and bureaucratic intrigue. And the star of the show was Lord Curzon, the Viceroy of India. Lord Curzon had grave doubts as to whether India could generate a sufficient number of high quality students to fill the institute rolls. Even if that were possible, could the country provide opportunities to those who had successfully completed their training? He was also suspicious of Jamsetji's motives: why did Jamsetji, for example, stipulate a linkage between the proposed institute and the Tata family? But the foremost issues were the availability of funds – overseas professors were expensive – and the utility of having departments for Philosophy, etc.

In 1899, Jamsetji resolved to dissociate his family from the proposed institute and pledged immovable properties in Bombay (now Mumbai) worth Rs.3mn towards its running costs. These were guaranteed to generate an annual income of Rs.1,25,000. Despite the gesture, the matter remained deadlocked for two years. Finally, the government proposed a critical evaluation of the scheme by one or two distinguished scientists, specially with regard to the location of the institute.

Enter Sir William Ramsay. The man destined to win the Nobel Prize for Chemistry in four years' time for his discovery of inert gases arrived in India on 7 December 1900. His role was primarily that of a real-estate hunter. So he undertook a whirlwind tour, along with his wife, and visited fourteen educational centres in two and a half months. In the report he wrote while sailing back, Sir William described his idea of an ideal location: it should have easy access to raw materials, should have some source of electric power, and its climate "should be such that it is possible to work with energy during the greater part of the year". Moreover, the location "should not be a very large centre of population, else social and administrative occupations from which it is so difficult to escape in a large city, would necessarily absorb the attention of the staff from their more immediate duties". Bangalore fitted the bill perfectly.

But what clearly clinched the deal for Bangalore, according to Sir William, was a welcoming administration. The Dewan of Mysore, Sir K. Seshadri Iyer, was sufficiently impressed by the project to recommend allocating it free land. The Maharaja, Krishnaraja Wodeyar IV, gladly accepted the idea and a triangular-shaped piece of land in the most elevated part of Bangalore was earmarked for the institute. The state further expressed a willingness to make an annual contribution on condition that the institute benefited the local people. Despite this lucky break, Ramsay's financial estimates predicted a shortfall of funds. The report failed to cheer Lord Curzon for other reasons as well. He found some of Sir William's recommendations difficult to accept. For example, he did not like the idea of a single institute taking up the responsibilities of teaching as well as fostering new industries. And he certainly did not want the Government of India to subsidise the scheme.

Meanwhile, Jamsetji approached the Secretary of State for India in London, Lord Hamilton, and obtained a verbal approval for a joint trust controlled by both the government and the Tata family. This did nothing to alter Curzon's mood. Thankfully for the Viceroy, a frown and a few telegrams later, Hamilton did a volte-face. A meticulous Curzon then asked for a second opinion from Professor Orme Masson of the University of Melbourne and Lt. Col. Clibborn of the College of Engineering, Roorkee. Upon visiting Bangalore, the duo found "the climate enervating even in November" and concluded that the "prevalence of both enteric fever and plague did not speak of its healthiness". Despite the bad review, Bangalore was chosen to be home to the Indian Institute of Science. And the only reason it won the race was the availability of free land.

Even as his dream was inching towards fruition, Jamsetji's health was waning. He passed away in May 1904 before the institute became fully functional.

The bureaucratic wrangling continued for two more years before the government consented to provide funds. That done, the first Director of the IISc arrived at Bangalore. He was Morris William Travers, who had been a Professor of Chemistry at the University College in Bristol. Significantly, Travers had been Sir William's research assistant and had aided him in the identification of krypton, neon and xenon in 1898. (Sir William had already discovered helium and argon.) And like Sir William, Travers discovered that the IISc was a good paymaster. His salary was £1,800 per annum for ten years and he was assured a pension of £500 per annum for life.

Travers' arrival resulted in a fresh round of disagreements. He seldom saw eye to eye with the Tatas and was particularly averse to the ideas of Padshah, the educationist. Padshah, for example, suggested including anthropological studies in the IISc; Travers simply refused to discuss the topic with him. Similarly, he refused to humour the Tatas on the issue of having a school for social studies at the institute. His years in Bangalore were punctuated by such episodes and his limited knowledge of the Indian milieu possibly added to the chaos. But Travers also had practical knowledge of running an educational institute. As one of his first deeds, he realigned the institute's constitution to mirror those of some of the British universities. He also supervised the construction of buildings, set up laboratories and willingly shouldered the bulk of the administrative responsibilities during the initial years. Even in this task, Travers' refusal to control the ever escalating expenditure led to a disagreement with V. P. Madhava Rao, the incumbent Dewan of Mysore. At one point, the Dewan even declined to sign cheques to pay the contractors. A slighted Travers responded by securing a loan from the Bank of Madras to fund the construction activities. By 1912, the situation had become messier. When Travers had gone to England on leave, Norman S. Rudolf had been the acting Director. Rudolf was now charged with purchasing manure worth Rs.2,600 out of the institute's funds and using it in his own garden. Moreover, the book on the history of the institute titled *In Pursuit of Excellence* states that "during his officiating Directorship, [Rudolf] had sown seeds of dissension among the staff".

What really damaged Travers' case was Rudolf's counter-charge that he was siphoning off funds himself. In March 1913, a Committee of Enquiry adjudicated that Travers "should go and it had passed no reflection on his honour". In other words, he was an honourable man who had committed no wrong, but the institute would benefit from his departure. Rudolf, too, was absolved of misconduct, though he was found to be incompetent.

The drama culminated with Travers' voluntary retirement. World War I was breaking out in Europe and he returned home to oversee the manufacture of glass. Among other things, Travers worked on cryogenics in his later years. He also did a splendid job as Sir William's biographer. His book titled *A Life of Sir William Ramsay* was published as late as 1956. Travers died in 1961 at the ripe old age of eighty-nine. Through those long years, he displayed a deep love and concern for the IISc. This is evident in his private correspondence with some of the IISc staff wherein he continually sought their reassurance that the institute was progressing well and that its achievements were well known. It would not be wholly speculative to state that the reason Travers has not been fully recognised in either India or Britain has more to do with his handling of situations than a larger flaw in his character.

At the very least, nobody can deny that Travers was heading the IISc when it admitted the first batch of students in 1911. The next two directors after Travers were also British. A. G. Bourne headed the institute for six years (1915-21) and he was followed by M. O. Forster (1922-33). Many professors of the era were British as well. The Indian takeover of the IISc happened in 1933 with the appointment of the Nobel laureate Sir C. V. Raman as the Director of the institute.

* * *

Although the great Jamsetji Tata did not live to see his beloved Indian Institute of Science gain a reputation, he oversaw the success of a different kind of enterprise – a silk farm – in Bangalore. Only the staunchest Bangaloreans still remember and celebrate the story of the Tata Silk Farm. It is a story nonetheless worth telling because it brings together philanthropy, vision, innovation and degeneration. And it runs like this:

Having studied the silk industries in Italy, France, China and Japan during his overseas visits, Jamsetji gradually grew convinced that cottage silk industries would do much to alleviate poverty in India. So he decided to venture into the industry, not as a pure entrepreneur, but as an experimenter. The first step was to decide upon the model to be replicated. The Japanese silk industry appealed to him the most because of its assimilatory nature. The industry had borrowed the silk egg production system from Pasteur (France). Its filature-related processes came from Italy. As a result, Japan was producing two-thirds of the world's raw silk (China is the top producer today). His farm, therefore, would run on the Japanese model.

The next step was finding a suitable location. Jamsetji did not look beyond the state of Mysore. He knew that Tipu Sultan's initiative more than a century ago had made Mysore the silk capital of India. The climatic conditions in the state were ideal for the growth of mulberry trees and the town of Channapatna already bred a "favourable" variety of silkworms. Of course, the state's silk industry was unorganised and ran on obsolete technologies. This meant low margins for all the stakeholders and a difficult existence for the labourers in particular. Clearly, the need of the hour was Japanese innovation. Unfortunately, the local Channapatna leaders disagreed with Jamsetji's assessment. It is said that they even discouraged him from proceeding further in the venture. So Jamsetji decided to shift the project to Bangalore and approached the Dewan of Mysore, Sir K. Seshadri Iyer, for help. The Dewan gave his full cooperation and helped set up the Tata Silk Farm in the Basavanagudi locality of Bangalore.

A little earlier, Jamsetji had finally found the people who could take charge of the project – a husband-wife team of sericulture experts named the Odzus. Some accounts claim that Mrs. and Mr. T. Odzu were initially Jamsetji's personal attendants. But what is certain is that the Odzus came to

Bangalore and revolutionised the silk industry with their scientific approach. They not only sold silkworm eggs to sericulturists, but also taught them advanced production processes. Many of the trainees went on to achieve fame in the industry. Within no time, the farm had become a mandatory stopover for sericulturists and a sort of tourist attraction for the masses.

Delighted with its success, Jamsetji approached the government once again. He now wanted to multiply the scale of operation so that more people could benefit from the venture. This time, the government's response was not as encouraging. So the scale and the model remained the same.

The Odzus continued the good work for the next eighteen years. In 1914, ten years after Jamsetji's death, his heirs handed over the farm to the Salvation Army. The move did not bring the desired results. Unequipped with Jamsetji's vision, the Army first and foremost terminated the services of the Odzus. The farm was then handed over to army officers with no exposure to sericulture. The slump that followed was inevitable. The crash was not far behind and it was initiated when the authorities decided to use the juicy mulberry fruits to make jams and pickles! Meanwhile, the buildings in the farm were vacated to accommodate automatic flyshuttle looms. The idea was to create employment for inmates of the Army's orphanage. Fair enough. But as acres of mulberry bushes withered, they were uprooted to make way for cereals like *ragi* and pulses like *avare*. Unfortunately, even the inmates did not benefit. The jams-pickles-cereals-pulses and the looms failed to deliver and the farm closed down forever.

* * *

As the nineteenth century ended, the need to expand the city became urgent, especially in the cantonment areas. As new localities emerged, they were promptly named after the administrators and prominent personalities of Bangalore. In 1906, Fraser Town was built with the money donated by noted citizens such as Rai Bahadur Annaswamy Mudaliar, Khan Bahadur Hajee Ismail Sait, Rutna Singh, Rao Bahadur Maigandeva Mudaliar and Kunnaswamy Naidu. Why then was the locality named after the penultimate Resident of the Civil and Military Station? One can only speculate. Perhaps the donors couldn't decide who among them should be commemorated. Perhaps they had no choice in the matter. Or, perhaps, they were simply unassuming and generous.

Fraser Town was followed by Richards Town, named after E. J. Richards, a District Magistrate and Collector of the Civil and Military Station. It is said that Richards took great interest in developing the town. Cox Town is named after another ICS officer who held the same positions as Richards. Richmond Town, which is now part of downtown Bangalore, is named after a leading Madras advocate.

Miller Road is named after a judge, Sir Leslie Miller, who ensured fair representation for the backward classes. Cooke Town and McIver Town are named after Collectors. Murphy Town is named after an engineer who built many beautiful buildings in the Cantonment area, Rhenius Road is named after a missionary. Cleveland Town and Wheeler Road are named after the same person – John Wheeler Cleveland. A French priest named Fr. Sarvanton, who is said to have rendered great service during the plague and cholera epidemics, has a circle near Coles Park named after him.

And of course, Sir Richard Sankey, the renowned Chief Engineer of Mysore, has a road and a tank named after him.

Sir Richard Sankey made many lasting contributions to Bangalore including the creation of the buildings housing the High Court (Attara Kacheri), the East Parade Church and the Museum. He also designed the Cubbon Park.

Interestingly, there is neither a Churchill Town, nor a Churchill Road.

Of War and Independence

There was this Englishman named Philip Spratt,' says Mr. Murthy of Select Bookshop in reply to my question. 'Certainly a very accomplished and prominent foreigner. Fits your bill. He wrote about communism, philosophy, sociology and many other topics. Used to edit *MysIndia*. A good friend of Stephen Spender's… and he gave me French lessons.'

Undoubtedly fitted the bill. So I went after his story and this is what I found:

As a young lad, Spratt was extremely introverted. His aversion for self-expression was such that he submitted blank pages instead of essays while in school. And in early youth, he became one of those shy men who take to idealism. His socialistic inclinations gained strength after he entered Cambridge and joined its Union and Labour Club. He had no desire to excel in academics and spent his time in various cerebral pursuits. He also made a nodding acquaintance with intellectuals such as Virginia Woolf. Enamoured of the Marxist ideology and driven by an unspoken desire to improve humankind, he drifted towards Communism. He was not alone. Around 1919, small revolutionary groups in Britain came together to form the British Communist Party. The Party soon secured an affiliation with the Communist International (Comintern), an umbrella organisation dedicated to spreading communism throughout the world. Spratt joined the Party soon after his haloed hero – Lenin – died.

In 1926, at the age of twenty-four, he received an interesting proposition from one of the first members of the Party, Clemens Dutt, who, incidentally, had a Bengali father and a Scandinavian mother. Dutt asked Spratt if he would be willing to go to India as a Comintern emissary. It was to be a six-month assignment, he would undertake no public work and act purely as a messenger and reporter. His anonymity perfectly suited the mission and he accepted.

Spratt's brief was to urge the Communist Party of India, formed the year before, to launch a Workers' and Peasants' Party as a legal cover. Members of this outfit were to get into leadership positions in trade unions throughout India. But before he left, a Russian Comintern representative in London named Petrovsky added a task to the mission – he asked Spratt to write a pamphlet urging India to follow the example set by China.

Upon reaching India, Spratt wrote the pamphlet and got it published under the title *India and China*. The act led him to the dock for the first time, but the judge dealt leniently with the charge of sedition and released him. In the next ten years, Spratt would be tried twice more and sentenced on both occasions.

Meanwhile, he took stock of the situation in India and found promise in the nascent communist movement. M. N. Roy was getting Indian recruits trained in the USSR with the help of the Comintern. Prominent communist leaders such as S. A. Dange, Muzaffar Ahmed, Shaukat Usmani and Nalini Gupta had already been jailed (1924) as propagandists. In fact, 1924 was a watershed for the Trade Unionists. The Girni Kamgar Mahamandal (GKM) had spearheaded a prolonged strike in the Bombay textile industry, but they had functioned by excluding communists from their ranks.

The situation changed soon after the arrival of Spratt and Bradley (another Englishman who came in 1927). Communism began dominating the Trade Union movement. Branches of the Workers' and Peasants' Party were set up in Bengal, Bombay, the United Provinces and several cities in Uttar Pradesh. When the GKM disintegrated, the communist-backed Girni Kamgar Union (GKU) took its place. And promptly led its 60,000 members into two strikes in 1928 and 1929. Dange and company joined the struggle after their release. Since the rail, iron and textile industries participated in the strikes, millions of working days were lost. Matters seemed to be getting out of hand. The recommendations of the Simon Commission did nothing to assuage the situation either. The Communists gained popularity by the day and threatened to form a potent force. The government had to set a stern example. On 20 March 1929, Spratt and Bradley were served non-bailable arrest warrants along with twenty-eight Indians including Dange, Usmani and Ahmed. All of them were taken to Meerut for a trial. As an afterthought, another Englishman named Lester Hutchinson, who later became a British Member of Parliament, was arrested. It didn't matter that Hutchinson was more of a journalist and an observer, and had activated himself only after the others were arrested.

The Meerut trial stretched from June 1929 to January 1933, generated a mountainous 2,600 documents and cost the taxpayer £120,000. It has other points of interest as well. The jury was dispensed with in favour of a "trained judge". One of the prisoners even died during the interminable trial process. Interestingly, the Labour Party replaced the Conservatives in Westminster before the trial began, but that did not alter the government's treatment of the case. Hutchinson's mother was told at the Brighton Labour Party Conference that her appeals for justice would be useless because Lord Irwin, the Viceroy of India, had declared that London's interference would result in his resignation.

When the trial began, the accused were charged with conspiracy to deprive the King-Emperor of the Sovereignty of India, incitement of antagonism between capital and labour and forming the Workers' and Peasants' Party in many venues. They were also generalised as Communists (not all of them were) who had the long-term plan of overthrowing governments everywhere by instigating strikes and armed uprisings. In short, the accused faced the same fate as British union leaders of a bygone regressive era. Although Spratt thought of his own role as that of a gadfly, the government saw him as an important and fanatical revolutionary. He was among the ones meted the severest punishment – transportation for a period of twelve years. The luckiest were

---

Workers of the Binny Mills Join the Action

The Binny Mills in Bangalore has seen many changes in names and ownership in its colourful history. It took its first avatar in 1875 as the Woollen Factory. It was then a carpet-making unit kick-started by S. Lee, the Principal of the School of Engineering. It later became known as the Bangalore Mill Ltd., and was then renamed as the Bangalore Woollen, Cotton and Silk Mills before finally becoming Binny and Co.

Following the popular trend in 1926, workers of the mill agitated against unfair management practices. They struck work and held demonstrations to demand recognition for their Labour Union and an enhanced salary. During

sentenced to four years rigorous imprisonment. The sentences were, however, reduced following an appeal in July 1933. Spratt's was curtailed to two years RI. But despite the government's best efforts, the trial did not produce the desired results. The Communist and freedom movements continued unabated in India.

During his imprisonment, Spratt slowly began confronting his doubts regarding Communism. He read the Mahatma's *Atmakatha* in Hindi and was struck by the shocking realisation that he had barely understood India. When he was released in 1934, he was certain that he no longer had a message for India. He was equally certain of being a misfit in England and had no wish to go back. He wavered in his loyalty to the Party, and told some of his friends that he intended to resign. It was at this juncture that Spratt went to Madras to marry Seeta, the daughter of a communist leader named Singaravelu. But the government interrupted conjugal bliss by arresting Spratt yet again. This time it was a precautionary measure taken to suppress the Civil Disobedience Movement initiated by the Congress Party. By the time he was released in 1936, he had read more of Gandhiji's writings and was inclined to think that when it came to Indian affairs, the Mahatma was "partly right". Philip Spratt had become not just an ex- but an anti-

---

one such demonstration, police fire killed four workers. An enquiry committee found the firing unwarranted and held Sir Mirza, who had just taken over as the Dewan of Mysore, responsible.

The mill workers developed a strong bond with the Congress Party and played a significant role in the freedom struggle, most notably during the 1942 Quit India Movement.

Sometime in the 1950s, Binny employed many Yorkshiremen who resided in plush Bangalore bungalows and spent the evenings in their own club. During the day, they taught Indians assembly-line spinning and weaving.

communist. And having transformed himself thus, he went to Bangalore.

Spratt's actions in Bangalore reveal the extent of Stalin's influence in his transformation. While Gandhiji was pulling him out of communism, Stalin had been the push factor. Like countless others, Spratt was appalled by the Russian leader's stentorian actions in his homeland. So after the Russian invasion of Finland in 1939, he began writing strongly against Soviet policy. He was by then the political voice behind *MysIndia*, a liberal weekly published in Bangalore. And on occasion, he allowed his work to reflect his obsession with Stalin. Trivial circumstantial evidence, at least, points in this direction – while writing about a popular Hindu preacher living outside Bangalore named Meher Baba, Spratt described him as having "Stalinish features with merry eyes"! Moreover, when Stalin died in 1953, Spratt wrote a sarcastic obituary in his editorial that began thus:

'The official announcement of the death of Stalin is conclusive proof that Soviet science has not yet conquered death, that Jewish doctors had no hand in it, and that he died in the natural course like almost everybody in the still

---

Miss Mayo Provides the Contrast

Katherine Mayo's much denounced book *Mother India* was released around the time Philip Spratt came to India. The book was controversial for many reasons. The American writer had opened Indian sewers and pretended that its putrid contents were not the refuse of Indian civilisation, but were in fact Indian civilisation itself. Among other things, Mayo ridiculed Mahatma Gandhi, Rabindranath Tagore and the Hindu practice of worshipping idols. It is contended that the British sponsored the book soon after she wrote *Isle of Fear* in defence of American imperialism in the Philippines. And the apparent motive for doing so was to swing American opinion against Indian self-rule.

The book gave rise to widespread criticism and protests. Among those who sprang to India's defence were Lala Lajpat Rai, Annie Besant and a plethora

unregenerate parts of the world groaning under the sway of capitalists, exploiters and warmongers.'

In the same piece, Spratt took Nehru to task for saying that Stalin was a man of peace. The Indian Prime Minister, in fact, regularly came under his hammer. He often made forceful arguments to allege that Nehru's sympathy to the communist cause was endangering India. To make himself clear on this count, he brought out *Blowing up India: Reminiscences and Reflections of a former Comintern Emissary* in 1955. Using a grave Orwellian voice in the latter part of the book, he conveyed his fear that Communism might conquer the world in three decades or so. His fear was very real and very human – upon hearing that Chiang Kai-shek had fled and Mao was now China's leader, Spratt spent a sleepless night, by his own admission.

His need to influence Indian politics, therefore, should be seen in this light. India was now his only home (he had even turned vegetarian). And he was concerned about its future. So he kept striving to forge an alliance with like-minded people. In 1951, he became the Secretary of Minoo Masani's Indian Congress for Cultural Freedom and regularly contributed to its bulletin *Freedom First*. As the years

---

of American and British nationals. Many of them wrote to the Mahatma to reiterate their support for India, or to urge him to correct the perception created by Mayo. But all he did was to write to Mayo and inform her that the book did not leave a nice impression in his mind. Writing in *Young India*, Gandhiji added:

'The carefully chosen quotations give it the appearance of a truthful book but the impression it leaves on my mind is that of a drain inspector sent out with the one purpose of opening and examining the drains of the country....The book is without doubt untruthful, be the facts stated ever so truthful...'

progressed, Spratt continually trotted away from the Left. The gallop came in 1959 with the formation of the Swatantra Party.

Founded by the peerless Rajaji along with Minoo Masani, N. G. Ranga, B. R. Shenoy, Piloo Mody, Khasa Subba Rau and A. D. Shroff, the Swatantra Party provided an alternative to the Nehruvian brand of socialism. These men were the first capitalists in Indian politics. They stood for competitive enterprise, land-owning peasants (as opposed to the cooperative farming model Stalin adopted in the USSR) and the right to pursue wealth wholeheartedly. So it naturally had the support of industrialists, ex-rulers, and agrarian leaders. The Congress tried to paint it as a rich man's party, but in post-liberalisation India, the Congress and other parties in power have been implementing ideas first espoused by the Swatantra Party. Spratt's association with the Party was inevitable. Not only were the Party's ideals a reflection of his own, he and Rajaji were also good friends who had shared a mutual admiration since 1938. In 1965 or thereabouts, Spratt even shifted from Bangalore to Madras to edit the Party's newsweekly *Swarajya*.

Such was the amazing journey of Philip Spratt. Although on the surface it seems to be a journey marked by reinventions, it was one of consistency. His reinventions ensured that he always remained honest with himself. Bangaloreans of yore fondly recall this inimitable Englishman cycling through the streets, often loaded with a stack of books. In the early 50s, another regular patron of Select Bookshop, Prof. Ramaswamy, kept bumping into him.

'I cannot claim his friendship, but I remember him vividly,' says the professor. 'Dishevelled hair, buttons missing on his coat, trousers crumpled, tie upside-down… he was a thorough introvert. But you could *see* that he was an intellectual who was dedicated to his work.'

'Did he come across as one who wrote frank and fiery editorials?' I ask.

'Not at all.'

All the same, Spratt wielded a prodigious pen that churned out editorials as well as books. He published a translation of Louis Renou's *Vedic India* in 1957. *Diamat (Dialectic materialism) As Philosophy of Nature* came out in 1958 and *Hindu Culture and Personality* was written sometime after that.

Philip Spratt died on 8 March 1971.

* * *

In the year 1940, Tatiana Adolphna began a long journey in search of love, dreams and... food. After she left the town of Kazan, south of Moscow, she travelled further south in an attempt to escape poverty as well as the imminent war. Many torturous months later, she reached Teheran and was promptly jailed for not possessing any papers. Perhaps she spent her time thinking about the uncertain future. Perhaps she thought nostalgically about the past... about her days as a well-known Russian actress whose beauty deserved a better fate.

After languishing behind bars for a couple of months, she found herself thrown on the Afghanistan border. She walked east. A few brisk weeks later, she arrived in Quetta in present-day Pakistan and allowed the British to take charge of her life. They first put her in a local refugee camp, but presently shifted her to Satara in Maharashtra. Tatiana had arrived in India. One fine day in the Satara camp, she met her future husband Gerhart Martin Jacoby.

As the only surviving member of his German Jewish family, Gerhart had an equally incredible story to tell. Having fled his hometown of Dresden, he had first reached Italy and found it equally unsafe. His next stop was Iceland. But even that remote piece of land was not safe. There was no option but to flee yet again, this time on a steamer heading for Australia. Gerhart never completed the trip. When the vessel docked in Bombay, he took one look at his surroundings and immediately disembarked.

His troubles weren't yet behind him. The British eyed the German citizen with suspicion. He was a Nazi unless proved otherwise. They jailed him in Delhi under the same roof as stalwarts such as Sardar Patel and Jawaharlal Nehru. In the three months that the British took to confirm his Jewish faith, Gerhart learnt Urdu. When he was released, he too was sent to Satara. One fine day in the Satara camp, he met his future wife Tatiana Adolphna…

Love softened the harsh fate meted out to the two young people. It did not matter that Tatiana spoke little English. It did not matter that Russian wasn't among the ten-odd languages Gerhart spoke. It mattered a lot to both that they got married. Their first daughter, Ingrid Jacoby, was born in the camp. By this time, Gerhart had managed to find employment as a manager in the Grand Hotel in Bombay. He was familiar with the line of work and his success meant that the family could move out of the camp. Over the years, Gerhart accepted assignments in Mussorie, where Ingrid's sister was born, and then Dehradun before returning to work at the Grand Hotel.

A Holocaust Survivor in Bangalore
Bangalore is home to a few Europeans who escaped the holocaust. When I rang up one of them, the person heard me out and took a fortnight to consider whether to give me an interview. Finally (s)he said:

'I don't want to remember how I lost my entire family. My life is the only thing that belongs to me. I don't want to know people and I don't want them to know me or my story.'

In the early 50s, a lucrative offer came his way. The Italian automobile giant Vespa had tied up with Bajaj India and the joint venture offered him the sole auto-rickshaw dealership for the whole of South India. Tatiana, not Gerhart, took up the offer and shifted to Bangalore along with the children. Gerhart joined them sometime later. The couple ran a prosperous dealership till 1958 before migrating to Canada. In a year, the family was back in Bangalore. Their precious savings had all but evaporated in the interim. Some money was lost to cheats, some to a dearer currency.

Tatiana and Gerhart now decided to make their Indianness official. So they obtained Indian citizenship in addition to restarting the dealership. But Gerhart also had plans for an alternate profession. One day, he opened a suitcase he had brought back from Canada and looked fondly at its contents – un-popped corn. Next, he learnt how to perform a magic trick with it. By roasting the corn over a slow *sigri* and topping it with Indian spices, he converted it into popcorn. And just like that, he was on the way to becoming the Popcorn King of India. Of course, *sigris* could only give so much output. He needed popcorn making machines like the ones he had seen in America. So he imported one and kick-started his business. But given the hungry clientele, one machine was hardly sufficient. He needed more. But why keep importing them? He could try and make them himself. Fearing patent issues, he made changes to the imported machine's design to create his own version, and then began

---

A Parallel

Tatiana apparently wasn't the sole transcontinental trekker to come to Bangalore. According to Ingrid Jacoby, a man named P. Louis walked his way to Bangalore from Greece. What is weirder, he came via Burma! After coming to Bangalore, Louis became the manager of the West End hotel, which was then run by Spencer's.

mass-producing them. Soon, he was selling both – popcorn and machines that made them. Forty-five years later, the plant is still running.

The harried couple had finally made it into the big league. Tatiana, for one, decided to let her flaming-red hair down. She took a fancy to the dance floor, became a regular patron of the Bangalore night clubs and could soon dance with the best. This was a time when ballroom dancing was still in vogue. When the British had left, elite Indians had stepped in to keep the floors packed. Seeing the ravishing Tatiana, young Indian men, well boys actually, would leave their girlfriends behind at their tables and cajole her to dance with them. She, in turn, indulged her "chokra boys".

Tatiana made an impression in the night clubs in other ways as well. She would often arrive with a companion clinging to her neck. A live python! She would order a beer for herself and an ice-cream for the snake. Bangalore's old-timers still talk about her and the python… During this phase of her life, she made friends with another Russian, Lara Belgresty, who used to give cabaret performances all over India. Lara eventually retired and settled in Bangalore.

Meanwhile, Gerhart was following mellower pursuits. He became a member of the Bangalore Amateur Dramatics Society and even gave a performance once. He also began organising Oktoberfest for the Max Mueller Bhavan. It cannot be confirmed now whether he served popcorn with the beer.

Tatiana died in 1980. Gerhart followed suit thirteen years later. Theirs is undoubtedly the best World War II story set in Bangalore. A story about a German man and a Russian woman getting together to stick their tongues out at European warmongering. Both Gerhart and Tatiana led fascinating lives that are windows to the world they occupied. A world where people like them were not just real,

but real enough to be accepted despite their idiosyncrasies.
As Ingrid points out:
  'People of that era had a larger sense of humour.'

* * *

In 1939, the same year that World War II broke out, an
Indian industrialist named Seth Walchand Hirachand
travelled to the United States on a business mission – to
discuss with Chrysler the possibility of starting an
automobile unit in India. Although the deal couldn't be
arranged, a chance encounter with William Douglas Pawley
during his return journey changed the aeronautical future
of India. Pawley was then the chairman of the New York
based Inter-Continent Corporation and a Director of the
Harlow Aircraft Company. More pertinently, he was planning
to establish an aircraft production factory in China. So when
Seth Walchand learnt that Pawley was a co-passenger on
his flight, he got himself introduced to him. In the course of
the conversation, Seth Walchand mooted the idea of
producing aircraft in India as well.

Pawley was a decisive man. He had made a pile of money
in American real estate in 1925-26 before shifting to
aviation. The move ensured that he escaped the ravages of
the American Depression of 1929, and simultaneously,
soared the heights of his new profession. By 1928, he had
already become the President of the Aircraft Company of
Cuba, and his next promotion happened as early as 1932.
Pawley's rise was meteoric and could be attributed to his
twin traits of energy and vision.

So, not surprisingly, he was as animated about the idea
as Seth Walchand. He thought little about the fact that India
lacked even a car-producing factory (Hindustan Motors was

established only in 1942 and the first indigenous Indian car – the Ambassador which is modelled after the Morris Oxford – rolled out only in 1948). All Pawley saw as a prerequisite was the government's support and patronage. That should have been easy, especially since the "mother" government in London had clearly asked India to make its own "arrangements for defence, especially in the air". Seth Walchand immediately despatched a telegram to the Indian government detailing his scheme. But neither his promise to get the first craft airborne in nine months nor the mention of Pawley enticed the government to respond; he spent nine fruitless months sending telegrams and trying to follow up the proposal. During this period, Japan's air attacks against China intensified. India, too, was facing the possibility of a Japanese invasion via Burma. Whether it was due to these developments or a sudden clarity of thought, the Indian government now stepped into high gear. Lord Linlithgow, the Viceroy of India, himself got involved in Seth Walchand's proposal. He asked the industrialist and Pawley to attend a high-level meeting with his officials at Simla (now Shimla).

Meanwhile, the Burmese government was frustrating Pawley's attempts to set up an aircraft plant in the country. So he gladly answered the summons from Simla. When he and Seth Walchand arrived at India's summer capital on 1 July 1940, they were accompanied by a top aviation expert from America named McCarthy Jr. McCarthy could both fly and design planes and would soon become the General Manager and mainstay of the Indian plant.

The Simla talks proved to be conclusive. Within seventy-two hours, the Indian government approved the proposal, and promised to buy fighters, trainers and twin-engine bombers from the new plant. The orders, once they materialised, would be worth $4.4mn.

A delighted Seth Walchand hurried away to begin the hard work. He roped in two of his friends, Tulsidas Kilachand and Dharamsey Khatau, as additional investors in the venture. Each of them purchased shares worth Rs.25 lakhs. In October 1940, Walchand contacted the rulers of the four princely states of Baroda, Gwalior, Bhavnagar and Mysore to raise further capital. The only positive response came from Mysore. Representing the Maharaja, the Dewan Sir Mirza Ismail said that the state of Mysore was willing to invest Rs.25 lakhs, provide land free of cost, supply water and electricity at subsidised rates and provide more assistance if required. The tacit stipulation, of course, was that the plant would be situated in the state of Mysore. There was absolutely no reason for Seth Walchand to disagree. After six days of sorties, Pawley and his team identified the most ideal site for the plant – a piece of land outside the Bangalore Cantonment. There was a cluster of five small lakes on the land, making it ideal for operating amphibian craft as well.

It was all falling into place. The Hindustan Aircraft Company was registered on 23 December 1940 and Pawley became its operational head. The very next day, a team began clearing termite hills from the site. In three short weeks, the factory's new building, service roads and the main runway were ready! At this time, the company employed 22 American technicians, 300 "specially selected and qualified" Indian engineers and 2,000 skilled workmen operating shifts round the clock. Pawley displayed a tremendous empathy for Indian aspirations and did everything possible to train Indian personnel. The Indians responded by surpassing all expectations. Before long, the Americans buried their doubts and admitted that "Indian workmen can absorb the techniques of aircraft construction far quicker than their Chinese counterparts". Both McCarthy and Pawley were thrilled by the progress. The plant seemed to have everything – a plethora of orders, funds, vision, a team with high morale and a comprehensive array of machine tools despite the wartime crunch of materials. It received another fillip when the Government of India increased its commitment to the venture by becoming a shareholder in April 1941.

Meanwhile, the Chinese government had become a desperate customer – the Japanese bombers had crippled many manufacturing units in the Chungking area of China. And the still functional units could come under fire any moment. So Pawley purchased the machinery and raw material stocks of these units on behalf of the Hindustan Aircraft Company. Each scrap of material procured made the journey that much easier.

On 29 July 1941, a pilot named E. R. Fenimore successfully tested the first craft produced by the company – a Harlow PC-5A trainer. The plant seemed to be on course for rolling out around 150 aircraft – including Curtiss 75A-5P Hawk fighters and Vultee V-12-D attack bombers in addition to the Harlows – by the end of 1942. Of course, it was not sufficient for a world gone crazy, but a significant contribution nevertheless.

All plans went awry with Japan's attack on Pearl Harbour in December 1941. America and Britain declared war on Japan. New Delhi became the Southeast Asia Command centre for the Allied forces. The action was getting nearer as well. Colombo was being bombed and Assam had been infiltrated by the Japanese. Due to all these factors, the Bangalore plant suddenly gained a global significance. That meant that it had to adapt. Fast.

Seth Walchand and his friends reluctantly agreed to sever ties from their beloved company in return for fair compensation from the Indian government. The state of Mysore retained its shares without having any management links with the company. Along with the change of guard, the purpose of the plant itself was modified. It was felt that overhaul and repair of aircraft would be of far greater value to the Allied cause than assembly. So the assembly programme was initially curtailed and then abandoned altogether by mid-1943. Meanwhile, the United States Army Tenth Air Force (USAAF) arrived in Bangalore in early 1942. They were to occupy the company premises "entirely on contingency basis" for the duration of the war. In July of the same year, American managers and supervisors were recruited to work in Bangalore. Accompanying them were those who had received honourable discharges from the American Volunteer Group (the Flying Tigers) after the retreat from China. The Indian technicians were retained on American funding.

Although the plant continued the good work in the new setup, the Tenth Air Force felt that the results could be better. So after negotiations, they took complete control in September 1943. The main entrance of the company flew the Union Jack, Stars and Stripes and the Mysore *gandaberunda* side by side for the next two years. The plant now employed 250 U.S. civilian experts, 600 USAAF technicians and nearly 15,000 Indian personnel! And it managed to keep all of them busy. It is said that one Pratt & Whitney Twin Wasp or Wright Cyclone engine came off the overhaul lines every 45 minutes. A war was truly on.

When Japan surrendered in August 1945, the USAAF packed its bags and went home to celebrate. It was time for the company to reinvent itself yet again. But rediscovering its prowess in manufacturing proved to be as challenging as doing it the first time – with the end of the war, orders weren't as plentiful. So retrenchment was inevitable. In fact, the company had to resort to building railway coaches and buses for a brief period! The company also renamed itself in

December 1945. It is now called the Hindustan Aeronautics Limited.

And just to put it in perspective again – the Ambassador hit the Indian roads three years after the end of the war.

* * *

As World War II was redefining the aircraft plant, it was making an impact on the city as well. While Madras and Colombo were operational centres, Bangalore acted as a rest and recreation centre for the soldiers. They were seen everywhere. Although there was no shooting and killing, the air was tight with a gravid expectancy. Reminiscing about those days in a newspaper article, Bangalorean H. F. Gonsalves says:

'Besides our own regiment, there were British and African troops, Australian Border Regiments and American soldiers (Dough Boys)... Convoys of armoured trucks lumbered through the streets daily. Trains were packed with soldiers. Sad to say, there was a dearth of armament! Coconut palms were cut down and fashioned into dummy anti-aircraft guns... strategically placed to frighten [Japanese] bombers away. At night, searchlights swept the sky. Everybody had to dig slit trenches. All conversation began, ended and was punctuated with the imminent [Japanese] invasion.'

The city prepared for the worst. Windowpanes and mirrors were pasted with brown paper. Blackouts were regularly observed. Bulbs were painted to allow only a pencil beam downwards. Vehicle headlights were given a similar makeover. Local boys and girls volunteered as clerks and nurses in the army. Schools presented certificates to prize-winning athletes instead of cups and medals – the money saved thus was donated to the war effort. A beautiful Muslim daughter-in-law belonging to a prominent family acted in plays to raise funds even as her mother-in-law observed the *purdah*. Petrol was rationed, water supply turned erratic and domestic help deserted their employers. One might have thought that the Japanese had already captured Madras. Bangalore might as well have been London on an agreeable, actionless day.

Meanwhile, hotels, butchers and vegetable vendors saw roaring business – after all, the soldiers needed to eat and keep their spirits high. *Funnels*, a now defunct dance club that had a live band and was located off M. G. Road, was quite popular with the troops. After a cheerful night in a joint such as this, British and American soldiers would regularly indulge in drunken brawls. Aware of this practice, a contingent of police forces from both countries patrolled the streets, ready to cart off their men to the barracks. Overall, the war brought a rejuvenating spirit to Bangalore – beer, billiards, racing and theatre caught the public's fancy.

So did two atypical expatriates named Gunboat Jack and Young Tarley. Gunboat Jack, who died in Bangalore, was especially popular with the children of Bangalore. He could shoot, ride, box, trick-shoot and trick-ride like a street performer. One account says that he was fond of the bottle and used to happily transfer ownership of his properties during a night of revelry.

It must have been easy to forget about the war, given the scale of merriment. The refugees, however, provided a sober reminder. Hundreds of them came from Malaya and Singapore and stayed in Bangalore for the duration of the conflict. So did Italian prisoners of war, most of whom had been captured in East Africa. 23,000 Italians came to India from Ethiopia alone. A considerate government promptly packed them off to salubrious cities – those who did not end up in Nainital or Dehradun came to Bangalore. The Maharaja of Mysore undertook the expense of looking after them. They lived in dysfunctional camps in the city outskirts of Jalahalli, Jakkur and Hebbal. Water mains supplying the camps often broke down, but it was a minor inconvenience compared to volunteering as targets for the Allied troops. And over time, their living conditions improved. Workshops were set up, allowing them to make violins and furniture. They were even issued paper money, and an occasional outing to watch Lawrence Olivier on the big screen was not out of the question.

* * *

World War II also brought women like Ray Raitt to Bangalore as part of the Women's Army Auxiliary Corps, or WAAC as it was popularly known. Although the WAAC came into existence in America, Ray was British. She worked as a nurse during the war and eventually married a planter. Ingrid remembers her as someone who was "ugly as sin" and who loved dancing and organising charity shows in support of the war.

Two years after the war ended, India gained its independence. Many British women, especially those who had spent a long time in India or lived on their own, faced a dilemma: should they go back home? Some of them eventually did. Ray was amongst those who preferred to stay in Bangalore till the very end. Ingrid, who has seen both the farewells and the funerals, nursed Ray during her last days and even brought her library books to read. The dying lady repaid the kindness by bequeathing her house to Ingrid!

Post-Independence

Svetoslav Roerich was the son of Nicholas Roerich – the renowned Russian artist, writer, archaeologist, philosopher and traveller. Devika Rani was the grand-niece of the Nobel laureate Rabindranath Tagore. Both took to and mastered different art forms, met each other when they were middle-aged, married and moved to Bangalore in 1945.

Devika Rani became associated with the Indian film industry in the late 20s. It was the era of silent films and the beautiful lady chose to work on costumes and production sets. In 1929, she married the well-known Indian producer Himanshu Rai and went to Germany to learn more about the nitty-gritty of film-making. Her transformation came with the introduction of talking pictures in the Western world. She came back to India and co-starred with her husband in *Karma*, the country's first talking picture. It became a runaway success. And thus began Devika Rani's journey as the First Lady of the Indian screen. Himanshu Rai's production house, The Bombay Talkies, kept featuring her as the leading lady during the next decade, and these performances were highly acclaimed, more so because the couple successfully used art to depict social evils such as the caste system. With Rai's death in 1940, Devika Rani stopped acting, but continued to be the production controller for the unit. More success came her way. And then, at the height of her career, she quit the industry to marry Dr. Svetoslav Roerich.

Meanwhile, Svetoslav Roerich was making a name for himself as well. Born in St. Petersburg in a family that cherished art, Svetoslav's sketches showed promise by the time he was five. By twelve, he was stretching canvasses onto frames and preparing paints for his father. He soon began accompanying his father on archaeological trips to ancient Russian cities and came to comprehend the history and culture of his country. The family moved to independent Finland in 1918 and while there, Nicholas began teaching his son painting. One of his earliest lessons was: don't imitate me.

A year or so later, Svetoslav left for his studies. He briefly went to London and then to New York, specialised in architecture and eventually completed his post-graduation from Harvard University. At the same time, he experimented with theatre, but mainly drew, illustrated books and created graphics. The young man was soon exhibiting his work and winning awards.

In 1923, the Roerichs landed in Bombay. Nicholas and his wife Elena embarked upon their life's work; Svetoslav and his elder brother George (who later became an Indologist) accompanied them as assistants. As the family undertook research expeditions in Sikkim, Bhutan and Nepal, Svetoslav developed a liking for Oriental art and local systems of medicine. Towards the end of 1924, the rest of the family left on an arduous Central Asian expedition while Svetoslav returned to the United States. Although he was just twenty years old, he was setting forth on his own mission.

As Head of Corona Mundi, the international art centre set up by his father in 1922, and Vice President of the Roerich Museum in New York, his mission was to draw the global art world closer together. And he did this by conducting international exhibitions and competitions. In the spring of 1928, the Roerichs came back from Central Asia and decided to settle down in the Kulu valley. Svetoslav returned to India to help his family found the Himalayan Research Institute – Urusvati. For the next four years, he shuttled between the institute and the western world. This was the time when he was doing his bit to persuade nations to ratify the path-breaking Roerich Pact. By 1932, he too settled in Urusvati to teach botany, ornithology, pharmacopoeia, crystallography and folk medicine. Eight years later, he exhibited a collection of his work named *Paintings of India*.

Svetoslav was proving to be a worthy son to an illustrious father – a rare occurrence, indeed, for a father and a son sharing an art form. The two Roerichs took this further by sharing their icy Muse. Both of them, over decades of dogged

---

The Roerich Pact

Nicholas Roerich initiated the Roerich Pact in response to the indiscriminate destruction caused by the Russian Revolution and World War I. The Pact was aimed at the preservation of art, culture, national monuments, and educational and scientific institutes at all times, including periods of war. Nicholas also designed a "Banner of Peace" that would adorn these edifices, just as the symbol of the Red Cross marks structures administering health care.

The Pact was ratified by the Baltic states, India (post-independence) and twenty-one countries of South, Central and North Americas. It officially came into effect in 1935.

persistence, have captured the Himalayas in every mood, colour, contour and dimension. Nicholas, in fact, would breathe his last at the Himalayan foothills on the eve of his departure to Russia in 1947. Svetoslav shared an equally obdurate love for the mountains, as can be inferred from his own words:

'I have seen many countries, but I have not discovered more beautiful a place as the Kulu Valley... Is it not strange that throughout the world, the great teachers of whatsoever race or faith have always gone to the heights to receive some of their greatest revelations? Does height, does eternal snow, the rarefied atmosphere contribute towards greater lucidity, or is it in order to rise above the sphere of the turmoil of life?'

It is hence all the more striking that he relocated to Bangalore and then stayed put for the remaining forty-eight years of his life. Of course, life in Bangalore had its compensations – the entire city adored him and Devika Rani. And the couple led an almost royal life. Although they often rented a room at the Ashoka hotel and maintained a residence in the city, they also owned the Tataguni Estate on the outskirts of Bangalore. After the death of the childless couple, the 457 acres of the estate would be a subject of prolonged litigation. But during their lifetimes, it was a haven of peace and creativity. Svestoslav produced many of his best works there – these perhaps include a portion of his work on Christian themes – and he felt that purchasing the estate had brought him luck.

Bangalore, too, benefited by his presence in many ways. He played a supervisory role at the Shri Aurobindo School of Art and was deeply committed to the Karnataka Chitrakala Parishad. Both forums brought him in regular contact with local artists. And he always found words of encouragement for each one of them. Pushpa Dravid, a city-based painter, experienced Svetoslav's warmth firsthand when she was pursuing her thesis on Nicholas Roerich's oeuvre on the Himalayas.

'Dr. Svetoslav Roerich was a delightful man,' she says. 'Had praise on his lips for everyone… and he used to chivvy us all to work hard. He could put me in a peaceful frame of mind with just a few words in his soft, lyrical voice.'

'What about Devika Rani?' I ask.

'She was a beautiful, wise lady,' she replies. 'Slightly dominating perhaps. I met them when they were both old. She used to be his manager during exhibitions… you could see that she inspired him. Yes, it was an excellent match.'

'Didn't they tire of Bangalore?'

'I shouldn't think so. Svetoslav Roerich loved the city. They spent their summers in Naggar in the Kulu valley, but otherwise stayed here.'

'Was he against God?' I ask, hinting at his Communist leanings.

'Not at all. Come to think of it, he was not against anything. He advocated self-belief and faith in the divine power.'

Svetoslav's writings and actions nevertheless show him to be a true communist and a patriotic Russian. When Germany invaded the Soviet Union during World War II, he and his brother sent word that they were ready to enrol in the Red Army as volunteers. They also sold paintings through joint exhibitions and raised money for the Soviet Red Cross and the Red Army. Furthermore, in his address over All India Radio, Lahore, in 1943, Svetoslav came down harshly on the German invasion, praised the leadership of Lenin and Stalin, and gave a stirring account of Russian valour. Similarly, he didn't flinch from supporting the Indian struggle for independence. He and Jawaharlal Nehru had forged a lasting friendship in 1942 and he later painted the Indian Prime Minister's portrait. Today, three of his portraits – those of Nehru, Indira Gandhi and S. Radhakrishnan – embellish the Central Hall of Parliament.

Given India's pro-Soviet tilt in the decades following its independence, Svetoslav's work attained a deep politico-cultural significance. When he held two very successful exhibition tours of the Soviet Union in 1960 and 1974, they were seen by some as the best possible method to further Indo-Soviet cultural ties. Perhaps it was – India did influence his work to a great extent. The man himself has described his loyalties towards India and Russia, and their effect on his work, thus:

'I am always striving to join India, where I have been living for years, to everything that I got in Russia or from Russia, and on the other hand, everything I do in India belongs to my Motherland.'

Svetoslav Roerich died on 30 January 1993. A year later, Devika Rani followed suit.

* * *

In the 1950s, a theatre group named BADS (Bangalore Amateur Dramatic Society), comprising British nationals, performed regularly for exclusive crowds in select venues. Their modus operandi, apparently, was to study all the happening plays in London while on home leave and then faithfully replicate them in Bangalore. Most members of the group were said to be well-educated, sophisticated and wealthy. And they preferred to stage modern plays, with themes that required little attention to costumes. Oscar Wilde seems to have been one of their favourite dramatists.

In 1960, close to the time BADS was dismantling, another troupe that called itself the Bangalore Little Theatre (BLT) came into existence. The BLT differed from BADS in the sense that it had a mixture of Indian and British actors. Author and translator, Professor Ramaswamy, who was the founding secretary of the troupe, has nostalgic memories of the thrice-a-week rehearsals.

'In my four active years with the troupe,' he says, 'the Indians and the Brits got along famously.'

The actors were employed in varied day jobs. Scott Todd was an important man in the telecom industry. His wife, Margaret, had a lovely voice and taught stage movement and speech to the rest.

'And then we had the Muirheads, Esther and Gordon,' he continues. 'I think Gordon was an attorney. I forget the daytime professions of the Leahs and the Meiklejohns. Oh yes, there was Dr. Roy Perry as well. But the most remarkable of the lot was David Horsborough. He was a wonderful human being and a fine actor. Was supposed to have been in the Royal Air Force. After he came to India as an English professor, he studied Sanskrit in Benares, learnt the *tabla* and wrote books.'

* * *

The eminent mythologist Joseph Campbell finally came to India in 1954 at the age of fifty. Had not the Depression of 1929 taken a toll on the American economy and his family's financial situation, he would have made the journey as a twenty-five year old and the story might well have been different. As it happened, Campbell was an accomplished man in his field by the time he arrived in India. And he was best known as the editor of Heinrich Zimmer's papers on Indian art and civilisation.

As was his practice, Campbell maintained a personal diary during his Indian journey, and after his death, it was published as a book under the title *Baksheesh and Brahman*. It is as close as he ever got to writing an autobiography. Reading through the journal, one is immediately struck by his disillusionment with India. And one can't help feeling that his use of the word *baksheesh* alludes not just to the alms a foreigner in the Orient is accosted for, but also to the economic aid that flowed from the US to India. That being the case, he was particularly distressed to find Nehruvian India packed with people who had the strongest anti-American views. Giving vent to his angst, he said:

'My own feeling, now, about Asia, world anti-Americanism, and so on, is that our do-goodism should now be definitely and absolutely stopped, since it is succeeding only in fostering a malevolence that may be our ruin, and any giving or helping should be precisely and firmly of the sort that it is everywhere said and thought to be – namely, carefully selfish; and also that I, personally, shall do nothing more to advertise, blurb, and explicate India, for India and Asia are obviously at the beginning of a prodigious boom and can be counted on to take care of themselves. Moreover, why should it be Americans who are always trying to create an understanding of others, when no one seems to feel the least impulse to seek to understand America? In fact, to hell with this whole "service-to-this-or-that-section-of-the-world" idea.'

Strong words indeed, especially coming from a scholar who preferred to be apolitical and was anything but a racist. Campbell was disgusted with what he saw as ingratitude and he had no doubts whatsoever that he was now on the other side of the Iron Curtain (interestingly, Campbell had nurtured Communist inclinations before Stalin committed his infamous excesses). Indians, he felt, were willing to shower their sympathies upon China, Southeast Asia, Russia, and perhaps even East Germany, but not the United States. According to him, Britain was flirting with China and France with Russia... America had lost the world, and would end up as a "fall guy"!

Much of his political predictions have not come true. His forte, it has to be remembered, was mythology. And his bitterness needs to be seen in the proper context. Here was a man who had dedicated a good part of his life to studying the ancient literature of India, in interpreting its age-old symbols and arts, and exploring the myths of the land before arriving at an informed opinion about (the evolution of) Indian civilisation. Moreover, he had come in search of Brahman – the transcendent.

What he experienced, instead, was the reality of India. In addition to the disenchantment caused by Indian politics, he encountered thieving roadside soothsayers and pick-pocketing urchins. He found text from his book used without acknowledgment in a newspaper article written by a certain Pyarelal Nayar. His visits to holy men of varying repute left him dissatisfied. He found Bollywood plagiarising Holly-wood. And, of course, he saw poverty as all-encompassing as Brahman.

It was all, perhaps, a shade too removed from what his scholastic pursuits had led him to expect.

Mercifully, the trip seems to have become progressively more rewarding and Campbell appears to have adjusted well to India. At any rate, his words become less acerbic. In addition to travelling extensively to cultural centres, he organised a dance tour for his wife Jean Erdman, who is believed to be the first modern dancer from America to visit India.

Four months after landing, Joseph Campbell had lunch with Jawaharlal Nehru, the fountainhead of Indian anti-Americanism. It softened his animosity and he relished the opportunity to "place on the level of human judgement a figure whose importance in the present world scene is perhaps paramount".

The climax, befittingly, came towards the conclusion of the trip. While in Trivandrum, Campbell chose to meet an ex-policeman (and not an ex-postal employee as Campbell believed him to be) named Sri Krishna Menon. The mythologist felt that Sri Krishna Menon (again, not to be confused with the Defence Minister in Nehru's cabinet) "seemed to represent a life pattern closer to the married sages of the Upanishads than to that of the life-and-flesh despising monks". At long last, Campbell had met a guru with whom he could converse on a refined intellectual plane.

'The chief value of my conversation with Krishna Menon,' said Campbell, 'is that it assures me that my own reading of the teaching coincides with the authority of at least one Indian sage. I know that the conversation and image of the teacher in his room of teaching will remain very clearly in my mind.'

Peace, it seems, descends upon seekers only after a hard penance. While watching an Indian film during the later part of his tour, it occurred to Campbell that:

'Seeing again in the movies what I had already seen with my own eyes, I had a very pleasant sense of the magnitude of the experiences that I have been having this year. In the course of my tour, I have been seeing India only piece by piece, little by little. Seeing it all again – as it were, all at once – I felt how big this whole thing is. The Orient is a vast natural phenomenon, like a continent of trees, mountains, animals and peoples.'

So now to the lingering question: where does Bangalore fit into all this? It doesn't, except that during the six-month sojourn, he made three brief stopovers in the city en route to Mysore, Halebid, Belur, Shravanabelagola and Hampi. That is all. Yet, Campbell formed some impressions of the city. He found Bangalore to be "cool, high and pleasant; a clean, attractive city but hardly Indian". He even put on his blue suit for dinner, partly because the atmosphere was that of a pleasant Anglo-Saxon resort.

And since he was a meticulous man, Campbell has not forgotten to mention that he visited a second-hand bookshop on M. G. Road where he met a "bookish Englishman". Perhaps, just perhaps, he was alluding to Philip Spratt. The bookshop, without a doubt, is Select Bookshop.

* * *

By the 1970s, expatriate Indians from East Africa, Malaysia and Hong Kong flocked to Bangalore to relocate or initiate businesses. This was probably the first indication of globalisation as applicable in the modern context. The 1980s saw West Asian students – mainly Iranians, but also Palestinians, Jordanians et al – filling the college rolls in Bangalore. Smriti Shrinivas, author of the magnificently presented *Landscapes of Urban Memory – the Sacred and the Civic in India's High-Tech City*, notes that many were fleeing repressive homeland regimes, but some were also seeking respite from military duty, war or marriage!

Even at this point, Bangalore was a garden city, a place where one could enjoy urban and hill-station pleasures together. Elderly walkers could still cross the road without worrying about palpitations.

In the late 70s and early 80s, Indian IT companies opened their offices in Bangalore. The city would never be the same again.

A few more noteworthy contributors

Innes Munro	–	Hyder Ali's chronicler. Has also described some remarkable manners and customs of Indians (before Abbé Dubois).
Eyre Coote	–	Brilliant British General who fought battles against Hyder and Tipu.
Rev. W. Reaves	–	Compiled the Kannada-English and English-Kannada dictionaries.
Rev. F. Kittel	–	German working in the Basel Mission in Mangalore. Published a Kannada dictionary in 1894.
Lewin Cunningham	–	As Commissioner, introduced the Indian Penal Code and the Code of Criminal Procedure in Mysore. Formed a regular police force in 1866, conducted the first state census in 1871.
Lord Wavell	–	The Viceroy of India who introduced the Civil Marriages Act in 1942. Before that, illegitimate children proliferated in the Cantonment area because inter-religious marriages were not recognised. Either the groom or the bride had to first convert to the other's religion.

Afterword

I had many reasons for writing this book. Because migration is an intriguing phenomenon (and a fundamental aspect of human evolution)… Because of my own brief experiences as an expatriate… And also because it is a pleasure to meet a stranger – more so an expatriate – and understand his motivations and opinions. But there is more to it.

Like a few of my colleagues in the IT industry, I was a reluctant immigrant. But a majority of them were willing (many wouldn't have minded taking the flight out of India as standees). In either category, the motive was the same. Financial benefits. I had little opportunity to meet immigrants with novel, even whacky, motives for relocating. It was disappointing and I resolved to meet, if not study, such people later. Then one day I paid a short visit to New York and understood, for the first time, what global diversity meant.

I took delightful subway rides and tried to absorb the vibrant diversity of the city (I recommend this exercise to anybody interested in human nature). At the same time, it struck me that newcomers to New York could make only infinitesimal additions to the variety. The city has seen it all. It displays it all. So I tried thinking of a city where expatriates would still be a novelty. A place which has recently begun attracting foreigners, but has accumulated enough of them for a meaningful study. Such a place, I decided, might exist in the developing world. That set me thinking – does/could India have such a city? Would I be able to find a new dimension of diversity in a land of a million conundrums and a billion people already diverse enough to numb sociologists?

On returning to Bangalore, I found my prayers answered. I saw foreigners everywhere I went. Never before in Independent India have foreigners existed in such large numbers. So I told myself: 'I need to tell this story.'

I plunged into it with a few hopes and assumptions about the expatriates:

- The diversity of India would ensure that they are a mixed bag.
- Recent experiments in globalisation would throw a few surprises.
- The milieu would prompt them to draw quaint and/or profound comparisons.
- The demands of India would place them at their introspective best.
- They would teach Indians a lot about themselves.
- And at the end of it all, they would still be puzzled about the land.

I'm happy to note that they have all come true. Had I believed for a moment that the IT revolution in Bangalore was solely responsible for bringing foreigners here, I would not have written the book. A combination of factors provides the impetus for the expatriate influx and that is what makes the topic interesting.

Let me now present a few of my conclusions and impressions, along with the various considerations that shaped this book—

Knowledge-Seekers and Problems-Solvers

Knowledge-seekers and problem-solvers have been visiting India for ages, but we see that their roles have now evolved. Patrick came to obtain a good education. Claudia came to learn about a phenomenon that hasn't been researched in such depth elsewhere. Sameer came because a shrinking world is reducing the time it takes for developed-world issues to impact the developing world. Caroline came not to create awareness of an Indian art, but to find a long-term solution for its preservation.

Expatriates taking to activism/social work, I feel, is a significant phenomenon. In the years ahead, urban India will need no external help for taking care of its economy. But who will address issues, especially rural issues, that require urgent resolution? A few amazingly committed Indians are stepping up. Unfortunately, they aren't sufficient in number. Perhaps the next generation of Indians, brought up with the same privileges as Westerners, might be adventurous and holistic enough to choose challenges beyond personal finances. For now, the help extended by the expatriates is priceless.

The Corporate Connection

Expatriates working in the world of business have evolved as well. After India gained independence, many foreigners, mainly the British, stayed back in big cities either to run their own businesses or because they held prominent positions in worthy enterprises. How were their relationships with Indian peers and subordinates? Knowing the social and financial state of the then inchoate nation, it would not be rash to assume that they were inequitable. *White worship*, which exists even today, was a lot more sacrosanct then. Few Indians could muster the confidence to break historical shackles. Moreover, Indians hadn't ushered in the Green Revolution, shown their ability to sustain democracy, or spread a large and illustrious diaspora. And oh – they hadn't entered the realm of IT.

The IT revolution has created a generation of Indians with the first *real* opportunity to exhibit its skills in front of a global audience. Having proved their credentials, Indians now find it possible to have a peer relationship with foreigners, more so when they don't share a client-vendor relationship. And with equality comes friction. In the case of the foreigner transplanted to an Indian work environment, the friction is caused by the demands on time and energy (not necessarily on the intellect) that an Indian organisation makes on an individual. Indians neither overstaff nor are they flexible about their deadlines. Therefore, foreigners transitioning from a lax work environment need to step up a gear or two. Other changes are required as well. For example, office politics and reward mechanisms are so different in India that a naïve foreigner is bound to feel frustrated.

Now a word about superior-subordinate relationships between Indians and expatriates respectively. They require a rare mix of tact and firmness. Many Indian bosses lack that. So they find it difficult to be strict with incompetent subordinates from overseas. The result – a single project might bring together an Indian who doesn't need to be told he will be working nights and an expatriate who will leave at 6 p.m. come what may. The problem, partially, is due to the fact that the job market requires more engineers than the Indian universities can deliver.

Of course, bright and innovative expatriates also come to India. Now, if they belong to a culture that encourages frankness, they fail to realise when to toe the line. Perhaps expatriates need to be prepared before being inducted into an Indian workplace. Just like Indians are trained in "cross-cultural sensitivity" before being posted abroad, foreigners need to be taught which sensitivities to adopt and which to shrug off.

Romance

After meeting many Indo-expatriate couples, I have reached the conclusion that the Indian family structure is resilient enough to accept the overseas bride or groom. Indo-expat marriages/relationships fail chiefly because of incompatibilities between the partners. In other words, they are no different from any other marriage. I also feel that the popular perception about such marriages – that they stand a better chance of survival when they are between Indian women and expatriate men – is incorrect.

Racism

Enough has already been said about the obsequiousness the Indian shows to the white man and the superiority he assumes towards the black. I would like to ponder over just one more point:

Is the Indian media still *white worshipping*? This is not something that one can conclude with certainty. And even if it is true, I personally prefer a media that pays excessive heed to the foreigner to one that ignores him. And – it speaks volumes about India's tolerance that a person like Bob Hoekstra can make strong statements against the political and administrative machinery.

Selecting My Stars

I selected my stars, the personalities featured in the book, based on three criteria:

- They should be first-generation immigrants.
- They should have made interesting and unusual journeys in life.
- And they should (therefore) have acquired perspectives that aid us in understanding the flux in society.

Restricting the scope to first-generation immigrants, I feel, makes a lot of sense. The second-generation immigrant belongs solely to the land to which his family has emigrated. But try as he might, the first-generation immigrant will never be able to integrate fully, much like an unbroken nutrient in the bloodstream. So he deserves to be inspected for what he brought, retained and absorbed. Here again, I did not hesitate to profile the short-term immigrant so long as he provided a unique perspective.

I have also deliberately not profiled foreigners who are here on purely religious pursuits. Instead, I have portrayed people who consider religion as an essential but partial aspect of their lives. Like Fr. Hank Nunn. In other words, I have chosen spirituality over religion. This approach also helps the book's objective of trying to find beauty in melting pots.

Also, I have made no attempt to rectify the factual errors committed by my stars. The idea was to present them exactly as they are – interesting people who are, quite naturally, fallible too.

People of Indian Origin Are Visitors

It would not have escaped the reader that People of Indian Origin featured in the book are treated as foreigners. Because that is who they are. Existing literature on the Indian diaspora deals predominantly with nostalgia. Even second-generation immigrants are treated as if India has given them roots. The truth is that it has merely provided the seed. That is why I have treated them as I have treated any other expatriate. That way, I could stress the contrasts they provide while keeping their Indianness in the background.

Celebrating the Underdog

One of the greatest challenges of the twenty-first century, I feel, will be our collective ability to think original thoughts (outside the realms of science and technology). I say this considering the way we analyse world events. All over the world, the media is turning increasingly strident. As a result, the loudest voices get maximum coverage. This kind of bombardment is quite effective – we subconsciously take rigid stances, fail to hear the other side of the story and seriously limit our tolerance and wisdom.

The solution would be to create a world where varied opinions – like those voiced by my stars – get due weightage. No single notion would drown the others. That way, we take nothing for granted. And we might even rediscover the story of the underdog. Because – and this book proves it – he has a significant story to share.

Material Comforts Take a Back Seat

A large number of expatriates in Bangalore appear willing to sacrifice material comforts during their stay here. Of course, a wonderful life awaits those who can afford it. But my point is.– improving roads and having more policemen on them will not succeed in retaining those who wish to leave. Europeans, in particular, don't seem to mind a little discomfort in exchange for a secure job. This is a clear corollary of the formation of the European Union. Global developments such as the EU, in fact, have enabled Bangalore to play host to a larger diversity of expatriates.

Hence one finds "bread-n-butter" expatriates, with the same hopes and aspirations as a middle-class Indian.

Bangalore Is Ideal

Expatriates find Bangalore an ideal city to live in. And this is due not just to the weather. Bangalore, despite its frenzied growth in the past decade, has remained a mellow city. The original inhabitants of the land are not very fussy about who comes here. Although some may disagree with me, I feel this is a great strength of the Kannadiga culture.

The expatriates are responding to this by making Bangalore, and India, their own. Just today, I heard an unusual request on a FM radio channel. An expatriate who was returning home called up from the airport to request a Hindi song. He said he would certainly be coming back, but meanwhile could the song be dedicated to the friends he had made in the city?

That is what I'm talking about.

Bibliography

Campbell, Joseph. *Baksheesh and Brahman – Indian Journal 1954-55*. New York: HarperCollins, 1995.

Churchill, Winston S. *My Early Years*. London: Fontana Books, 1930.

Dubois, Jean-Antoine. *Hindu Manners, Customs and Ceremonies*. (translated by Beauchamp, Henry K.). New Delhi: Asian Educational Services, 1986 (3rd edition).

Gidwani, Bhagwan S. *The Sword of Tipu Sultan*. New Delhi: Allied Publishers, 1978.

Government of Karnataka. *Karnataka State Bangalore District – Gazetteer of India*. Bangalore: Government of Karnataka, 1990

Hindustan Aeronautics Limited. *Diamonds in the Sky – Sixty years of HAL*. Bangalore: HAL, 2000.

Jain, Sanjeev. "The History of Asylums in India". (In: *The Confinement of the Insane 1800-1965: International Perspectives*, Ed. Roy Porter and David Wright).

Cambridge University Press, 2003.

Jayapal, Maya. *Bangalore – The Story of a City*. Madras: EastWest Books, 1997.

Kausar, Kabir. *Secret Correspondence of Tipu Sultan*. Bangalore: Karnataka State Archives, 1998 (2nd edition).

Kirsur, Mukund V. *Indian Silk*. Bangalore: Central Silk Board, Ministry of Textiles, Feb 2001.

Murthy, Sridhara P. S. *Rajaji*. (Kannada): Other information not available.

Nair, Janaki. *Bangalore's Twentieth Century – The Promise of the Metropolis*. Delhi: Oxford University Press, 2005.

NIMHANS. *Golden Jubilee Commemorative Volume*. Bangalore: NIMHANS.

Roerich, Dr. Svetoslav. *Reflections*. Bangalore: International Roerich Memorial Trust, 1992.

Simo, Anthony. *History of the Archdiocese of Bangalore: Volume One, From Its Origin up to 1971*. Bangalore: Published by the Author.

Spratt, Philip. *Blowing Up India – Reminiscences and Reflections of a Former Comintern Emissary*. New Delhi: Prachi Prakasan, 1955.

Srinivas, Smriti. *Landscapes of Urban Memory – The Sacred and the Civic in India's High-Tech City*. Hyderabad: Orient Longman, 2004.

St. Martha's Hospital. *Down the Arches of the Years*. Bangalore: St. Martha's Hospital, 1986.

Subbarayappa, Dr. B. V. *In Pursuit of Excellence*. New Delhi: Tata McGraw Hill, 1992.

Select Source Citations

Articles from the *Hindu*, the *Times of India*, the *Deccan Herald*, the *Statesman*, the *Telegraph*, *Mid-Day*, the *Tribune*, the *Sportstar*, the *Hindu Business Line*, the *Guardian* and the *New York Times*.

Websites of:

Aim25 (Archives in London and the M25 area)

Avatar Meher Baba

Canada Tibet Committee

http://www.cartage.org.lb/

Centre for Civil Society

Centre for the Study of Culture and Society (Bangalore)

ESPN-Star

GandhiServe Foundation (Mahatma Gandhi Research and Media Service)

Hindustan Motors

Indian Institute of Science

Indian Liberal Group (liberalsindia.com)

Indian National Congress

India Together (Civil Society Information Exchange Pvt. Ltd)

NASSCOM

National Galleries of Scotland

Office of Tibet, The (the official agency of His Holiness the Dalai Lama, in London)

People's Health Movement

rediff.com

Roerich & Devika Rani Roerich Estate Board

Roerich family Museum and Institute in St. Petersberg, The

Ronnie Johnson's website on Bangalore (children-of-bangalore.com)

Sangama

Tribute to Hinduism, A

University of Richmond

Working Class Movement Library (UK)